Identity Before Identity Politics

In the late 1960s identity politics emerged on the political landscape and challenged prevailing ideas about social justice. These politics brought forth a new attention to social identity, an attention that continues to divide people today. While previous studies have focused on the political movements of this period, they have neglected the conceptual prehistory of this political turn. Linda Nicholson's engaging book situates this critical moment in its historical framework, analyzing the concepts and traditions of racial and gender identity that can be traced back to late eighteenth-century Europe and America. She examines how changing ideas about social identity over the last several centuries both helped and hindered successive social movements, and explores the consequences of this historical legacy for the women's and black movements of the 1960s. This insightful study will be of particular interest to students and scholars of political history, identity politics, and US history.

Linda Nicholson is Susan E. and William P. Stiritz Distinguished Professor of Women's Studies and Professor of History at Washington University in St. Louis.

Cambridge Cultural Social Studies

Series editors
Jeffrey C. Alexander, *Department of Sociology, Yale University*, and Steven Seidman, *Department of Sociology, University of Albany, State University of New York.*

Titles in the series

List continues at end of book

Identity Before Identity Politics

Linda Nicholson

CAMBRIDGE
UNIVERSITY PRESS

CAMBRIDGE UNIVERSITY PRESS
Cambridge, New York, Melbourne, Madrid, Cape Town, Singapore,
São Paulo, Delhi

Cambridge University Press
The Edinburgh Building, Cambridge CB2 8RU, UK

Published in the United States of America by Cambridge University Press,
New York

www.cambridge.org
Information on this title: www.cambridge.org/9780521680486

First published 2008

Printed in the United Kingdom at the University Press, Cambridge

A catalogue record for this publication is available from the British Library

Library of Congress Cataloguing in Publication data
Nicholson, Linda J.
Identity before identity politics / Linda Nicholson.
    p.   cm. – (Cambridge cultural social studies)
ISBN 978-0-521-86213-4
1. Group identity – United States – History.   2. Women – United States –
Identity – History.   3. African Americans – Race identity –
History.   4. Women's rights – United States – History.   5. Civil rights
movements – United States – History.   I. Title.   II. Series.
HM753.N53   2008
305.48′896073–dc22
                                                            2008020506

ISBN 978-0-521-86213-4 hardback
ISBN 978-0-521-68048-6 paperback

To Gil

Contents

Acknowledgements

This book has been with me over the last ten years as I have moved among different cities and different institutions. The book began in the late 1990s when I was a faculty member at the State University of New York, Albany. Colleagues there, and also in Sofphia, helped me as I struggled with early versions of what would evolve into this book. In 1998–99, I was awarded a fellowship with the Center for the Study of Values in Public Life at the Divinity School of Harvard University. That fellowship enabled me to devote large amounts of time towards writing first drafts of several chapters. It also provided me with audiences and colleagues – particularly Janet Jakobsen – who provided useful feedback on these early drafts.

In 2000, I moved to Washington University in St. Louis. My colleagues in Women and Gender Studies and in the History Department have provided a stimulating and supportive environment as I continued work on it. The monthly workshop in political theory run by Andrew Rehfeld at Washington University provided me with a space to present drafts of various chapters over the years. I am grateful to participants in that workshop for all of their comments. I am also grateful to my colleagues Howard Brick, Leslie Brown, and Gerry Izenberg for some helpful reactions to various chapters.

And finally I would like to thank Alison Jaggar, Steve Seidman, and my brother Philip Nicholson for reading through many chapters, on occasion many times. Their support of this project, with that of my husband, Gil Nussbaum, kept me going as the book moved towards completion.

Introduction

During the late 1960s, certain political phenomena appeared on the US landscape that altered the terms of public debate about social justice. The political movements on behalf of African Americans and women took a distinctive turn. Both of these movements had been a force in United States politics prior to the late 1960s, most visibly in the earlier civil rights and women's rights movements. In these earlier incarnations, these movements had fought for legislation aimed at expanding the access black people and women had to opportunities long denied them for reasons of race and sex. But in the late 1960s, a new kind of emphasis emerged within both movements. While many within these movements continued to work for the above goals, others, particularly those who were younger and angrier, began to articulate different kinds of aims. Those who started calling their movement "Black Power," instead of "Civil Rights," and "Women's Liberation," as distinct from "Women's Rights," created a politics that went beyond the issue of access and focused more explicitly on issues of identity than had these earlier movements. Other activists, such as those who replaced "Gay Rights" with "Gay Liberation," made a similar kind of turn. The more explicit focus of these groups on issues of identity caused many to describe this new politics as "identity politics."

Identity issues had not been totally absent from the political movements of women and African Americans prior to the emergence of "identity politics." In these earlier movements, activists had struggled against prevailing ideas about who women and black people were, ideas that had often been used to prevent members of both groups from occupying social spaces open to men and to whites. But mostly such struggles had involved denying that blacks and women were naturally different from whites and men, and thus naturally unable to live and to work in those places open to whites and to men.

But the younger activists found this mere denial of difference inadequate. While such denial broke down barriers against the participation of some blacks and women in public life, it also worked to maintain a privileging of certain values and practices of middle-class public life, a privileging that functioned to exclude many. As younger feminists began to focus on issues of private life, and as African American activists began to identify more with the values and practices of poor and working-class African Americans, the privileging of such values and practices seemed at best to benefit only some already advantaged members of their own groups. Changes that would reach wider numbers seemed to demand a revolution in the norms and values of US society, including a radical rethinking about how differences between blacks and whites and women and men were to be understood. While differences between blacks and whites and women and men had earlier been associated with what was supposedly inferior about the former groups, these younger activists began to associate such differences with what was positive, if not superior, about these groups. This self-conscious attempt to reframe the meaning of these identity categories was reflected in such political slogans as "Black is Beautiful" and "Sisterhood is Powerful." This proud assertion of difference became viewed by these younger activists as linked with a more radical restructuring of the social order than was demanded by the earlier movements, a restructuring that could address the needs of greater numbers of blacks and women.

This move to reframe the meaning of these categories of identity was accompanied by a focus on group specific problems. Whereas older political movements of the left had struggled for the kinds of things everyone could be expected to want – such as voting rights or access to educational and employment opportunities – the younger activists focused on problems specific to the situations of their particular groups. Women and black people examined their experiences for answers to questions about what it meant to be a woman or black. They articulated political demands based on those experiences and the specific needs emerging from them. As articulated by the Combahee River Collective in the early 1970s, "identity politics" was a politics emerging out of a group's distinctive experiences and expressed the needs it saw as following from those experiences. The Combahee River Collective contrasted this kind of politics to one earlier prevalent on the left where activists fought for supposedly universal ends on behalf of those who lacked the abilities or resources to fight for them themselves:[1]

---

[1] This recognition that different social groups had different perspectives and needs was not completely original with identity political activists. Marxists had long recognized the differences between the perspectives and needs of the working class from that of members of other social classes. However, Marxists had also tended to view the working class as a universal class. It was universal firstly because its members would come to represent the great majority of the population as capitalism developed. Secondly, Marxists held that its

This focusing upon our own oppression is embodied in the concept of identity politics. We believe that the most profound and potentially the most radical politics comes directly out of our own identity, as opposed to working to end somebody else's oppression.[2]

Members of these new political movements believed that focusing on their group's distinct experiences was necessary not only to understand their group's unique needs. It was also necessary to redefine the goals of a just society. Social justice meant not only that women and black people should have access to that which had previously been understood as desirable, but it also meant changes in existing social beliefs about what should count as desirable. One of the slogans of the Women's Liberation Movement expressed this point in the following way: "Women who strive to be equal to men lack ambition."

"Identity politics" generated strong and diverse reactions across the political spectrum. Those who supported it believed that a new day was dawning in terms of sex roles and race relations. Others viewed it very differently. Conservatives attacked identity politics as too "radical," labeling those associated with it as "extremist." Some conservative critics of feminism distinguished between a feminism that stressed women's equality with men, and a "gender feminism" that emphasized women's unique experiences and needs. While claiming to support the former, these critics attacked the latter.[3] But, even among many of those on the left and among more moderate thinkers, identity politics was sharply criticized. Leftists sometimes credited identity politics with causing the left to dwindle in effectiveness from the 1960s to the present. They described identity politics as a type of interest group politics, where people who previously had been intent on transforming society as a whole now became concerned with their own limited ends. They argued that while an earlier left aimed at the real, common needs of people for a decent standard of living and political control over their lives, identity politics was a more culturalist, self-oriented politics. More moderate actors also took issue with identity politics' suspicion of universal rights and with many of its radical challenges to the existing social order. For such actors, identity politics

perspectives would alone not be distorted in the ways in which the perspectives of members of other social classes would be distorted. And finally, Marxists believed that the needs of the working class would, at base, represent the needs of humanity as a whole. In short, while Marxists did critique what they saw as the false universalism of bourgeois social thought, Marxists maintained a kind of universalism in their own political views.

[2] "The Combahee River Collective: A Black Feminist Statement," pp. 63–70 in Linda Nicholson, ed., *The Second Wave: A Reader in Feminist Theory* (New York: Routledge, 1997), p. 65.

[3] See Christina Hoff Sommers, *Who Stole Feminism?: How Women Have Betrayed Women* (New York: Simon & Schuster, 1994).

invited tribal forms of identification which courted social division and moral relativism.[4]

Both conservative and more centrist critics sometimes equated the "identity politics" of the post-1960s left with any political struggle where a group promotes its own specific interests. In accord with this understanding of "identity politics," the identity politics of the post-1960s left was viewed as identical to the turn any national, ethnic, or religious group takes when it defines the needs of its own group as paramount over the needs of society as a whole.

Identity politics seems now to be largely dead, or, at minimum, no longer able to command the kind of public attention that it did from the late 1960s through the late 1980s. And not surprisingly, this public diminishment of identity politics is understood in very different terms by different segments of today's population. Among many of those who had been active in its promulgation, and even among some younger activists today, the identity politics of the 1960s, 1970s, and 1980s is seen as a lost nirvana, a social revolution that somehow got prematurely stalled. But among those who had criticized it in the above kinds of ways, this public diminishment is experienced with grateful relief. For these commentators, identity politics represented a wrong turning point in United States history, a turning point that is now best left forgotten.

One premise of this book is that neither of these two responses is justified. Identity politics was not a nirvana. The ideas about identity promoted by identity politics were often misguided. Moreover, proponents of identity politics too frequently generalized the needs of the many from the perspective of the few. But, on the other hand, identity politics caused neither the demise of the left, nor can it simply be equated with an interest group politics. Rather, it represented a serious attempt to reconfigure our understanding of social difference. While some of the ways in which it depicted social identity were limited, it also inaugurated a very useful discussion about identity, a discussion that we continue to need today.

A second premise of this book is that we can best understand this complicated contribution of identity politics by placing it within history. We are now far enough away from the excitement and anger that identity politics generated, to begin to gain some objectivity about the forces that caused it to come into being, that shaped its nature, and that contributed

---

[4] For criticisms from the left and from a more centrist position see respectively, Todd Gitlen, *The Twilight of Common Dreams: Why America Is Wracked by Culture Wars* (New York: Henry Holt and Co., 1995) and Arthur M. Schlesinger, Jr., *The Disuniting of America* (New York: W. W. Norton & Company, 1992).

to its present state. Such a history might help us begin to grasp not only why activists involved with identity politics felt the need to challenge existing beliefs about social identity in the ways that they did, but also why the movements were limited in the ways that they were. This kind of assessment might also help us in better understanding where we need to go today in thinking about social identity.

Thus, this book is centrally historical, and particularly in its first three chapters, is a history of ideas. I want to illuminate the historicity of some of the ideas about social identity that have organized the lives of women and black people in the history of the United States and that motivated activists to challenge those forms of organization and the ideas behind them. Because the intention of this book is to illuminate the prehistory of identity politics, this book will focus on those forms of identity that were central in this politics, that is, on race and sex. I will examine other forms of identity such as religion, nationality, class, etc. only in so far as these relate to the histories of these other two forms of social identity. And while similar phenomena emerged outside of the United States at this point in time, the focus of this book will be primarily on the prehistory of that politics in the United States.

In the opening chapter I focus on one particularly powerful way of thinking about the identities of women and those of African descent that emerged in the middle of the eighteenth century in northern and western Europe and that has played a very important role in United States history. This way of thinking used nature to explain differences between men and women and between blacks and whites, differences that earlier had been explained by other means. While this new turn to nature was theoretically race and gender neutral, in practice, its use was accompanied by a greater degree of naturalization of the identities of women and those of African descent in comparison to those of white men. Because of this difference in the degree of naturalization, the identities of women and those of African descent became perceived in less individualistic and more generalizable ways than those of white men. The identities of members of the former groups were also perceived as less subject to change and modification through the exertion of reason and will. In this chapter I look at some of the ideological mechanisms that made possible this differential degree of naturalization of the identities of members of these groups.

This differential degree of naturalization was pervasive in the United States by the late nineteenth century. Adherence to it was so extensive that even many of those in the United States who began to rebel against existing social arrangements for black people and for women assumed it in their movements against such arrangements. But during the first few decades of the twentieth century, certain groups within the population began to articulate and defend a different stance on social identity, one where human identity was assumed to be more similar among all human beings, with most characterological differences claimed to be individual in nature.

To illuminate the full contours of this new stance, in chapter 2 I turn to the writings of Sigmund Freud. Freud, of course, was Austrian and therefore a focus on his writings takes the narrative of this book outside of the United States. But his work had a strong impact on public consciousness in the United States as well as in other parts of the world. And my focus on Freud is not so much on the specificities of his theoretical contributions as on how his writings reflected broad-based changes in ways of thinking about social identity among intellectuals and academicians across much of Europe and North America.

Particularly, in the development of his ideas we can see tensions between the hold of older, more naturalistically based ways of thinking, and the development of newer ideas about identity. Freud developed many of his core ideas about social identity in a period of time when many intellectuals still adhered to the older, more naturalistically based models. In focusing upon Freud's partial move away from these models and his arguments against those who still more fully adhered to them, we gain a glimpse into some of the key issues that divided proponents and detractors of these changing positions at this moment in time. Secondly, though Freud's move away from these older ways of thinking was only partial, the brilliance of his work reveals many of the important political ramifications of some of the newer ways of thinking. In particular, a focus on his work enables us to see how a rejection of naturalistically based understandings was related to a more socially egalitarian and individualistic understanding of human nature. But, as Freud's writing also illustrates, even to the extent such a rejection was present – which for Freud was not always the case – such a move towards egalitarianism could still be limited by the continued influence of unjustified heirarchical judgments about human behavior, judgments conceptually distinct from but historically associated with that naturalism.

If Freud's work illuminates a particular kind of political alternative to naturalistic understandings of human differences, the work of a different group of United States thinkers slightly later in the century illuminates a different kind of challenge with different political implications. In chapter 3 I focus on certain shifts in the discipline of anthropology in the United States in the period from the 1920s through the 1950s and in particular on the ways Franz Boas, Ruth Benedict, and Margaret Mead helped elaborate a new concept of "culture." This concept explains practices common to members of a group neither by reference to nature nor by reference to individually specific influences of the environment. Instead it allows for the fact that members of a social group may share traits as a result of common environmental conditions. But as a naturalistic model of organizing social identity, and Freud's more individualistic reaction against it, contained political implications, so too did this new concept of "culture" also contain political implications. The new concept of "culture" challenged the hierarchical model of social group differences that had been justified by naturalistic accounts and that were even left in place by a more environmentally individualistic approach.

Both types of challenge to naturalistic explanations became part of the cultural landscape of mid-twentieth-century America. The writings of some of these anthropologists, especially the writings of Benedict and Mead, like the writings of Freud, had wide circulation outside of the academy. Thus, the work of these intellectuals, in conjunction with the contributions of other scholars and writers introducing related ideas, contributed to the availability of alternatives to naturalistic accounts in popular culture. The question, however, is when and why these ideas became used by activists struggling to change existing social arrangements affecting African Americans and women. In chapters 4 and 5 I turn away from a history of ideas and to a history of the social movements engaged with such change. As I argue, structural shifts in the history of the United States caused some groups of women and some groups of African Americans at particular moments in time to turn away from the older naturalistic accounts and towards those ways of thinking about social identity that were exemplified in these intellectual challenges. In these two chapters I focus on these structural shifts to help explain changes in the history of these movements and to explain why each of these alternative ways of thinking about social identity found certain groups of adherents at certain moments in time. These kinds of stories will provide us with an understanding of why identity politics emerged when it did and what issues around identity this politics was created to address. These stories will also give us some insights as to why some aspects of identity politics and not others have been able to survive into the present.

In the epilogue I elaborate on this last issue, focusing on the legacy of identity politics in the early twenty-first century. Identity politics caused many to recognize the importance of social identity without supplying acceptable means for conceptualizing this type of identity. One legacy of identity politics has been, in fact, a very extensive recognition in social thinking about the importance of societal differences in affecting people's attitudes and people's lives. This recognition is manifest in a variety of ways, from increased attention to "the gender gap" in politics and the growth of such organizations as "Emily's List," to the expansion of cable television stations that specifically target black, women, and gay and lesbian audiences; and to an educational system focused as much as ever on "multiculturalism." Such phenomena continue to remind us of the importance of social difference. However, we still are not quite sure about how to think about such difference. Rather, we tend to oscillate between an early twentieth-century model that proclaims that "we are all just individuals" and a model that explains social differences in overly homogeneous ways. In the epilogue, I suggest some ways of thinking about social identity that may help us get beyond both of these alternatives and thus better approach societal problems connected to social difference.

As the reader can conclude from the above, this is not a typical kind of history. This study covers a broader sweep of time and a more diverse type of subject matter than is covered by many, more academic histories. While there are many dangers to this kind of broad-based approach, I hope it will enable us to focus on some of the large shifts in ways of thought and in political movements that more focused narratives do not as easily allow. In particular, I hope that it gives us a more historical sense of why identity politics emerged when it did and a degree of insight into some of the conundrums about social identity that we still face today.

1   The politics of identity: race and sex before the twentieth century

In contemporary usage, the categories of "race" and "sex" share a common, curious feature. On the one hand, these appear as neutral categories: "natural" ways of organizing the human race. Thus, theoretically, everyone belongs to some race or another; everyone has a "sex." But, on the other hand, when examined more closely, the neutrality of the social organizing function of these categories dissipates. White men and women do not seem to belong to a "race" in quite the same ways as black men and women do. Similarly, men as a group are not defined by their status as men in quite the same ways as women as a group are. For both black people and women, their racial and sexual status appears to provide a richer, more elaborate content to their social identities than do the categories of "white" and "male" provide to white people and women. Generalizations about black people qua black and women qua women abound; many fewer such generalizations about white people qua white and men qua men can be found in our social lexicon.

In this chapter I want to focus on the evolution of the social categories of race and of sex from the late eighteenth to the late nineteenth century in western Europe and North America. As I will argue, this curious feature in contemporary understandings of these two forms of social categorization in the west has its roots in this period. At this time and place, science was emerging as a powerful tool for providing answers to questions about why the natural and social worlds were as they were. Consequently, scientists began to elaborate frameworks that accounted for the social divisions that were readily apparent in everyday life. These frameworks, because created by science, possessed an aura of objectivity and neutrality. The distinctions scientists described seemed distinctions independent of evaluative judgment and applicable to all.

But, the social distinctions that scientists described were distinctions already deeply enmeshed in evaluative judgments, in judgments about differences between women and men and blacks and whites and about the proper social functions of all. Science not only provided a neutral gloss to these judgments but, in taking over the job of explaining such distinctions, employed nature as the means to justify such judgments. In short, nature came to occupy a role previously occupied by other sources, such as the Bible, in serving as the reason why existing divisions of social life had to be as they were.

But, existing judgments about divisions of social life possessed a particular bias. They were very much about social exclusion, particularly about excluding women as a group from non-domestic spaces and about excluding black men and women from political and civic spaces occupied by whites. But this meant that nature had to do heavy work in elaborating the identities of women and black people. The categories of female and black had to be descriptively rich, and since these categories were understood as categories of nature, this meant that they had to be descriptively rich in naturalistic terms. The categories of white and male, since not required to do as much exclusionary work, could be thinner in natural content and more easily brushed aside in favor of other identities, such as being American or a wage earner, in providing more elaborated content to the identities of white males. Such forms of self-description as wage earner or American, since not linked to nature in the same ways as were race and sex, enabled white men to think of their own identities more in terms of choice or accomplishment. In short, while nature now determined who all of us were, for some of us it determined this more extensively than for others.

The above points suggest that the histories of the male/female distinction and of race cannot be told as isolated histories. These forms of social categorization evolved in complex interplay with a host of other forms of categorization, some metaphysical, such as between nature and choice, and some political, such as between citizen and not citizen. In this chapter I hope to map out some aspects of this complex interplay between the development of these two forms of social categorization and the development of other forms of categorization over this period. I do so firstly as a means for giving us some insight into the curious ways in which we use these two forms of social categorization today. But also, in better understanding how these two categories came to function by the late nineteenth century, we are better equipped to understand why many of the twentieth-century struggles against existing boundaries took the forms that they did.

To some extent, the stories of the categories of race and of sex from the late eighteenth to the late nineteenth century share overlapping features. To some extent, however, the stories of these forms of categorization diverge. Because of the remarkable degree of overlap in these stories in this period, I am dealing with both as part of the same chapter. But because of the divergence in many of the specifics of these two stories,

I need also to deal with these two histories in different sections. Let me begin by first focusing on the category of race.

Race, nature, and nation

As many scholars have pointed out, our modern understanding of "race" arose during the latter part of the eighteenth century. At this point in time, "race" came to mean a division of the human species into a small number of groups distinguished from each other by observable physical differences. The word "race" had originally entered western languages during the sixteenth and seventeenth centuries when it referred to a more narrow sense of ancestry, that of a particular family line:

Between the expulsion of the Jews and Moors from Spain and the landing of the first Negro in the North American colonies in 1619, the word "race" entered Western languages. It originally had a multiplicity of meanings that mostly related to running, mathematical or astrological lines, millstreams, ships' wakes, marks and courses. The word also denoted being of good, noble, and pure lineage, and in Christian Europe directly related to membership in an ancient and exclusive noble order of kings and bishops and to a particular time sequence (*cursus*) that had its authority (*auctoritas*) and origin (*origino*) in a historical past stretching back to Rome. This order was at the outset resistant to any counterclaim from Trojan, Saxon, Arthurian, Celtic, Gallic, Frankish, Jewish, and Moorish sources, which were regarded as mere legends and fables.[1]

But from the sixteenth to the late eighteenth century, the term "race" gradually came to refer to larger segments of the world's population.[2] By the late eighteenth century, it had come to mean a division of the human population reflective of major geographical divisions, roughly correlated with differences in physical appearance. Late eighteenth-century natural philosophers differed among themselves about which divisions and differences were significant. Thus, they differed in terms of how many "races" there were and how they were to be labeled.[3] However, despite such

---

[1] Ivan Hannaford, *Race: The History of an Idea in the West* (Baltimore: The Johns Hopkins University Press, 1996), p. 147. Michael Banton claims that the word "race" first entered the English language in 1508 in the poem *The Dance of the Sevin Deadly Sins* by the Scotsman, William Dunbar. Banton emphasizes the centrality of the idea of lineage to sixteenth-, seventeenth-, and eighteenth-century usages of the term. See Michael Banton, *Racial Theories* (Cambridge University Press, 1987), pp. 1–27 and p. 17 for the reference to Dunbar's poem.

[2] Nicholas Hudson, "From 'Nation' to 'Race': The Origin of Racial Classification in Eighteenth-Century Thought," pp. 247–64 in *Eighteenth Century Studies* 29, no. 3 (1996), p. 248.

[3] Philip Nicholson, *Who Do We Think We Are: Race and Nation in the Modern World* (New York: Sharpe, 1999), pp. 113–14.

differences in specifics, this new idea of race became widespread enough through the early nineteenth century so as to begin to appear in French and English dictionaries by the middle of this century.[4]

These new forms of racial classification emerged in a context where Europeans already viewed certain segments of the world's population as inferior to themselves. Thus, long before the late eighteenth century, Europeans viewed Native Americans and Africans as "savage" and thus lesser human beings than they. However, earlier beliefs about inferiority were centered less on the idea of physical differences than later became the case. Philip Nicholson notes that as late as 1656 an African American woman was granted freedom from slavery by a Virginia court on the grounds that she was a Christian. Later rulings made religious status immaterial.[5] Winthrop Jordan makes a related point when he claims that it was not just the physical differences between Africans and Europeans that, from a European perspective, initially justified African slavery. That Africans were, according to Europeans, "heathens," that their social practices were seen as strange and "primitive," and that their physical characteristics were also different, made it possible for Europeans to justify slavery for Africans, as well as to a lesser extent for Native Americans, in ways they appeared never able to justify it for white Christians with more similar social customs.[6] And the rationale for such differential evaluations could easily be found independent of appeals to physical differences. Many Europeans, invoking the Bible, described people from Africa as more intensely degenerate products of humanity's decline from Adam and Eve than Christian Europeans.[7] Other, more "enlightened," theorists invoked the inferiority of cultural resources.[8]

But, during the eighteenth and nineteenth centuries, as "the book of nature" expanded its credibility as a source of explanation, so were physical differences more frequently employed, firstly as criteria for differentiating groups, and then later, particularly by the mid nineteenth century, as signals of the deep-seated nature of such differentiations.

This change in the use of physical differences is reflected in the growing adoption of the doctrine of polygenism over monogenism.

[4] Hudson, "From 'Nation' to 'Race,'" p. 247.
[5] Nicholson, *Who Do We Think We Are*, p. 76.
[6] Winthrop Jordan, *White Over Black: American Attitudes Toward the Negro, 1550–1812* (Chapel Hill, N.C.: University of North Carolina Press, 1968), pp. 217–18.
[7] Stephen Jay Gould, *The Mismeasure of Man* (New York and London: W. W. Norton & Company, 1996), p. 71.
[8] Gould points to Benjamin Franklin as one believing in the importance of culture. He notes, however, that such an "enlightened" attitude did not in Franklin's case, as it did not in many others, entail a belief in racial equality. *Ibid.* p. 64.

Eighteenth-century monogenists thought of humans as divided into different groups, with each group marked by differences in physical characteristics. But, for monogenists, the physical characteristics that separated
human beings, like other differences, were understood as the result of
relatively transient phenomena, such as shifts in climate, or of people's
actions. Consequently, physiological racial designations were seen as
fluid. Thus some natural philosophers, such as the late eighteenth-century
naturalist, Johann Friedrich Blumenbach, while employing physical features to differentiate racial groups, also stressed the transient nature of
physical differences as well as the commonalities among humans and the
differences between all humans and animals.[9]

However, during the nineteenth century, polygenism gained increasing
support. Polygenists claimed that the physiological characteristics that
constituted racial differences were not superficial and transient but deep
and abiding, of the same order of depth as those which separated human
beings from animals. To depict such physiological differences as deep and
abiding, polygenists invoked God and the idea of an original, multiple
creation. The idea of an original, multiple creation suggested that beneath
the observable differences that humans could see was a natural organization or order, established by God. This underlying natural order was the
cause as to why some traits were either not present or present only in
transient form among some, and, in contrast, commonly found, and
found together, among others.

But, as Nancy Stepan notes, this kind of position entailed an important
shift in the idea of human "nature." It entailed a shift from a view where
biology was thought of as epiphenomenal to accidents of culture or
climate to one where culture became epiphenomenal to biology:

In short, a shift had occurred in which culture and the social behavior of man
became epiphenomena of biology. Races were no longer thought of as the superficial and changeable products of climate and civilization, as the first monogenists
had claimed, but stable and essential entities which caused or prevented the
flowering of civilised behaviour.[10]

---

[9] Nancy Stepan, *The Idea of Race in Science: Great Britain 1800–1960* (Hamden, Conn.:
Archon, 1982), p. 9. As Richard Popkin points out, for Blumenbach also, as for other
theorists of the time, such as Lord Kames, Oliver Goldsmith, and Count Buffon, the
differences that did exist could be accounted for, and perhaps overcome, by changing
people's environments. See Richard Popkin, "The Philosophical Basis of Racism,"
pp. 245–62 in Harold E. Pagliaro, ed., *Racism in the Eighteenth Century* (Cleveland and
London: The Press of Case Western University, 1973), p. 251.

[10] Stepan, *The Idea of Race in Science*, p. 4. Ludmilla Jordanova makes a similar point about
the emergence of a new foundational view of nature in relation to gender in *Sexual Visions:
Images of Gender in Science and Medicine Between the Eighteenth and Twentieth Centuries*
(Madison, Wis.: University of Wisconsin Press, 1989), pp. 27–28.

This further elaboration of race contained, however, some discrepancies with widely held views about human beings. Because it asserted that race generates a range of human differences, from differences in physical appearance to differences in behavior, and because it implied that all of these differences are rooted in God-given differences in underlying human "natures," it appeared to deny the possibility of free choice to human beings, that is, choice that is the result of rational thought. It also denied the attribution of individuality to human beings.

Even before the nineteenth century, some intellectuals had become aware of such problems in classifying human beings like plants or animals. Both the late seventeenth-century philosopher, Leibniz, and the mid-eighteenth-century theorist, Buffon, argued against certain forms of naturalistic classification precisely on these grounds. Buffon himself argued for a dynamic understanding of "race" as a way to overcome such problems.[11]

But as the idea of racial differences as deep and abiding became more widely adopted, others reconciled such inconsistencies in different, less intellectually vigorous ways. One common nineteenth-century strategy was to portray the different racial classifications as themselves differing in natural content. Thus, while all racial categories were "natural," some of these linked human beings more closely to nature than did others. Placing "race" within nature, in effect, came to mean depicting some groups of humans as more "natural" than others.

A particularly important idea in making possible this differential deployment of race was that of a "great chain of being." This idea, while an old one in European thought, was first revived by early eighteenth-century naturalists as a way to place humanity as a whole within nature.[12] This idea enabled naturalists to tie human beings to the rest of nature by showing how humans shared some characteristics with other natural phenomena. These naturalists could assert the "naturality" of human beings while also asserting the privileged position of human beings as the highest form of "nature." This revived use built upon older Catholic cosmological beliefs that placed human beings halfway between nature and angels, sharing their bodies with nature but their souls with that which transcended nature.

This idea of a great chain of being is not inherently racial. But, when combined with racial thinking, it added a powerful conceptual support to

---

[11] Hudson, "From 'Nation' to 'Race,'" pp. 252–55.

[12] Stepan, *The Idea of Race in Science*, p. 6. Stepan points to this revival by referencing the historian of this idea, Arthur Lovejoy, author of *The Great Chain of Being: A Study of the History of an Idea* (Cambridge, Mass.: Harvard University Press, 1936).

such thought. If all of nature could be situated along a great chain of being, then why could not the different types of human beings be understood as occupying different places on such a chain? Many late eighteenth- and early nineteenth-century naturalists rejected this addition to racial thought, claiming that the idea of a great chain of being provided a poor framework for understanding and classifying natural phenomena.[13] But, despite the rejection of this way of thinking by many naturalists of the late eighteenth and early nineteenth century, the idea of a great chain of being reemerged to occupy a central role in racial science by the middle of the nineteenth century.

As Nancy Stepan points out, the appeal of this idea lay not only in politics. The idea of the great chain stressed the gradual nature of differences among natural phenomena. To claim, on the contrary, that human beings shared more in common with each other than human beings did with animals seemed to suggest that a great gulf separated human beings from animals. But gradualism was to be found everywhere in the natural world. Denying gradualism seemed also to mean denying naturalism.[14] And when Darwinian theory drew adherents in the late nineteenth century, and contributed towards moving the study of nature away from description and towards explanation, the idea of a gradual evolutionary ascent of nature became even more compelling. Even today, in much popular thought, evolutionary theory is linked with the idea of a hierarchical ordering within nature, with humans "at the top" and the rest of nature existing in a descending order of complexity.

A curious feature of this idea of a great chain of being, and of its elaboration in Darwinian theory even continuing into the present, is that while it roots humanity within nature, it does so by illuminating the connections that human beings share with those "below" them; there are no natural phenomena deemed higher than human beings. This means that if different types of human beings are placed on the chain, some types of human beings end up closer to "nature" than others. Those who are placed at the top of the chain get to occupy a kind of bridge position between lower forms of nature and that which goes beyond nature. However, those at the bottom are more completely explained by their "naturalistic" classification.

This is how the idea of the great chain of being functioned within nineteenth-century racial science. Whites, because at the top of the chain, were understood as both a part of nature and as not part of it. While sharing certain bodily features with other types of human beings,

---

[13] Stepan, *The Idea of Race in Science*, pp. 9–12.   [14] *Ibid.* pp. 12–13.

whites also displayed attributes that allowed for rationality, individuality, and choice. Non-whites, on the other hand, and Africans in particular, were portrayed as a human type midway between whites and those forms of animal just below humans, specifically, apes and monkeys. Denied those attributes that placed whites outside of nature, blacks were more thoroughly described by their natural classification than were whites.

This analytic framework was so conceptually appealing that much time and energy went into "proving" its truth. All manners of measurements were developed to establish that whites stood "higher" than blacks and that blacks stood midway between whites and other animals on a great chain of being. Those features measured included, among others, those of skull size, skull shape, and facial angle. As many commentators have pointed out, these studies reveal a multitude of scientific flaws. These flaws reveal the power of widely shared assumptions to skew the use of evidence. As Stephen Jay Gould concludes from his study of the work of Paul Broca:

Conclusions came first and Broca's conclusions were the shared assumptions of most successful white males during his time – themselves on top by the good fortune of nature, and women, blacks, and poor people below. His facts were reliable (unlike Morton's), but they were gathered selectively and then manipulated unconsciously in the service of prior conclusions. By this route, the conclusions achieved not only the blessing of science, but the prestige of numbers. Broca and his school used facts as illustration, not as constraining documents. They began with conclusions, peered through their facts, and came back in a circle to the same conclusions.[15]

Such studies thus "proved" intellectually what those who conducted them had already assumed – that some races were closer to nature than others.

But if we wish to understand how the differential deployment of race operated in even more widespread ways, we need to focus on mental processes that functioned in even less explicit ways. Here, I would suggest that, for whites, what made race, and thus nature, less determinative of their own identities, had also to do with differences in the role racial identity played in their own self-understandings in comparison with the role it played in their understandings of African Americans. From the perspective of whites, race served to differentiate blacks from themselves. This meant that from the perspective of whites, race was the most interesting and important aspect about blacks; for whites, race encompassed

---

[15] Gould, *The Mismeasure of Man*, p. 117. For ways in which politics similarly affected the observations and conclusions of scientists in their studies of women's closer associations with nature, see Cynthia Eagle Russett, *Sexual Science: The Victorian Construction of Womanhood* (Cambridge, Mass. and London: Harvard University Press, 1989), pp. 36–39.

the identities of blacks. But whites were not only concerned about their relationships with blacks; they were also concerned about their relationships with each other. In the period of the late eighteenth and nineteenth centuries, when race was being elaborated as a naturally defining form of identity, another social category, that of national identity, was changing its nature as the means by which many Europeans were coming to understand certain important relationships with each other. As a consequence of the spread of social contract theory, such Europeans were coming to understand national identity less as a consequence of regional ancestral legacy and more as a consequence of thought and will. Thus, while whites were increasingly defining blacks through categories of nature, many were coming to define themselves in relation to each other through the language of reason and choice.

Whatever the role of social contract theory in changing understandings of national identity in Europe in the late eighteenth century, in the United States at this time its impact is quite clear. The language of this theory is embedded in the founding documents of the nation. This meant that national identity became identified with popular sovereignty, with the idea of government of and by the people. National identity consequently became something which added to one's sense of being a rational, thoughtful human being, one capable of making informed decisions for which one could be held accountable.

But, in the late eighteenth century in the United States, as some were gaining this type of a sense of national identity, others were being denied any sense of national identity, either in terms of regional ancestry or in terms of providing evidence of one's reason and will. As Nicholas Hudson points out, one consequence of African enslavement, both in the colonies and in the newly formed United States, was to eliminate from the consciousness of those doing the enslavement any sense of the national identities of those being enslaved. While there was some recognition among planters of differences in place of origin, "in general, however, the process of shipping and marketing slaves literally stripped the signs of national difference from the bodies of Africans."[16]

Replacing nationality as an identity signifier for slaves was race. And when the United States became a nation, creating a new national identity for some, those now racialized as black were denied this identity because of their racial status. In 1790, the US Congress limited naturalization to "free white persons."[17] In 1792, when Congress established a national

---

[16] Hudson, "From 'Nation' to 'Race,'" p. 251.
[17] Matthew Frye Jacobson, *Whiteness of a Different Color: European Immigrants and the Alchemy of Race* (Cambridge, Mass. and London: Harvard University Press, 1998), p. 25.

militia, the participants of this militia were defined as "each and every free able-bodied white male citizen of the respective states."[18] In such early laws, it is quite clear that a large part of the meaning of citizenship is "not black."

That a slave could not be a citizen was self-evident to those who established the early republic. But, as Matthew Jacobson points out, the more telling question was the citizenship status of freed blacks. And in late eighteenth- and early nineteenth-century debates about the possible abolition of slavery, few assumed that such abolition would entail the integration of freed blacks into US society as equal citizens with whites. The common assumption was that blacks would disappear, for some, as a consequence of the loss of their distinctive physiology through long-term exposure to a temperate climate, or for many, as a consequence of deportation and colonization elsewhere.[19] Most early nineteenth-century politicians who opposed slavery combined this opposition with support for colonization.[20] In a famous, and widely quoted debate with Stephen Douglas in 1858, Lincoln denied allegiance to the view that blacks and whites could live in political equality with each other.[21]

Lincoln's prewar disbelief in the possibility of political equality between blacks and whites was widespread in the north. A few northern states provided suffrage to blacks, but by 1840, 93 percent of northern blacks were effectively denied the vote.[22] Even when blacks were not denied the vote, their citizenship rights were denied in other ways. By 1860, in all states but Massachusetts, blacks could not be jurors.[23]

One might question how much the adoption of the Fourteenth and Fifteenth Amendments to the Constitution following the Civil War provides evidence of a great shift in attitude among northern whites towards the idea of black citizenship rights. A skeptical answer to this question is suggested by the north's lack of concern with the enforcement of such rights in the south in the post-reconstruction era. That lack of concern gives credence to such claims as George Fredrickson's that the very adoption of these amendments had more to do with the political needs of the north in the immediate period following the Civil War, than it had to

---

[18] *Ibid.* p. 25.   [19] *Ibid.* p. 28.

[20] David Brian Davis, *Inhuman Bondage: The Rise and Fall of Slavery in the New World* (Oxford University Press, 2006), p. 256.

[21] Thomas F. Gossett, *Race: The History of an Idea in America* (Dallas, Tex.: Southern Methodist University Press, 1963), p. 254.

[22] Michael Goldfield, *The Color of Politics: Race and the Mainsprings of American Politics* (New York: The New Press, 1997), p. 90.

[23] *Ibid.* p. 91.

do with a change in attitude among northern whites about the fitness of black people for US citizenship.[24]

One cannot, however, give definitive answers about the "citizenship" status of blacks in the post-Civil War period without recognizing the complexities of what "citizenship" means. Legally, the Fourteenth and Fifteenth Amendments established citizenship rights for black people. But this did not mean that white people, in the north or south, understood black people to be truly Americans, able to participate in public life in the same kinds of ways as whites. The 1896 Supreme Court ruling establishing the acceptability of "separate but equal" provides evidence that at least through the late nineteenth century, a very powerful attitude among whites was that blacks were members of the body politic only in very circumscribed ways.

The limits of this membership are further indicated by the continued ways in which whites labeled blacks. During the last decades of the nineteenth century, while some blacks were beginning to adopt versions of the label "African American" or "Afra American" to describe themselves, whites continued to use words that emphasized racial characteristics.[25] The persistent use by whites of such labels as "colored" or "negro" with a small "n" put emphasis upon the physiological characteristics of those who were not white. It continued to make nature, not nation, the defining aspect of identity for some.

In sum, racial identity and national identity in the United States context were not unrelated concepts.[26] Possessing a particular form of racial

---

[24] George Fredrickson, *The Black Image in the White Mind: The Debate on Afro-American Character and Destiny, 1817–1914* (New York: Harper and Row, 1971), p. 183.

[25] Thus, for example, Sterling Stuckey claims: "From the late 1880s down to the opening years of the new century, the term Afro-American, frequently used, easily competed with Negro as the most popular designation for black people. Especially then, Afro-American began appearing in the titles of black organizations," in *Slave Culture: Nationalist Theory and the Foundations of Black America* (New York and Oxford: Oxford University Press, 1987), p. 239. Stuckey notes in a footnote to the above that the most prominent organization bearing the phrase "Afro-American" was the Afro-American League founded in 1890. Stuckey in turn references Herbert Aptheker, ed., *A Documentary History of the Negro People in the United States* (New York: Citadel Press, 1964 [1951]), Vol. II, p. 679.

[26] Philip Nicholson argues that these concepts have never been unrelated, that the concepts of nation and race emerged and have changed always in relationship with each other. Nicholson uses the metaphor of a double helix to describe this interdependence. By this metaphor, Nicholson suggests not only that these concepts have often existed in opposition to each other, but that even when they have come together – as in the case of Germany in the twentieth century – the meaning of one establishes the meaning of the other. Nicholson adds to this stress on the conceptual interdependence of race and nation, an emphasis on the economic factors that form many of the key fibers of the double helix. As the above story of the "denationalization" of Native Americans and Africans suggests, those who lost their national identities in the New World did so as part of a process by which they also lost claims to land, to other natural resources, and to their selfhood. Thus,

identity meant that one could *not* possess a national identity. While the category of "white" easily coexisted with "American" – indeed so over-lapped with the latter category as to lose much of the natural content it might otherwise possess – the category of "black" made national identity impossible. To be white was to be American, that is to be, at least as a consequence of one's racial identity, able to create through reason and will the laws which governed one. To be black, however, was to be a creature of nature, and thus governed by laws not of one's own, or of any human's creation.

The above discussion provides clues about the kinds of cultural strug-gles that black people needed to wage in the late nineteenth and early twentieth century. Black people needed to accomplish two tasks. Firstly, they needed to "de-racialize" themselves. This meant that they had to minimize that view of who they were that linked physiology with a distinc-tive grouping of mental and behavioral traits. They had to become "indi-viduals" in the same kinds of ways that white people were. But secondly, and linked with this first task, was that they needed to become "Americans." They needed to make that aspect of identity which was linked in the United States with pride, choice, and accomplishment a more central aspect of how white people understood who they were. As we will see in a later chapter, these tasks were more easily attainable for some groups of blacks than others. And these differences led to important class tensions within African American politics over the course of the twentieth century. But before we begin to focus on the twentieth century, let us continue our focus on the pre-twentieth-century period by turning our attention now to the category of sex.

Sex, nature, and the family

In the above I have argued that two types of mechanism operated to make "race" more determinative of the identities of black people than of whites: (1) intellectual/scientific frameworks that differentiated blacks from whites in terms of their closeness to nature, and (2) less conscious mech-anisms that made "race" less emotionally salient for whites in relation to other forms of identity and more central for blacks from the perspective of whites. But I would claim that very similar mechanisms operated in the use of the category of "sex" in the period of the late eighteenth through the

Nicholson underlines the point that the story of the interlocking history of race and nation is not an abstract story of changes in concepts, but is grounded in the real material transfer of bodies and wealth. Ideas about membership in racial groups or nation-states only provided the psychological and legal justification for such transfers of bodies and wealth. See Nicholson, *Who Do We Think We Are*, pp. 7–8.

late nineteenth century. Here also, as science was emerging as an important tool for making sense of the social world, so science became employed in ways that situated women as a group closer to nature than men.[27] But in addition, as was the case with race, other more general societal changes also functioned to differentially associate women's and men's identities with nature in less explicit intellectual ways. Social structural changes occurring in this period led to changes in the meaning and centrality of social roles, with those becoming more central to the identities of women – particularly that of mother – and those becoming more central to the identities of men – particularly that of wage earner – themselves differentially associated with nature. As with "race," so with "sex," while everyone was assigned a "sex," some became associated with their "sex" more intensively than others.

Beginning with the role of science in establishing women's closer connection to nature, we need first to acknowledge the increasing position of physiology as foundational. As with race, the late eighteenth-century science of sex did not inaugurate a view of women as inferior to men; that thesis had been well argued throughout western history. Aristotle's arguments about the inferiority of material to efficient causes had long been used to establish the point.[28] Biblical references to Eve's creation out of the rib of Adam established the same claim. But already apparent in seventeenth-century natural law theory, and elaborated in the Enlightenment celebration of science, was a developing focus on natural phenomena to explain why things were as they were, including why differences in male and female behaviors were as they were. Whereas the early seventeenth-century writer, Sir Robert Filmer, would invoke the Bible to ground claims about the roles of women and men within the family, the more modern and enlightened natural law theorist, John Locke, would invoke differences between women's and men's bodies to do the same.[29] And as the authority of natural scientific observation increased during the course of the eighteenth and nineteenth centuries, so did claims about the role of the body become more elaborate and a larger part of ordinary discourse. Thus, Rosalind Rosenberg points out that prior to the middle

[27] The category of woman, of course, intersects with other categories of identity, such as racial ones. In the following we will see how this general categorization was sometimes modified to excuse white, urban, middle-class women. For black women, however, this general categorization concurred rather than conflicted with a similar hypernaturalization that came with being categorized as black.

[28] Thomas Laqueur, *Making Sex: Body and Gender from the Greeks to Freud* (Cambridge, Mass. and London: Harvard University Press, 1990), pp. 151–52.

[29] See my discussion of Filmer and Locke in Linda Nicholson, *Gender and History: The Limits of Social Theory in the Age of the Family* (New York: Columbia University Press, 1986), pp. 133–66.

of the nineteenth century, while most physicians credited the uterus with some power over women's lives, this belief was mitigated by beliefs about the greater power of personal and divine will. By the latter part of the nineteenth century, the relative weight of these two kinds of beliefs had shifted. Exemplary of this shift are differences in the advice doctors gave to pregnant women about how to produce healthy children:

> Early nineteenth-century medical authorities urged pregnant women to think sweet thoughts and adopt a pious manner to insure that they would remain healthy and that their unborn children would develop well. By the latter part of the ninetenth century, however, doctors were minimizing the power of free will to affect physical development ... This significant change in thinking, shifting medical and hereditarian responsibility from human and divine actors to impersonal and largely uncontrollable biological forces, reflected the growing appreciation among doctors, as well as intellectuals, of how remote could be the determinants of individual behavior.[30]

In sum, as natural scientists gradually turned from texts such as Aristotle and the Bible, and away from beliefs in the power of divine and personal will, the evidence from the body took on a growing importance in explaining differences between women and men. This meant that in the case of sex, as in the case of race, physiology emerged as the basis of the male/female distinction.

The question in regard to sex, as with race, though, was how this greater emphasis on the body functioned to explain and thus police behavior for women in more extensive ways than it did for men. The first point that needs emphasis here is that with sex, in distinction from race, there existed no simple analogy of women as a group with nature and men as a group with civilization. Complicating factors were the two issues of race and social class. As many US historians have noted, a significant cultural distinction operating in this period was that between the "lady" and the rest of the female population. A "lady" was distinguished from others of her sex for a variety of reasons, but predominant among them was her lack of animality. The newly urban, white, middle-class wife and mother was distinguished from black, working-class, and rural members of her sex by such factors as her distance from physical labor, her diminished need to bear a multitude of children, and by a supposed lesser susceptibility to the power of sexual desire. Moreover, this lesser susceptibility to the power of sexual desire and an alleged superior moral and aesthetic sensibility distinguished her not only from black, rural, and working-class women, but

---

[30] Rosalind Rosenberg, *Beyond Separate Spheres: Intellectual Roots of Modern Feminism* (New Haven and London: Yale University Press, 1982), p. 6.

also from men, both those of other races and social classes as well as from her own.

However, an interesting aspect of the concept of "lady" was how it was used to erase the otherwise strongly naturalistic associations of "woman."[31] The naturalization of this latter concept was established in complex ways. On the one hand, there were the scientific accounts that, as with "black," served to intellectually establish the closer association of "women" to nature than man. One such late nineteenth-century intellectual framework that supported this kind of claim was provided by the elaboration of evolutionary principles into recapitulation theory, the theory that claimed that all living organisms recapitulated in their own individual development the history of evolution. Recapitulation theory was closely linked with the German Darwinian Ernst Haeckel, who introduced the well-known phrase that "ontogeny recapitulates phylogeny."[32] That women as a whole represented a phase of evolutionary development that men had passed beyond was argued by highlighting the features that women shared with children and adolescents. Thus women's smaller and narrower skulls, shorter extremities, and longer trunks were physical facts that were highlighted to make the analogy; women's supposed greater impulsiveness, timidity, emotionality, deficiencies in abstract reasoning, and weakness of will were psychological indicators used to make the same analogy.[33] That recapitulation theory sometimes led scientists to make claims about women that ran counter to accepted stereotypes of Victorian womanhood points to the occasional lack of consistency in scientific constructions of Victorian womanhood:

Though most of the scientific description of feminine peculiarities reads like a transcription of familiar Victorian wisdom, this was not always the case. To anyone acquainted with the nineteenth century stereotype of exquisitely sensitive, vaporous womanhood, one of the more startling assertions in the literature was that of woman's physical insensibility relative to man. In this once again women resembled primitive peoples.[34]

Apart from recapitulation theory, evolutionary theory in general was widely used to explain sexual differences. And one frequently cited claim elaborated from evolutionary theory was that men's more evolved state

---

[31] When 1960s feminists began using the word "woman" as the opposite of "man," some speakers had trouble abandoning "lady" for "woman." My sense is that this difficulty in part stemmed from the naturalistic associations "woman" still held for these speakers.

[32] Russett, *Sexual Science*, p. 50.

[33] *Ibid.* p. 56. See also Nancy Leys Stepan, "Race and Gender: The Role of Analogy in Science," pp. 38–57 in David Theo Goldberg, ed., *Anatomy of Racism* (Minneapolis: University of Minnesota Press, 1990), pp. 39–40.

[34] Russett, *Sexual Science*, p. 56.

caused a greater variability among men than among women. This claim about the greater variability of men was widely accepted in late nineteenth-century sexual science, being advanced by such writers as Charles Darwin, Havelock Ellis, W. K. Brooks, and even by such feminist authors as Charlotte Perkins Gilman and Anna Garlin Spencer.[35] Ellis elaborated Darwin's initial claim about physical variability to include mental characteristics, using the supposed greater variability of men to explain why there existed so few women geniuses; Gilman and Spencer accepted this elaboration.[36] This particular claim directly deals with one of the problems entailed by using nature to explain racial or sexual differences – that such uses end up denying the individuality of white men as much as they deny the individuality of blacks and women. By claiming that nature itself is the cause of the greater individuality of white men, one gains the authority of nature without assuming the liabilities that appeals to nature impart.

While evolutionary theory provided one intellectual framework for placing women closer to nature than men, other types of frameworks achieved similar ends. One could begin, as many did, with more of a "separate but equal" way of thinking about men and women's "natures" and still end up with explanations that naturalized women more than men. One author of particular influence who illustrates this point is Edward Clarke in his widely read book, *Sex in Education; or A Fair Chance for the Girls*.[37] Clarke did not make claims about women's inherent inferior mental abilities. Instead he began his book with an explicit statement about the equality of the sexes:

Neither is there any such thing as inferiority or superiority in this matter. Man is not superior to woman, nor woman to man. The relation of the sexes is one of equality, not of better and worse, or of higher and lower. By this it is not intended to say that the sexes are the same. They are different, widely different from each other, and so different that each can do, in certain directions, what the other cannot.[38]

But the difference that Clarke stresses is a difference that has consequences for women's education as serious as any entailed by claims about women's inferiority. Clarke argues that the human body is dominated by three systems: the digestive, the nervous, and the reproductive. He argues that while the first two of these is the same for women as for men, the third is vastly different.[39] Of particular relevance for women's education, is that

---

[35] *Ibid.* pp. 92–97.   [36] *Ibid.* pp. 96–97.
[37] Edward H. Clarke, MD, *Sex in Education; or A Fair Chance for the Girls* (Boston: James R. Osgood and Company, 1873; reprinted in 1972 in New York by Arno Press and The New York Times Press in the series, Medicine & Society in America).
[38] *Ibid.* p. 13.   [39] *Ibid.* pp. 32–33.

the female reproductive system makes demands on the female body that the male system does not. These demands are particularly strong on girls between the ages of approximately fourteen to nineteen:

The principle or condition peculiar to the female sex is the management of the catamenial function, which, from the age of fourteen to nineteen, includes the building of the reproductive apparatus. This imposes upon women, and especially upon the young woman, a great care, a corresponding duty, and compensating privileges. There is only a feeble counterpart to it in the male organization ...[40]

Clarke, like many of his time believed that the human body has at its disposal only a certain amount of energy.[41] For girls, if this energy is too much devoted to mental activity when their reproductive systems require it, the female body becomes subject to a wide variety of forms of break-down. On the one hand, their reproductive systems may not properly develop, generating such consequences as painful menstruation and possible infertility. On the other hand their nervous systems may suffer, causing such symptoms as insomnia, "neuralgia," and "hysteria."[42] They may also become more masculine in their skin texture, bone structure, and instinctual responses.[43] Clarke summarizes some of the diverse and terrifying consequences that can ensue:

It has been reserved for our age and country, by its methods of female education, to divest a woman of her chief feminine functions; in others, to produce grave and even fatal disease of the brain and nervous system; in others, to engender torturing derangements and imperfections of the reproductive apparatus that last a lifetime.[44]

Clarke's book is a frightening book. It is sprinkled with case studies which describe young women with serious diseases, some of which end in death. Particularly frightening is Clarke's argument that the kinds of bodily breakdowns he describes do not immediately follow intensive mental activity, but often only appear much later. Thus, the book strongly points to the conclusion that too much higher education for women is a very risky idea. The forcefulness of his argument and the frightening nature of the dangers it raises makes it not surprising that the publication of the book generated widespread attention. Not everyone responded favorably to Clarke's argument. The publication of Clarke's book was followed by the publication of several books critical of his position.[45]

[40] *Ibid.* p. 120.
[41] Russett discusses how the principle of the conservation of energy pervaded much late nineteenth-century sexual science in *Sexual Science*, pp. 104–29.
[42] Clarke, *Sex in Education*, pp. 96–103. [43] *Ibid.* pp. 92–93. [44] *Ibid.* p. 116.
[45] Rosalind Rosenberg lists some of these books, including Julia Ward Howe's edited collection, *Sex and Education: A Reply to Dr. Clarke's "Sex in Education"* (Cambridge,

However, that the argument was considered at least plausible is indicated by its very large sales, and by the fact that some saw the need for a response.[46] That it could stir up such debate suggests that the premises of its argument were not too far outside of the mainstream of late nineteenth-century thought.[47]

One premise of the book that is particularly relevant to the argument of this chapter is the importance given to the female reproductive system in placing constraints on female behavior. Clarke states that the female reproductive system makes demands of girls and women that the male reproductive system does not make of boys and men. Because this is the case, men can use their minds in ways that women cannot. Boys and men, in short, can employ that faculty, the brain, which takes human beings beyond the rest of the natural world, in ways that girls and women cannot. Thus, while Clarke begins with a claim about the equality of the sexes, his argument leads him to naturalize girls and women in the same more extensive ways as did those who began with a more explicit "great chain of being" framework for thinking about women's relation to men.

In my earlier discussion of race, I made the distinction between scientific claims that supported a view of black people as closer to nature than whites, and less conscious ways of thinking that led in similar directions. Clarke's book, while extremely popular for a learned treatise, was still only read by a relatively small part of the population. Yet, one of the central tenets of the book – that women's reproductive systems were more determinative of their identities than were men's reproductive systems – was a tenet not limited to scientific discourse. It was part of ordinary common sense. To understand why this was the case requires that we give some attention to how women's and men's social roles had diverged in significant ways in the course of the nineteenth century.

Since the emergence of women's history in the early 1970s, scholars have devoted much attention to the rise of "separate spheres" as an

Mass.: Roberts Bros, 1874); Anna C. Brackett, *The Education of American Girls* (New York: n.p., 1874); and Eliza Bisbee Duffey, *No Sex in Education: Or, An Equal Chance for Both Girls and Boys* (Philadelphia: Stoddart and Co., 1874). These references are found in Rosenberg, *Beyond Separate Spheres*, pp. 13–14, footnote no. 29.

[46] The numbers and stature of those who supported Clarke are indicated by Rosalind Rosenberg's claim that "At the University of Michigan where women had been studying for only three years [in 1873 when *Sex in Education* was published] it was reported that everyone was reading Clarke's book and that two hundred copies had been sold in one day." Rosenberg also notes that the regents of the University of Wisconsin invoked a Clarke-like argument in 1877 to back up their opposition to coeducation. See Rosenberg, *Beyond Separate Spheres*, p. 12.

[47] That Clarke's position overlapped with many others of his time is illustrated by Charles E. Rosenberg in "The Female Animal: Medical and Biological View of Women," pp. 54–70 in Charles E. Rosenberg, *No Other Gods: On Science and American Social Thought* (Baltimore and London: The Johns Hopkins University Press, 1961, 1962, and 1976).

important aspect of nineteenth-century US history. As many have pointed out, the emergence of an economy more centered in cities and less dominated by agriculture meant the creation of an ideology which construed women as ideally domestic beings and men as workers supporting the family through non-domestic labor. I want to extend this discussion of separate spheres by focusing on some of the identity implications of this new ideology. The idea of "separate spheres" suggested not only a physical separation between the kinds of places where women and men most appropriately labored, but also a distinction between the kinds of people who most appropriately inhabited those spaces. And one set of identity implications that this idea generated was that of women as ideally mothers and men as ideally wage earners. Prior to the emergence of separate spheres, women had, of course, been mothers and men had responsibilities as family providers. But the idea of separate spheres generated some important changes in the meanings of both of these functions. Let me focus first on mothering.

The emergence of separate spheres ideology changed the meaning of mothering by eliding childbearing with childrearing. In all mammalian species, women give birth. And among humans, women are usually responsible for the care and feeding of infants, though sometimes that care and feeding is performed not by the biological mother but by servants, relatives, or other members of the community. But childrearing, in the sense of preparing young children – and particularly young boys – for acceptable participation in adult society, has not always been a female identified activity. In colonial America, this task was largely understood as primarily the responsibility of male heads of the household. Given the dominance of patriarchal family structures, it is not surprising that the important task of providing practical and moral guidance to children – and particularly sons – would be the responsibility of the male head of household. Wives might be expected to assist, but as "helpmeets," their participation in this task would not be different in kind from that which was practiced by the male head of household.[48] While it was assumed that women would give birth and take responsibility for the care of infants, these tasks were viewed as part of women's God-given burden rather than

---

[48] On the implications of seventeenth- and early eighteenth-century US family structures on views of men, women and their roles in parenting, see Ruth Bloch, "American Feminine Ideals in Transition: The Rise of the Moral Mother, 1785–1815," in *Feminist Studies* 4 (1978), pp. 101–26, and on this issue in particular, pp. 105–07. For a discussion of the implications of the decline of patriarchal family structures in England see Randolph Trumbach, *The Rise of the Egalitarian Family: Aristocratic Kinship and Domestic Relations in Eighteenth Century England* (New York: Academic Press, 1978).

tasks to be particularly celebrated.[49] Up until the late eighteenth century, "motherhood was singularly unidealized, usually disregarded as a subject, and even at times actually denigrated."[50]

But, beginning in the late eighteenth century, a new view of mothering began to emerge. As the work of some fathers became less connected to the household, so also did the male association with childrearing begin to decline.[51] Motherhood, on the other hand, expanded beyond its earlier more limited functions to signify a more encompassing and valued activity. While this growth in the valuing of mothering was in part due to the declining participation of some fathers in childrearing, it also was related to changing ideas about the nature of childrearing itself. Whereas childrearing had earlier been more understood as a task centered on providing practical and moral guidance to a child already possessed of certain rational faculties, it now became viewed in terms of childhood socialization, a process extending from infancy into adulthood. New Enlightenment ideas had begun to undermine an earlier Calvinist doctrine of infant depravity. Such newer ideas stressed the idea of the infant as a blank slate whose character would be shaped by influences beginning at birth.[52] These, and other emerging viewpoints, made the care of infants a morally significant activity.[53] As Jan Lewis points out, an early nineteenth-century mix of "evangelical Protestantism, late-Enlightenment political thought (both republican and liberal) and sensationalist psychology" conjoined to make of mothering an activity of tremendous public importance.[54]

The new alignment of childrearing with childbearing and early infant care was justified by extending elements of the natural function of childbearing to the task of childrearing. What was biological about being a mother came to describe a larger part of women's activity and thus a larger part of women's identities. To be sure, "mothering" maintained a highly

---

[49] Jan Lewis notes how mother's love prior to the Revolution, particularly in the Puritan colonies, was perceived with a bit of mistrust. See Jan Lewis, "Mother's Love: The Construction of an Emotion in Nineteenth-Century America," pp. 209–29 in Andrew E. Barnes and Peter N. Stearns, eds., *Social History and Issues in Human Consciousness* (New York University Press, 1989).

[50] Bloch, "American Feminine Ideals," p. 101. See also her comments on this point on pp. 104–05.

[51] Thus Bloch makes the following comments about this change: "The structural change that altered parental roles the most, however, was the gradual physical removal of the father's place of work from the home, a process already under way in eighteenth-century America among tradesmen, craftsmen, manufacturers, and professionals (if not the majority of farmers), and one that in England was rapidly accelerating with the beginnings of industrialization." *Ibid.* p. 114.

[52] Lewis, "Mother's Love," pp. 210–11.   [53] Bloch, "American Feminine Ideals," p. 110.

[54] Lewis, "Mother's Love," pp. 212–13.

moral dimension in the sense that mothers, like fathers, were assumed to perform tasks that required skill and moral strength. It was never assumed to be an activity that could not be improved with guidance. What became "naturalized" however was the idea that women's inclinations and instincts led them to desire this task and to perform it with greater ease and skill than men.[55] Features that had long been associated with women in general, such as a greater inclination to emotionality, became less an object of mistrust and more a feature perceived as benefitting women's role as caretakers and teachers of children.[56] "Mothering," in the sense of childrearing, thus became an activity that women did "naturally" and that defined women's God-given purpose in life.

In short, changing ideas about women's proper tasks cohered well with new scientific ideas about the importance of women's reproductive systems in shaping women's identities. This stress on the importance of women's reproductive systems thus emphasized the idea of women as dominated by their physical makeup. But the rise of separate spheres ideology was associated with some very different kinds of conclusions regarding masculinity, following from changes in ideas about men's roles as family providers.

Beginning in the late eighteenth and early nineteenth century in the United States, the nature of the work of many men evidenced some important changes. For one, as cities grew, farming became less dominant as a means of providing family income. But even non-farming occupations – such as trade, artisanship, and professional occupations – began to undergo some important transformations in this period. Prior to the late eighteenth century, these occupations, like landownership, mostly followed from family membership.[57] For those who inherited such farms or occupations, male work identity had a given, stable character that was more connected to family ties than to a perceived sense of individual talent or accomplishment. And successful performance of these occupations meant fulfilling the duties and obligations associated with these occupations more than in accumulating individual wealth. Anthony Rotundo, focusing particularly on the social world of colonial New England, labels

---

[55] Lewis also makes this point that what tied nature and God to mothering was mother's love. *Ibid.* p. 205.

[56] *Ibid.* pp. 210, 213–15. Bloch, "American Feminine Ideals," p. 116.

[57] E. Anthony Rotundo, *American Manhood: Transformations in Masculinity from the Revolution to the Modern Era* (New York: Basic Books, 1990), pp. 12, 194. Michael Kimmel makes a similar point when he describes American manhood at the turn of the nineteenth century as "rooted in landownership (the Genteel Patriarch) or in the self-possession of the independent artisan, shopkeeper, or farmer (the Heroic Artisan)." Michael S. Kimmel, *Manhood in America: A Cultural History*, second edition (New York and Oxford: Oxford University Press, 2006), p. 6.

the type of masculinity associated with this form of social organization as "communal manhood." He describes it in the following way:

> There, a man's identity was inseparable from the duties he owed to his community. He fulfilled himself through public usefulness more than his economic success, and the social status of the family into which he was born gave him his place in the community more than his individual achievements did. Through his role as the head of the household, a man expressed his value to his community and provided his wife and children with their social identity.[58]

But beginning in the early nineteenth century, as the United States became a country of expanding geographical boundaries, of increased commercial activity, and of new industrial production, the meaning of what it meant to be a family provider also began to shift. Many commentators have described the early nineteenth century as giving rise to a new version of economic manhood in the United States: "the self made man."[59] "The self made man" chose more than inherited his means of economic livelihood; and he judged his success more in terms of the accumulation of individual wealth than in terms of the fulfillment of inherited duties and obligations. In comparison with his eighteenth-century predecessors, and also in comparison with many of his compatriots in Europe, he was more economically and geographically restless, and saw his own worth as an economic provider more as a function of his own talents, courage, and energy than in terms of his inherited station in life. Economic gain became a sign of one's worth and, in the opening economic and geographical frontiers of the times, a possibility theoretically open to many:

> Men in the nineteenth century learned quickly to view and to use economic gain as a means of proving something both to themselves and to other men, namely that money was the measure not only of the ability to endure risk and hardship but to defeat other men. ... Some rushed to the West for gold and furs; others challenged a different kind of economic frontier in the East, one every bit as brutal and forbidding, by gambling in industry and commerce. ... And for those who survived this world, material possessions provided the symbols of their success and prowess, a phenomenon culminating in the gaudiness of the Gilded Age among those who were the children of the Age of Jackson.[60]

All of this entailed certain shifts in the meaning of what it meant to be a good man. Certain character traits – such as perseverance, hard work, and courage – rose in importance while others – such as loyalty, service to

---

[58] Rotundo, *American Manhood*, p. 2.
[59] Kimmel, *Manhood in America*, pp. 11–30 and Rotundo, *American Manhood*, pp. 18–25.
[60] David G. Pugh, *Sons of Liberty: The Masculine Mind in Nineteenth Century America* (Westport, Conn. and London: Westport Press, 1983), pp. 26–27.

community, and knowledge of one's place – diminished. The dress and habits associated with an older aristocratic elite now became associated not with superior social status but with an effeminate and decadent type of masculinity, one prone to debauchery and the excesses of self-indulgence. The self-made man of the nineteenth century was, on the contrary, simpler and plainer in his dress and habits; he was industrious, efficient, and able to exert self-discipline over the desires of the flesh. Like the young country he symbolized, he was portrayed as rugged and enter-prising, able to conquer new horizons with action and determination.[61]

This new ideal of the self-made man provides certain insights into the implications of the emerging ideology of separate spheres for norms of masculinity and for new understandings of differences between women and men. As women were coming to be defined more extensively as mothers, man's role as economic provider was also changing. But here the role was becoming less, not more, associated with inherited givens. On the contrary, work outside the home was coming to be seen as more chosen and changeable. More possibilities were available but associated with these possibilities was also a greater risk of failure. Success in this more open, uncertain, and competitive economic world was more pre-carious than that assured by adherence to community-given standards of appropriate behavior. Consequently, success required the very diligent employment of such traits as perseverance, hard work, and courage combined with whatever talent and intelligence one might be lucky to possess. While women, as mothers, were being urged to merely avoid going against instincts that were natural and given to all women, men, as wage earners, were being urged to draw on strengths randomly assigned among men, and to uphold character traits viewed as not easy to sustain.

Such generalizations must, of course, be interpreted properly. They capture only part of a social order much more complex than they describe. Thus, as earlier noted, while women were being described as dominated by their reproductive functions, class status could also constitute some of them as, in many respects, less subject to animalistic urges than men. And coexisting with the new ideal of "the self made man" were older ideals which depicted a too intense need for the accumulation of wealth as reflecting an unattractive greed. Thus, these generalizations must be understood as indicative only of threads in a social tapestry composed of many other threads, some in direct contradiction to these, and many of which were themselves in flux. To point them out is only to highlight elements of a social order that, for a certain period of time, achieved a

---

[61] Rotundo, *American Manhood*, pp. 178–85. See also Kimmel, *Manhood in America*, pp. 30–33.

certain new prominence and that account for otherwise inexplicable phenomena.

One such phenomenon that the above generalizations help us understand is the differential explanation of social failure for white women than for white men. For the former, failure was more typically linked to life decisions that ran counter to women's biologically assigned role as wife and mother. For men, on the contrary, failure was more commonly linked to life decisions that showed an inappropriate application of such character traits as hard work and perseverance, often too little, but sometimes too much. One example of this difference is in how the late nineteenth-century disease of "neurasthenia" was explained. Neurasthenia was a common late nineteenth-century disease to which both women and men were subject. But, a recent study of over three hundred cases of neurasthenia reported in medical journals between 1870 and 1910 found that while the symptoms presented by men and women were identical, the diagnoses differed sharply. Whereas physicians explained the symptoms of women by reference to breakdowns of their genital/reproductive organs, they explained the symptoms of men by reference to poor decision-making concerning voluntary behavior, most typically, in the case of professional men, to overwork. This study leads E. Anthony Rotundo to draw the following conclusion:

This sex-typed interpretation of the same symptoms reflects the common medical wisdom about gender in the nineteenth century: men were active and created their own fates by assertions of individual will; women were passive, imprisoned by the demands of their bodies.[62]

In sum, the ideology of separate spheres explained the different suitability of women and men for different types of work as following from the different "natures" of women and men. Women were best suited for childrearing because of their biologies. Male natural instincts, such as an instinct for aggression and competition, also played a role in the greater suitability of men for participation in a market economy. But success in this economy was also associated, much more than was mothering, with attributes seen as differentially possessed by men – such as intelligence and talent – and with the forceful application of such character traits as diligence and perseverance.[63]

[62] Rotundo, *American Manhood*, describes this study and draws this conclusion on p. 189. The study is by F. G. Gosling, *Before Freud: Neurasthenia and the American Medical Community, 1870–1910* (Urbana, Ill.: University of Illinois Press, 1987), p. 55.

[63] David Pugh quotes one early nineteenth-century speechwriter as making the following claim: "it is character alone, that can lift a man above accident – it is that alone which, if based upon good principles and cultivated with care, can render him triumphant over

Thus, within the ideology of separate spheres, both men and women had a sex. And each sex was viewed as given by nature. But women's sex resulted in a social role that was closely linked to women's biology. This meant that women were perceived as highly governed by their sex and less differentiated by individual differences. Men's "sex" allowed them, on the other hand, to be more varied, more individual, and more able to employ brain and will in the direction of their destiny. Biological sex differentiated women and men but it explained women more than it did men.

From the above history of sex, we might deduce those identity premises that women needed to challenge if they were to significantly alter their social position in twentieth-century US society. Women – white women as mothers and black women as mothers and black – needed to "denaturalize" themselves, that is, challenge the view that their bodies were significant determinants of who they were and what they could be. This challenge would enable them to be seen more as individuals, as different amongst themselves as were white men. It would also make possible a view of all women as governed as much by their will and reasoning abilities as were white men. But for others to see women as individuals and as governed by will and reason required that women's roles as mothers be reduced in significance. The "naturalization" of women was inseparably linked to the view that women had responsibilities in childrearing that necessarily dominated their lives and set limits to what they might accomplish.

Conclusion

Debates about "nature" vs. "nurture" in the twentieth century and continuing into the present have often been posed as though the issue was about human beings in general. Thus, when people have argued about the influence of biology versus environment, it has often appeared as though they were talking about the determinants of human character as a whole. But the preceding discussion should make us question the extent to which this debate has been primarily a sex or race neutral debate. I pose the following thought experiment: Would the nature/nurture debate have been so important in public discussion and generated so much intense disagreement throughout the twentieth century and continuing into the

vicissitudes and prosperous even in adversity." See Pugh, *Sons of Liberty*, p. 33. This quote is taken from O. L. Holley, *The Connexion Between the Mechanic Arts and the Welfare of the States* (Troy, N.Y.: n.p., 1825), p. 4. Pugh notes the citation of this quote also in John William Ward, *Andrew Jackson: Symbol for an Age* (New York: Oxford University Press, 1962), p. 170.

present, if the only identities that were being examined for the causes of their nature were those of white men?

The answer to this hypothetical question is, I believe, no. And the reason is because it has been mostly black men and women as well as women of other races who have had to fight for the recognition that biology plays a relatively minor role in affecting who they are and how they act. The legacy of late eighteenth- and nineteenth-century views about the meaning of race and sex was that black men and women and women as a group entered the twentieth century with significant "identity obstacles" towards changes in existing social arrangements. The exclusion of women from extensive participation in non-domestic activity and the view of black men and women as second class citizens, was justified on the grounds of the biological nature of all. This biological nature supposedly grounded the truth of a variety of claims about women and about black people, truth claims that were used to justify the maintenance of certain social arrangements. As we will see in the following chapters, a variety of intellectual shifts was necessary for the credibility of these truth claims to be significantly reduced. Certain social structural shifts were also necessary to cause those who fought on behalf of blacks and women to use these intellectual shifts in the service of struggles for social change.

Introduction to chapters 2 and 3

The "naturalization" of black and female identity that developed in the late eighteenth and nineteenth centuries in the United States and other western countries remained a major current in popular consciousness throughout the twentieth century and even until today. But beginning in the first half of the twentieth century, certain new ways of thinking about identity emerged in Europe and North America to seriously challenge such naturalization. Most importantly, environmentalism became less the position of a small band of intellectuals and more a widely accepted current in popular consciousness. In the process, environmentalism became a more widely available antidote to claims about natural differences.

Environmentalism became a widely accepted current in popular consciousness in part because it became elaborated by various schools of thought that wielded influence both within academic thought and within popular literature. In the next two chapters I will focus on two schools of thought that played an important role in this elaboration and popularization of environmentalism. One such school of thought was dynamic psychology. Dynamic psychology focused on the individual but portrayed individual development less as a function of inborn, natural givens and more as a function of environmental influences. Dynamic psychology was developed in a variety of ways and by a variety of thinkers in the early part of the twentieth century. But I focus on one particularly important contributor, Sigmund Freud, both because of the power of Freud's thought and because of its timing. Freud developed his theory at a time when naturalistic explanations still dominated much of academic thought. In seeing how he partially broke with such kinds of explanations, we gain a useful lens into larger cultural shifts.

In Freud's writing, the inputs from the body are described as more similar among human beings than they had been in naturalistic, late nineteenth-century accounts. This greater homogeneity of bodily inputs is illustrated in Freud's treatment of sexual desire. Within Freudian theory, sexual desire becomes a factor influencing human development in highly similar ways among men and women and among peoples of different ancestries. But this lessening of bodily inputs as a differentiating factor opens up space for environmental factors to play a greater role in differentiating human beings. In Freud's case, it is the specific circumstances of childhood interactions that are largely brought in to fill this space.

Thus, dynamic psychology as reflected in Freudian theory allows for character to be more differentiated by the specific circumstances of individual development and less determined by bodily type. This turn undermines the credibility of appeals to bodily type to reinforce existing social boundaries. As I have argued, such appeals to bodily type were more elaborated in regard to explaining the behavior of women and blacks than they were of men and whites. Thus, one consequence of the widening appeal of dynamic psychology was to allow for a more individualistic view of women and blacks, and thus to allow for a view of women and blacks as more similar in this respect to men and whites.

But as Freud's body of work also illustrates, the political consequences of this kind of turn could be limited by certain gaps within the theory. Freudian theory, and dynamic psychology in general, attempts only to explain human behavior. It leaves largely unexamined questions about the moral worth of the behavior so generated. Indeed, in Freud's own work, when such moral questions emerge, the answers provided tend often to merely reflect prevailing views. Thus, while this kind of intellectual shift does much to challenge appeals to the body as a means of limiting the behaviors of women and blacks, it does little to challenge prevailing views about the worth of behaviors associated with either group. For this kind of challenge to be put forward required a different kind of intellectual shift.

In chapter 3, I look at such a different kind of intellectual shift. I turn to the elaboration of environmentalism carried out not by psychologists but by early twentieth-century anthropologists. Focusing on the work of Franz Boas and some of his students, I point to some of the consequences of the elaboration of an environmental position when the behaviors being examined are those of social groups rather than individuals. Members of this anthropological school rebelled against earlier anthropological positions that explained the practices of diverse societies as a consequence of inherited differences, describing such practices instead as reasonable adaptations to environmental conditions. But this kind of perspective on *social* practices raised questions about those assumptions of inherent superiority that were attendant upon earlier views of social group differences. Thus, as dynamic psychology had the political consequence of reinforcing the social maxim that "we are all just individuals," so did this kind of environmentalist approach to social group differences also have political consequences. It gave legitimacy to the idea of the possibly arbitrary nature of existing evaluations of social differences. If the practices of all social groups were reasonable adaptations to particular social environments, how can some practices be described as superior to others? These anthropologists did not provide conclusive or even necessarily coherent answers to these questions, but helped in making these questions more a part of public discussion.

These two intellectual movements influenced the climate in which the political movements centered on race and sex flourished in the United States in the twentieth century. As we will see in later chapters, both the idea that "we are all just individuals" and the idea that the practices of particular groups are not necessarily superior to those of others became an important part of the struggles on behalf of women and African Americans over the course of this century.

2   Freud and the rise of the psychological self

> On or about December 1910 human character changed.
>
> (Virginia Woolf, *Mr. Bennett and Mrs. Brown*)[1]

Two stories predominate for characterizing the period from the late nineteenth to the early twentieth century in western Europe and the United States. There is an older story, represented in this quote by Woolf, which sees changes in the early twentieth century as representing a radical break with late nineteenth-century ways of life. Many of those who were proclaiming themselves modern in the early twentieth century saw themselves and their lives as dramatically different from those of their parents in joyous and exhilarating ways. According to the account they and later chroniclers told of the transformation, late nineteenth-century middle-class life was characterized by sexual repression and moral hypocrisy. Members of the middle class shrouded sex in silence, while if male, nevertheless indulging secretly, or if female, becoming repressed and neurotic. Such repressed and hypocritical attitudes towards sexuality were part and parcel of lives which were overly regulated, motivated by conformity, and restricted in joy. Old fashioned and rigid understandings

---

[1] The exact statement made by Woolf is the following: "And now I will hazard a second assertion, which is more disputable perhaps, to the effect that on or about December 1910 human character changed." The statement was made by Woolf in the context of her distinguishing two groups of writers: those she classified as Georgians, including Forster, Strachey, Joyce, and Eliot, and those she classified as Edwardians, including Wells, Bennett, and Galsworthy. In elaborating on the shift in social relations allied with the new group of writers she makes the following comment: "All human relations have shifted – those between masters and servants, husbands and wives, parents and children. And when human relations change there is at the same time a change in religion, conduct, politics, and literature." See Virginia Woolf, *Mr. Bennett and Mrs. Brown* (London: The Hogarth Press, 1928), pp. 4–5. The reference to this quote was provided to me in Peter Stansky's *On or About 1910*. Stansky claims that the specific date of December 1910 most likely arose from Woolf's memory of the exhibition held in London in November and December 1910 of "Manet and the Post-Impressionists." See Peter Stansky, *On or About December 1910: Early Bloomsbury and Its Intimate World* (Cambridge, Mass.: Harvard University Press, 1996), pp. 2–3.

of women's "proper place" placed unnecessary restrictions on women's intelligence and their contributions to society. Such understandings also placed unnecessary obstacles in the way of men's abilities to achieve companionate marriages. To those who came to call themselves flappers, who were taken with the ideas of Freud, or became excited about cubism in art, a new day was dawning. This new day was captured by the enthusiasts of all of these changes in the phrase, "the modern."

Central elements of this story have come under attack. Michel Foucault eloquently rejected that twentieth-century self-understanding which saw itself as progressively "liberating" itself from previous shackles on its sexuality, and doing this through greater openness and talk of sex. In opposition to those who would characterize the Victorians as overly silent about sexuality, Foucault pointed out a high degree of verbosity around sex since about the end of the sixteenth century in western societies. Foucault characterized the last several centuries as a period where a new form of power emerged, a power involving the discipline and control of bodies and pleasures. This power exerts itself not only through legal mechanisms but also through social practices legitimated through the new social sciences, such as psychology. The "regime of power" represented in these practices has demanded not silence around sex but increased talk about it. Foucault described this incitement of talk about sex as follows:

A first survey made from this viewpoint seems to indicate that since the end of the sixteenth century, the "putting into discourse of sex," far from undergoing a process of restriction, on the contrary has been subjected to a mechanism of increasing incitement; that the techniques of power exercised over sex have not obeyed a principle of rigorous selection, but rather one of dissemination and implantation of polymorphous sexualities.[2]

But, according to Foucault, the "liberatory" characterization of the twentieth century was problematic not only because of its failure to recognize the similarities between nineteenth- and twentieth-century verbosity about sex, but also because it failed to recognize the controlling nature of much of the twentieth-century talk. While early moderns saw in the new, scientific talk about sex a means to free themselves from nineteenth-century hypocrisy, Foucault pointed to the continuities between such talk and older mechanisms of control, such as the confessional.[3]

---

[2] Michel Foucault, *History of Sexuality, Volume I: An Introduction*, trans. Robert Hurley (New York: Pantheon, 1978), p. 12.

[3] *Ibid.* pp. 65–70. On p. 119 of this work, Foucault strongly praises psychiatric discourse for challenging "the perversion-heredity-degeneracy system" of the late nineteenth century.

But Foucault has not been alone in rejecting the Woolfian story. Other cultural historians have questioned characterizations of the twentieth century as a century of unfolding human freedom. Common to many of those who have shared in this more pessimistic assessment of the twentieth century is a shared negative assessment of psychological talk. Instead of describing this new type of language as the means by which we moderns have freed ourselves from the inhibitions of our predecessors, these historians have described it, like Foucault, as the means by which we have tied ourselves to new gods. Writers such as Christopher Lasch, Joel Kovell, T. J. Jackson Lears, and Warren Susman have linked an increased focus on the psyche to the development of a consumeristic, individualistic, narcissistic self who cares more about managing the impressions others have of him or her to doing good, who desires fame more than respect, and who is caught within the hopelessly self-defeating cycle of trying to fill up a fundamentally empty interior life with more and more commodities.[4] This negative assessment of the impact of psychological ways of thinking on twentieth-century culture has been echoed by social critics outside of the academy on all sides of the political spectrum. Critics on the right have described the spread of "psychobabble" as causing us to turn away from the language of character and morality while some critics on the left have pointed to the controlling, normalizing, and socially conservative role of this discourse.[5]

In this chapter I want to illuminate what was right in the original Woolfian position. Certainly this position needs to be modified by many of the insights made by Foucault and other critics. However, there are also important truths in the original sense of Woolf and other early moderns that some liberatory understandings of human nature were emerging in

However, Foucault also describes such discourse as representing a shift in the techniques of the deployment of sexuality and thus as part of the medicalization of sex discussed in other parts of this work.

[4] See Christopher Lasch, *The Culture of Narcissism: American Life in an Age of Diminishing Expectations* (New York: W. W. Norton & Company, 1979); Joel Kovell, "The American Mental Health Industry," in David Ingleby, ed., *Critical Psychiatry: The Politics of Mental Health* (New York: Pantheon, 1980), pp. 72–101; T. J. Jackson Lears, "From Salvation to Self Realization: Advertising and the Therapeutic Roots of the Consumer Culture, 1880–1930," in Richard Wightman Fox and T. J. Jackson Lears, eds., *The Culture of Consumption: Critical Essays in American History, 1880–1980* (New York: Pantheon, 1983), pp. 1–38; Warren I. Susman, *Culture as History: The Transformation of American Society in the Twentieth Century* (New York: Pantheon, 1984).

[5] One left theorist who has written about the controlling aspect of psychoanalysis in general is Jacques Donzelot, *The Policing of Families* (New York: Random House, 1979). Among feminists, some who view particularly Freudian theory as reflecting culturally conservative perspectives include: Betty Friedan, *The Feminine Mystique* (New York: Dell, 1963); Kate Millet, *Sexual Politics* (New York: Doubleday, 1970); and Shulamith Firestone, *The Dialectic of Sex: The Case for Feminist Revolution* (New York: William Morrow, 1970).

the early years of the twentieth century and that the kind of thinking Freud and others like him were introducing was contributing to these understandings. Virginia Woolf's statement, that "on or about December 1910 human character changed," while obviously made and needing to be understood with a certain tongue in cheek, does seem to capture something important that was happening in the broad cultural landscape of the time.

And one thing that was happening to "human character" in the early twentieth century was that new psychological kinds of explanation were beginning to challenge older models of social identity that linked character to natural differences. As I argued in chapter 1, these older models were particularly employed to place limits on the behavior of women and blacks, thus construing the identities of members of both of these groups in more stereotypical ways than they construed the identities of men and whites. But, as I will show in this chapter, as these new psychological explanations undermined the credibility of such older models, so they made the basic identities of all human beings increasingly similar, explaining differences in more individualistic terms. These explanations replaced appeals to a differentiating physiology with appeals to a combination of common structures and environmental influences. Consequently, character could be seen as more a random collection of traits, rather than as a coherent collection of traits "naturally" associated with each other and with particular types of bodies.

While the above claims can be made about many of the psychological explanations that were being developed in the early part of the twentieth century, they can be illustrated most dramatically in the work of one theorist, Sigmund Freud. As scholars have pointed out, some of what is taken as the unique contribution of Freud was being articulated by others of his time. Many dynamic medical psychologies were being created in Europe and America between 1885 and 1909, the date when Freud gave a series of lectures at Clark University which introduced Freud to the United States psychological community. As Nathan Hale writes: "Many conceptions often regarded as Freud's original contributions were a common part of these international developments."[6]

However, if Freud's work overlapped in part with others of his time, Freudian theory elaborated these new ideas in particularly powerful and comprehensive ways. Consequently, the theory can serve as an especially useful case study; in one body of work we are able to make connections among ideas being introduced in less systematic ways by others. Moreover, in considering the challenge that dynamic psychology made

---

[6] Nathan G. Hale, Jr., *Freud and the Americans: The Beginnings of Psychoanalysis in the United States, 1876–1917* (New York: Oxford University Press, 1995), p. 98.

to older accounts of identity, Freudian theory is especially useful for another reason. Freud began his training as a neurologist, as one who looked to physiology to explain abnormality. But, in perceiving limitations in that earlier training, Freud went on to develop types of explanation that were distinctively psychological. Consequently, in Freud's turn to psychology, we can see, through changes in one person's ideas, larger shifts in the appeal of new types of knowledges. To be sure, Freud, as a very early exponent of dynamic psychology, did not completely abandon elements of late nineteenth-century physicalist accounts. But even in his retention of such elements, we can see the identity implications of such incompleteness. In short, Freud developed his ideas in a time of radical cultural change; since his own developing theory occurred in the midst of that change, it can be used as a very good case study of it.

The challenge of Freud: the commonality of desire

In chapter 1, I described some of the ways many late nineteenth-century thinkers used descriptions of the bodies of blacks and women as arguments to reinforce existing social rules. Thus the skull sizes of women and African Americans were described as smaller than those of white men to justify arguments about the limits of education in expanding the cognitive abilities of both groups. Women's reproductive systems were described as making demands on women's energy that men's reproductive systems did not make, descriptions again used for justifying arguments about the different effects of educating women than of educating men. Such descriptions did not imply that environmental factors exerted no influence. Rather, they were part of arguments which claimed only that the constitutions of both groups affected the extent and ways in which environmental factors were influential.

Freudian theory challenged such claims not only by increasing the importance of the environment in ways I will analyze in later sections, but also by abandoning nature as a differentiating force even when nature remains for him a causal element. This point is illustrated in Freud's use of instincts. From the perspective of many forms of contemporary psychoanalysis, Freud's commitment to instinct theory represents the most outdated and useless aspect of his work. During the course of the twentieth century, deviations from orthodox Freudianism have mostly entailed rejection of Freud's reliance on instinct theory and towards more culturalist and interactionist modes of explanation.[7] Instinct theory is therefore

---

[7] Stephen A. Mitchell and Margaret J. Black, *Freud and Beyond: A History of Modern Psychoanalytic Thought* (New York: Basic Books, 1995).

that aspect of the master's thought that fits least well with contemporary understandings. Without wishing to resurrect this aspect of Freudian theory, I would, however, like to point to the increased egalitarian and thus historically important role even this part of Freud's theory played in relation to his time. This aspect of his theory functioned not only as a remnant of nineteenth-century somatic perspectives, but also as an important means by which some of the social uses of those perspectives became undermined.

To obtain a sense of how Freud's use of instinct theory was challenging, let us begin by considering Freud's focus on sex and the differences between his focus and the concern with sex that is evident in much late nineteenth-century thought. Foucault is right that Freud did not inaugurate a concern with sex; late nineteenth-century medical treatises were obsessed with the topic. Why was it then that when Freud began to emphasize sex as a dominant cause of neurosis, many people, including himself, saw what he was doing as shocking? To answer this question, we need to understand some of the subtle shifts in Freud's use of sex. While Freud did not inaugurate a concern with sex, some of the ways in which Freud elaborated this concern evidence change.

As many commentators have pointed out, sexuality in late nineteenth-century western society was understood as a normal and healthy part of human functioning. The dangers emerged only when it was not kept within certain boundaries. Such boundaries not only excluded sex outside of heterosexual marriage, but also certain kinds and intensities of sex even within the context of heterosexual marriage. It was widely believed that the purely sensual aspect of sex had be to kept within limits lest it overwhelm those spiritual and social ties upon which marriage was more importantly based:

> Victorian advice authors acknowledged sex and the pleasures accompanying it as a legitimate aspect of marriage. They simultaneously defined love as a spiritual relationship which is the essential meaning of marriage. This created a dilemma. Insofar as sexual feeling easily evoked sensual desires, the norm of sex in marriage threatened to undermine its spiritual basis … Sensual desire did not of course simply disappear. Rather, it was supposed to be sublimated into the quest for spiritual and social companionship between the husband and wife.[8]

Sexuality which moved beyond such boundaries could have dire consequences: not only undermining the spiritual connection between husband

---

[8] Steven Seidman, *Romantic Longings: Love in America, 1830–1980* (New York and London: Routledge, 1991), p. 31.

and wife but potentially causing individual breakdown and mental illness.[9]

Freudian theory was shocking, not because of its focus on sex per se, but because it pushed the boundaries of "normal" sex, arguing that sex was naturally and appropriately both a stronger and more animalistic force than many had claimed. Freudian theory linked strong sexual desire not with perversion, but with ordinary human functioning. Thus, as one noted psychologist of the period expressed it, the kind of sexual desire that had before been associated with "perverts and erotomania or other abnormal cases" was now being regarded as normal.[10] Particularly scandalous to some, was that what had previously been linked with perversion was now being described as the basis for some of the most admired achievements of human civilization.[11] The line between the pervert and those who made up the highest stratum of human society was being blurred.

Freud's move towards generalizing and thus normalizing "abnormal" sex can be seen as a steady and core thread in his early writings, taking different forms in different shifts. An example of one such shift is Freud's replacement of actual seduction with the fantasy of seduction as the initial cause of breakdown in some of his patients. Contemporary writers, such as Jeffrey Masson, have strongly criticized Freud for this move, describing it as a cowardly retreat from awareness of the pervasiveness of child abuse in the middle classes.[12] From a feminist perspective, it indicates Freud's greater reluctance to believe the stories of his mostly women patients. This same reluctance is present today in anti-feminist arguments about the commonality of "false memory syndrome."

Without necessarily disagreeing with such assessments of Freud's shift, I would like to complicate them by adding an additional point. It was in part Freud's desire to stress the commonality of the kind of sexual desire that had been thought improper that at least partly lay behind this turn. Freud wanted to make some type of thought of a childhood sexual interaction a common phenomenon. The very commonality of this thought is threatened if it is forced to depend on the occurrence of actual events. It is worthwhile looking at Freud's words directly:

[9] Hale, Jr., *Freud and the Americans*, p. 296.
[10] G. Stanley Hall, *Journal of Abnormal Psychology* 10 (1915–16), p. 82. This remark of Hall's was brought to my attention by Hale, Jr., *Freud and the Americans*, p. 296.
[11] Hale, Jr., *Freud and the Americans*, pp. 297–98. Hale quotes a remark by Pierre Janet that the Freudian doctrine of sublimation confused "the highest tendencies of the human mind with instincts which are common to all the animals."
[12] Jeffrey Moussaieff Masson, *The Assault on Truth: Freud's Suppression of the Seduction Theory* (New York: Simon & Schuster, 1984).

I will confide in you at once the great secret that has been slowly dawning on me in the last few months. I no longer believe in my *neurotica* [theory of the neuroses]. This is probably not intelligible without an explanation ... So I will begin historically from the question of the origin of my reasons for disbelief. ...Then came surprise at the fact that in every case the father, not excluding my own, had to be blamed as a pervert – the realization of the unexpected frequency of hysteria, in which the same determinant is invariably established, though such a widespread extent of perversity towards children is, after all, not very probable. (The perversity would have to be immeasurably more frequent than the hysteria, since the illness only arises where there has been an accumulation of events and where a factor that weakens defense has supervened.)[13]

Certainly Freud is here shifting the source of perversity from the act of the father to the fantasy of the daughter, and Freud's willingness to make such a shift can at least partly be attributed to sexism or cowardliness. But we also need to take into account Freud's desire in this period to generalize the presence of "perversity." Of note is that Freud was not abandoning an awareness that sexual seduction of children takes place; he continued to reference childhood seduction as a cause of problems he encountered.[14] What he abandoned was a belief in the pervasiveness of seduction, looking instead for causes that could be found more easily not only in the pasts of all hysterics but in all humans.

This point is reinforced by a later account Freud gave of this move. In *On the History of the Psychoanalytic Movement*, Freud talks about how he came to understand the phantasmic nature of these memories as cover-ups for the autoerotic activity of early childhood:

If hysterical subjects trace back their symptoms to traumas that are fictitious, then the new fact which emerges is precisely that they create such scenes in *phantasy*, and this psychical reality requires to be taken into account alongside practical reality. This reflection was soon followed by the discovery that these phantasies were intended to cover up the autoerotic activity of the first years of childhood, to embellish it and raise it to a higher plane. And now, from behind the phantasies, the whole range of a child's sexual life came to light.[15]

[13] Sigmund Freud, Letter to Wilhelm Fliess, Letter 69, September 21, 1897, in *The Standard Edition* of the *Complete Psychological Works of Sigmund Freud*, translated from the German under the general editorship of James Strachey, 24 vols. (London: Hogarth Press and the Institute of Psycho-Analysis, 1953–74), Vol. I, pp. 259–60.
[14] See, for example, Sigmund Freud, *Fragment of an Analysis of a Case of Hysteria* (1905 [1901]), *The Standard Edition*, Vol. VII, p. 57, footnote no.1. He also continues to reference seduction as cause of later problems on pp. 190, 234, and 242 in *Three Essays on the Theory of Sexuality* (1905), *The Standard Edition*, Vol. VII. He also references it in "Female Sexuality" (1931), *The Standard Edition*, Vol. XXI, pp. 232, 242. Finally, there is a reference to seduction as cause in his last written work, *An Outline of Psychoanalysis* (1940 [1938]), *The Standard Edition*, Vol. XXIII, p. 187.
[15] Sigmund Freud, *On the History of the Psychoanalytic Movement* (1914), *The Standard Edition*, Vol. XIV, pp. 17–18.

Of note is that Freud is not talking here about the sexuality of unusual children but rather about childhood sexuality in general. Freud's move towards understanding his patients' stories about seduction as fantasy cannot be separated from his desire to generalize the perverse, that is, in this case, to generalize the presence of sexual desire in children.

Moreover, if one reflects upon what else Freud was doing in 1897, the year he penned the letter to Fliess announcing his shift, one realizes that this is the time when the material for *The Interpretation of Dreams* was fresh in Freud's mind.[16] But this work, unlike Freud's writing in the prior period, is not an analysis of the unusual person, but an analysis of what is unusual in all of us, our dreams. And Freud in this work is making strong sexual desire a part of all of us, as an important component of dream content.[17] He is thus making strong sexual desire a part of the normal psyche. But strong sexual desire had been viewed as at least dangerous. There is no absolute shift here. As noted earlier, the Victorians, like Freud, thought of sexual desire as a normal, indeed desirable, part of the human psyche.[18] And Freud, like the Victorians, thought of sex as a potential source of problems. But by suggesting that a very strong element of sexual desire is part of the normal psyche, Freud was undermining the credibility of strong sexual desire as distinguishing the abnormal from the normal.

In other words, Freud, in his writings from the late 1890s through the first decade of the twentieth century, was taking what had been considered by many as at least a possible sign of perversity – the existence of strong sexual desire in adults and the mere presence of sexual desire in children – and making both of them common and thus "normal" aspects of human life. Thus, he was undermining the power of strong sexual desire as a criterion for differentiating *types* of people. If strong sexual desire plays an important part in the psyches of all, then strength of desire becomes less useful as a way to explain differences not only between the mentally disturbed and the rest of the human race, but also, as was commonly thought at the time, between men and women and between people of African and European backgrounds.

---

[16] Thus, also in *On the History of the Psychoanalytic Movement*, Freud states that *The Interpretation of Dreams* was finished in all of its essentials at the beginning of 1896 but was not written out until the summer of 1899. *Ibid.* p. 22.

[17] Freud's move to make sexuality basic to dreams is explicitly stated in the following passage from *The Interpretation of Dreams*: "The more one is concerned with the solution of dreams, the more one is driven to recognize that the majority of the dreams of adults deal with sexual material and give expression to erotic wishes." *The Standard Edition*, Vol. V, p. 396.

[18] For a useful discussion of the complex ways in which Victorians viewed sexual desire, see Seidman, *Romantic Longings*.

Supplementing the common Victorian belief that different groups of people possess different inherited intensities of sexual desire, was also the belief that different groups of people possess different inherited *types* of desire. But here also Freudian theory moved in a new direction. Freud's writings after the mid 1890s began to elaborate the ways in which the strong sexual desire we all possess is the same among us. The strong sexual desire that Freud finds everywhere – in the dreams of the ordinary human being, the symptoms of the hysteric, and the acts of the sexual pervert – is the same sexual desire.

This claim first begins to surface in *The Interpretation of Dreams*. Here Freud depicts the sexual desire that is part of all of our psyches, and that finds its distorted expression in dreams, as the basis for the way we are all a bit "psychotic." In this work, Freud explicitly connects dreams and psychoses. While he acknowledges that the precise nature of the connections are yet to be known, he states that it is in exploring the nature of one that we will also uncover knowledge about the other.[19]

However, it is not until the *Three Essays on the Theory of Sexuality* that Freud extensively elaborates on the commonality between the sexual desire that generates abnormal behavior and the sexual desire that is part of us all. Freud starts off the first essay of this work by introducing two terms he wishes to distinguish from "the sexual instinct." These terms are "the sexual object" and "the sexual aim." In distinguishing between sexual instinct, object, and aim, Freud was undermining commonly held beliefs that the sexual deviant possesses a different type of sexual instinct from the one who is not deviant. Freud instead suggests that the basic sexual instinct is the same while its object and aim can differ.

Freud elaborates on this point in his discussion of the sexual "invert." Freud makes the claim that inversion is better understood as reflecting a connecting series rather than as a composite of distinct "types."[20] He notes that inversion can take place in various degrees, from absolute inverts who exclusively desire as sexual objects persons of the same sex, to what he calls "amphigenic" inverts, those today we would call bisexuals, to what he calls "contingent" inverts, those who take as their sexual

[19] Freud, *The Interpretation of Dreams* (1900), chapter 1, "The Scientific Literature on Dreams," *The Standard Edition*, Vol. IV, p. 92.
[20] His words are the following: "Many authorities would be unwilling to class together all the various cases which I have enumerated and would prefer to lay stress upon their differences rather than their resemblances, in accord with their own preferred view of inversion. Nevertheless, though the distinctions cannot be disputed, it is impossible to overlook the existence of numerous intermediate examples of every type, so that we are driven to conclude that we are dealing with a connected series." Freud, *Three Essays on the Theory of Sexuality*, pp. 137–38.

object someone of the same sex only under certain circumstances.[21] He also points out that inversion can vary in other respects, such as in how the invert regards his or her desire and in the time of its original onset.[22] Freud states that thinking about inversion as a connected series sets his views apart from others who focus on the differences between types of inversion rather than on their similarities.[23]

That differences among "inverts" are differences in degree, suggests, of course, that differences between inverts in general and heterosexuals are also differences in degree. In a 1915 footnote to the *Three Essays on the Theory of Sexuality*, Freud makes this suggestion explicit:

Psychoanalytic research is most decidedly opposed to any attempt at separating off homosexuals from the rest of mankind as a group of a special character. By studying sexual excitations other than those that are manifestly displayed, it has found that all human beings are capable of making a homosexual object-choice and have in fact made one in their unconscious. Indeed libidinal attachments to persons of the same sex play no less a part as factors in normal mental life, and a greater part as a motive force for illness, than do similar attachments to the opposite sex. On the contrary, psycho-analysis considers that a choice of an object independently of its sex – freedom to range equally over male and female objects – as it is found in childhood, in primitive states of society and early periods of history, is the original basis from which, as a result of restriction in one direction or the other, both the normal and the inverted types develop. Thus from the point of view of psycho-analysis the exclusive sexual interest felt by men for women is also a problem that needs elucidating and is not a self-evident fact based upon an attraction that is ultimately of a chemical nature.[24]

And in the original version of the *Three Essays*, Freud makes a similar claim about what he calls "the perversions." As he states, "Everyday experience has shown that most of these extensions, or at any rate the less severe of them, are constituents which are rarely absent from the sexual life of healthy people …"[25]

Not only does Freud argue that no sharp line can be drawn between the normal and the abnormal in regard to sexual practice, he also extends the range of the sexually abnormal by making a theoretical connection between sexual perversion and psychoneurosis. As Freud states, "*neuroses are, so to say, the negative of perversions.*"[26] The processes which result in sexual perversion and those which result in neurosis overlap. But since no strong line separates the neurotic from the non-neurotic, this means, again, that no strong line separates the sexual pervert from the rest of humanity. Freud explicitly draws this conclusion:

[21] *Ibid.* pp. 136–37.   [22] *Ibid.* p. 137.   [23] *Ibid.* pp. 137–38.
[24] *Ibid.* pp. 145–46. This is a footnote added in 1915.
[25] *Ibid.* p. 160.   [26] *Ibid.* p. 165.

By demonstrating the part played by perverse impulses in the formation of symptoms in the psychoneuroses, we have quite remarkably increased the number of people who might be regarded as perverts. It is not only that neurotics in themselves constitute a very numerous class, but it must also be considered that an unbroken chain bridges the gap between the neuroses in all their manifestations and normality. After all, Moebius could say with justice that we are all to some extent hysterics. Thus the extraordinarily wide dissemination of the perversions forces us to suppose that the disposition to perversions is itself of no great rarity but must form a part of what passes as the normal constitution.[27]

Freud's suggestion that a common thread ties together the neurotic, the pervert, and everyone else, and this common thread is a common sexual instinct, is more fully elaborated in the second of the *Three Essays* where Freud focuses on infantile sexuality. Freud begins this essay by tying together the amnesia that hysterics experience with the amnesia that all of us experience about our first years. He makes the connection between these two cases in the common phenomenon of a repressed sexuality.[28] In later parts of this essay, Freud shows how the component parts of what later becomes the sexual instinct in normal development can be transformed into neuroses or perversions. Thus the experience of sucking can become in later life perverse kissing, hysterical vomiting, or other eating disorders.[29] The pleasures of bowel elimination can become neuropathic constipation.[30] In these examples, as in earlier ones, the appeal to sexual desire is used to express what we have in common rather than to illustrate underlying constitutional differences.

The play between desire and the environment

But if Freud employed sexual desire not to differentiate but to unite, what does cause differences among humans? And here the turn that was important in Freud, and what makes his theory a form of dynamic psychology, was his emphasis on our complex relationships with our social environments as a major source of differentiation. Again, the issue is one of degree. As noted in chapter 1, late nineteenth-century physiological theories did not completely ignore the social environment. And, as we will see later, Freud did not himself completely abandon reference to biological phenomena as a cause of differences. But, there are important differences in regard to degree. If late nineteenth-century theorists recognized the influence of environmental factors, the more prevailing emphasis

---

[27] *Ibid.* p. 171.   [28] *Ibid.* pp. 173–76.   [29] *Ibid.* p. 182.   [30] *Ibid.* p. 186.

was on the inherited, underlying physiology.[31] Now, the emphasis shifts; bodily factors are granted some degree of importance while intellectual energy becomes directed towards the social environment.

The type of environmentalism evidenced in early twentieth-century dynamic psychology is also different from that present in earlier, non-physiological accounts. Enlightened thinkers such as René Descartes, Mary Wollstonecraft, Harriet Taylor, and John Stuart Mill had long appealed to environmental factors as the cause of many of the observable differences between human beings. But the arguments in such cases were abstract and philosophical. Before the advent of dynamic psychology, there were few theories which provided systematic accounts of the environmental acquisition of specific traits. But late nineteenth-century physiological theories did claim such systematic specificity: women's inferior mental acuity could be demonstrated by direct measurement of their skull sizes in comparison to men's. Dynamic psychology replaced the abstract, philosophical appeals to the social environment with accounts about how particular traits are acquired. In this sense, dynamic psychology provided greater challenges to physiological accounts than earlier philosophical arguments had done.

To understand how this shift occurs in Freud's work, we need to begin with Freud's turn away from people's bodies and to their thoughts as the immediate cause of illness. As is well known, an important phenomenon of Freud's early career was his interest in Josef Breuer's use of hypnosis as a cure for hysteria. Distinctive about this method of cure from others in widespread use at the time – such as diet, exercise, rest, or massage – was that it aimed to change patients' thoughts rather than their physiological states. Equally significant was Freud's fascination with certain directions taken by the French neurologist Jean-Martin Charcot with whom he went to study in Paris. In his autobiographical study published in the mid 1920s, Freud talks about his attraction to Charcot's investigations into hysteria. He notes that one of the features he found exciting about this work was that it showed that hysteria could be brought on by suggestion and, moreover, when induced in this way, appeared in all respects identical to hysteria brought on by physical trauma. He also states that he found Charcot's work exciting for its demonstration that hysteria was frequently found in men. This finding contradicted the position that the cause of hysteria was malfunctioning of a woman's reproductive organs,

---

[31] For informative discussions about how environmental factors played some role in late nineteenth-century somatic accounts, but of how this was a minor role, see Hale's useful analysis of these accounts in *Freud and the Americans*, pp. 47–97.

which meant, therefore, that hysteria could be found only in women. Similarly, he mentions that upon leaving Paris he talked with Charcot about his wish "to establish the thesis that in hysteria paralyses and anaesthesias of the various parts of the body are demarcated according to the popular idea of their limits and not acording to anatomical facts." The demonstration of such a thesis would prove that it was the idea of the body, rather than the body itself, which was causing the paralysis.[32]

The issue of how one interprets what is distinctive in Freud's turn to ideas rather than physiology as the immediate cause of hysteria is complex. Freud's focus on ideas and their storage in memory did not mean that Freud explicitly abandoned nineteenth-century views of the body as the storehouse of past environmental influences. It is rather that Freud began "bracketing out" the physiological as analytically helpful in functioning as such a storehouse. Steven Marcus elaborates this point by claiming that after Freud abandoned "The Project for a Scientific Psychology" in 1895, he kept from his previous scientific training a neurophysiological hydraulic model while abandoning a neuroanatomical model. Because Freud retained the hydraulic model, he could, in his own mind, view the psychic apparatus he began constructing as merely a temporary substitute for the underlying physiological structures he believed science would one day find:

What he does is to retain the neurophysiological "hydraulic" model of energy, resistance, discharge, inertia, storage and so on – but what he gives up is the *neuroanatomical* model, and the concomitant effort to locate such physiological processes in determinate anatomical positions in the central nervous system. Instead of that he substitutes a virtually or conceptually spatial "psychic apparatus" which acts as a kind of functional isomorph of the abandoned neuroanatomical model ... Yet he never at the same time gave up on the primary model except, as he said, "for the present." He believed that some day – in the neurosciences of

---

[32] Frank Sulloway argues that this position of Charcot's was widely accepted in Vienna at this time. Consequently, Sulloway disagrees with Freud's explanation of the poor reception he received following his report on his work with Charcot to the "Gesellschaft der Aerte" (Society of Medicine). In his autobiography, Freud describes the poor reception his report generated as due to opposition to the ideas that hysteria could be found in men and that it could be caused by suggestion. Sulloway claims that the poor reception was due rather to the lack of novelty in Freud's ideas. Sulloway's arguments are irrelevant to my own, since my use of Freud is as a case study of developments happening within the more general social milieu. Whether Freud's ideas here are new or not is not important. What is interesting, however, and relevant to my argument, is that Freud saw these positions as importantly different from what he had earlier assumed to be the case. For Sigmund Freud's autobiographical claims see, *An Autobiographical Study* (1925 [1924]), *The Standard Edition*, Vol. XX, p. 13. For Sulloway's argument see Frank J. Sulloway, *Freud, Biologist of the Mind: Beyond the Psychoanalytic Legend* (Cambridge, Mass. and London: Harvard University Press, 1992), pp. 35–42.

the twenty third century perhaps – the systems of his psychic apparatus would in fact, in some as yet unimagined way, be localized.[33]

In other words, to the extent that Freud was analytically replacing physiological concepts with psychological ones for the purposes of understanding how past influences remained within us, this was only, he believed, as a temporary measure. At some point in time, when our knowledge of the physical body had much advanced, physiological concepts could be brought back in.

Yet, if Freud's focus on ideas does not mean he was simply rejecting the idea of the body as the storehouse of previous environmental influences, nevertheless, there are important ways in which his focus on ideas soon differentiated his study from earlier accounts. Most importantly, what Freud could do, first by focusing on ideas as immediate cause, then soon, in constructing the unconscious as the site where past ideas could be seen as stored and continuing to function as cause, and finally in developing various hypotheses to explain the paths by which past ideas caused present actions, was to provide accounts which were "scientific" in the ways that prior physiological accounts claimed to be, but which introduced very different types of elements as causal determinants. Such accounts made possible a "strong" environmentalism, meaning that they admitted more complex reference to an individual's past social interactions than had been the case in earlier physiological theories, and more specific references than had been the case in earlier, more philosophical ones.

This "strong" environmentalism is apparent in Freud's and Breuer's case histories in their co-authored work *Studies on Hysteria*. These case histories offer complex accounts of patients' interactions with relatives, friends, and strangers over periods of time. Breuer and Freud tell stories which reference a wealth of social interactions of their patients ranging from early childhood to the time when analysis ceases. Indeed, as at one point Freud himself confusedly acknowledges, the case histories he writes sound very much like short stories and therefore appear to "lack the serious stamp of science":

I have not always been a psychotherapist. Like other neuropathologists, I was trained to employ local diagnoses and electro-prognosis, and it still strikes me myself as strange that the case histories I write should read like short stories and that, as one might say, they lack the serious stamp of science. I must console myself

[33] Steven Marcus, *Freud and the Culture of Psychoanalysis: Studies in the Transition from Victorian Humanism to Modernity* (Boston: George Allen and Unwin, 1984), p. 11. For another useful discussion of the relationship of Freud's concepts to physiological ones see Gerald N. Izenberg, *The Existentialist Critique of Freud: The Crisis of Autonomy* (Princeton University Press, 1976), p. 34.

with the reflection that the nature of the subject is evidently responsible for this, rather than any preference of my own. The fact is that local diagnosis and electrical reactions lead nowhere in the study of hysteria, whereas a detailed description of mental processes such as we are accustomed to find in the works of imaginative writers enables me, with the use of a few psychological formulas, to obtain at least some kind of insight into the course of that affection.[34]

This quote suggests that Freud was led to a "strong" environmentalism almost in spite of himself.

Most scholars acknowledge that it is in the period after *Three Essays on the Theory of Sexuality* that Freud began to develop a comprehensive theory of the mind, developing earlier ideas and generating new concepts to construct a theory of human development. Freud elaborated on previously identified mechanisms, such as repression and defense, and constructed new structures, such as the ego, id, and superego, to account for both general patterns of human behavior and for why some of us depart from those general patterns in the ways in which we do.

I would like to focus on Freud's last major theoretical text, *The Ego and the Id,* as a means to understand what is historically distinctive about such accounts. This text provides some important clues about what it means to describe Freud as a dynamic psychologist and about why this form of psychology represents something new. Reading this text, one is first struck by its abstract and philosophical character. Freud appears struggling to construct a "master plan" of the psyche, a plan that clearly delineates the psyche's basic structures and forces. In this respect, this work replicates earlier philosophical psychology, a psychology that also attempted to delineate the basic structures of the mind. What is different, however, about this work is that two of the three structures that Freud elaborates here, the ego and the superego, are presented as developmental accomplishments. Eighteenth- and nineteenth-century philosophers understood the basic faculties of the mind, such as reason or will, as given to the individual – and thus differentially given to different individuals and groups. But, for Freud, ego and superego are developmentally acquired. But this means that crucial aspects of who we are come from interactions with our external environments.

Indeed for Freud, the ego *is* that part of the id which has been modified by the individual's experiences with the external world:

It is easy to see that the ego is that part of the id which has been modified by the direct influence of the external world through the medium of the Pcpt.-Cs; in a sense it is an extension of the surface-differentiation. Moreover the ego seeks to

---

[34] Josef Breuer and Sigmund Freud, *Studies on Hysteria* (1893–95), *The Standard Edition,* Vol. II, pp. 160–61.

bring the influence of the external world to bear upon the id and its tendencies, and endeavors to substitute the reality principle for the pleasure principle which reigns unrestrictedly in the id. For the ego, perception plays the part which in the id falls to instinct.[35]

The experiences that modify the id to form the ego include firstly, and most basically, the experiences of the body:

The ego is first and foremost a bodily ego; it is not merely a surface entity, but is itself the projection of a surface.[36]

The ego also makes external love objects part of itself. It does this partly through processes of identification:

Since then we have come to understand that this kind of substitution [the substitution of an identification for an object-cathexis] has a great share in determining the form taken by the ego and that it makes an essential contribution towards building up what is called its "character."[37]

So important are such relationships with external love objects that Freud claims that "the character of the ego is a precipitate of abandoned object-cathexes and that it contains the history of those object choices."[38] And, it is from the complicated history of the ego's relationship with parents that there emerges that powerful extension of the ego, the superego.

The above are familiar ideas to those with any knowledge of Freud. I draw attention to the above passages only to highlight an aspect of this text that may now be so taken for granted as to go unnoticed, which is that for Freud, who we are is largely a function of the world we experience and the external objects our desire seeks. Our character, for Freud, is not given, but developmentally acquired through the interaction of the id with the world around us. Twentieth-century psychoanalysis will elaborate more the environmental aspect of this equation as the instinct part of Freudian theory is minimized. But in making it possible for psychoanalysis to go in such a direction, Freud represents an important stepping-stone from the past.

Implications for identity

Freud's adoption of an elaborated form of environmentalism made possible a radically revised understanding of human differences. When character becomes largely the outcome of the interaction of mostly common instincts with the varying influences of the environment, then the ways in

---

[35] Sigmund Freud, *The Ego and the Id* (1923), *The Standard Edition*, Vol. XIX, p. 25.
[36] *Ibid.* p. 26.   [37] *Ibid.* p. 28.   [38] *Ibid.* p. 29.

which humans are different from each other become less either/or, more a question of degree than of an essential nature. Thus, in the above, we saw how for Freud the attributes of homosexuality shade off into those of heterosexuality as the attributes of all the perversions shade off into those of normality in general. A similar blurring of the boundaries between traits associated with normality and those associated with deviance is apparent in other aspects of Freud's thought. Consider Freud's 1908 paper "Character and Anal Eroticism." In this essay, Freud links together the character traits of being orderly, parsimonious, and obstinate with the sublimation of anal eroticism and suggests that other complexes of traits can also be linked to particular erotogenic zones:

We ought in general to consider whether other character-complexes, too, do not exhibit a connection with the excitations of particular erotogenic zones. At present I only know of the intense "burning" ambition of people who earlier suffered from enuresis. We can at any rate lay down a formula for the way in which character in its final shape is formed out of the constituent instincts: the permanent character-traits are either unchanged prolongations of the original instincts, or sublimations of those instincts, or reaction-formations against them.[39]

To suggest that aspects of character associated with normality, i.e. being orderly, parsimonious, and obstinate, are formed in the same kinds of ways as are abnormalities, is, however, to make problematic the line that separates the character trait from the "symptom," or what is in accord with "the natural order" and what represents a distortion of it. If the abnormal is formed from the same sexual desire and in accord with the same types of processes that generate the normal, then the abnormal no longer stands to the normal as "freak" to "pure form." Rather the abnormal and the normal exist as variations on a continuum of possibilities with different individuals developing their characters at different points along the continuum.

But another consequence of the adoption of this more elaborated environmentalism is that it undermines the idea of character as a unified phenomenon. Within the older, constitutional model, character traits were viewed not only as naturally attached to particular types of bodies but as naturally coming in a package, each kind of package associated with a particular kind of body. In chapter 1, I noted how classifying human beings racially and sexually in the same kinds of ways as plants or animals are classified ended up denying individuality to human beings, a denial which affected women and blacks more than it affected men and whites in so far as sex and race played a more prominent role in descriptions of

---

[39] Sigmund Freud, "Character and Anal Eroticism" (1908), *The Standard Edition*, Vol. IX, p. 175.

women and blacks. But in dynamic psychology, this aspect of the older form of explanation is also undermined. To the extent that environmental influences replace differentiating biological structures as causes of our differences, then all of our differences – and not just those of men and whites – become more idiosyncratic, less type-based. This is because accidents of environmental influence are themselves episodic, occurring in varying degrees of strength, and in many possible combinations with each other.[40] Consequently, human differences become not only more disassociated from specific types of bodies, but also more disassociated from other differences with which they previously had been associated. Character becomes more the idiosyncratic conglomeration of various traits, each neither necessarily associated with any other nor with specific types of bodies. To use a Freudian example, one component of our common sexual desire, the desire for oral gratification, can, through the accidents of environmental influence, produce some who are obsessed with the pleasures of the mouth, some who are repulsed by such pleasures, and many of a range in between. And the one who is obsessed with the pleasures of the mouth can in turn be male or female, homosexual or heterosexual, intelligent or not. In short, explaining character through appeal to the union of common forces with the contingencies of environmental influences makes character less the manifestation of bodily based groupings of traits and more a unique collection of an assortment of traits. What is good about us, and also what is bad, is not only a question of degree but also is independent of who else we are. And if what is good and bad is no longer type-based, then both can occur to any among us. Eli Zaretsky makes a related point in speaking of the distinction between dependency/independency in Freudian theory:

Specifically, his work implied that the "problems" – hysteria, passivity, dependency – that Victorians had assigned to women, to the working class, or to "inferior" or "uncivilized" people were universal – and, indeed, were not problems at all but rather timeless characteristics of human psychology. Thus, the logic of the distinction between those in control (white businessmen and professionals) and those

---

[40] Elizabeth Lunbeck notes a similar difference in the relation of nineteenth- to twentieth-century psychiatry. As she states: "Nineteenth century psychiatric knowledge was organized around the distinction between insanity and sanity; symptoms were discrete and delimited, and diagnoses were premised on individuals exhibiting symptoms and behaviors that, psychiatrists hypothesized, differed qualitatively from those displayed by persons not afflicted. Only in the twentieth century would psychiatrists cast as symptoms behaviors that differed only quantitatively from traits anyone might exhibit – too much of this (abnormal selfishness, for instance), too little of that (insufficient willpower) – and only then would they reject the term insanity as too rigid and posit that the abnormal was but a variation on the normal." Elizabeth Lunbeck, *The Psychiatric Profession: Knowledge, Gender, and Power in Modern America* (Princeton University Press, 1994), p. 344, note 7.

in need of control (women, blacks, homosexuals, and Jews) began to break down. In a sense, Freud can be described as "outing" the white, male professional's passive and dependent wishes.[41]

This move to undermine group-based characteristics is also revealed in some of Freud's further claims about homosexuality. At the time when Freud was writing, the term that was often used to describe what we today label homosexuality was "inversion." The "invert" was a person whose sexual desire and gender were "inverted" in relation to their external body parts. The idea of "inversion" typifies the kind of association between "nature" and character that was elaborated in chapter 1. Though the invert's external body parts were known not to match his or her sexual desire, an anomaly that some tried to resolve by assuming a connection between inversion and hermaphroditism, an association was still made between sexual desire and gender. Thus, while an invert was considered to be a freak of nature in the sense that genitals did not match sexual desire, the invert was like everyone else in uniting a kind of inborn desire with a particular type of sexed character.

Freudian theory, however, undermines the association between sexual desire and the rest of character. Consider the following chart where Freud is reflecting upon the causes of homosexuality:

> It [the mystery of homosexuality] is instead a question of three sets of characteristics, namely –
>> Physical sexual characters
>> (physical hermaphroditism)
>> Mental sexual characters
>> (masculine or feminine attitude)
>> Kind of object-choice
> which, up to a certain point, vary independently of one another, and are met with in different individuals in manifold permutations.[42]

Noteworthy about this chart is not only that it separates gender, in the sense of character, from sex, in the sense of body type, but that it also separates both from sexual desire. The chart constructs as a developmental possibility the masculine gay man and the feminine lesbian. But this kind of separation of gender and sexual orientation makes possible one of the distinctive features of the twentieth-century term "homosexual." The term "homosexuality" picks out only same-sex practice as an indicator of identity and, unlike "inversion," suggests no necessary connection

[41] Eli Zaretsky, *Secrets of the Soul: A Social and Cultural History of Psychoanalysis* (New York: Vintage Books, 2005), p. 61.
[42] Sigmund Freud, "The Psychogenesis of a Case of Homosexuality in a Woman," in *The Standard Edition*, Vol. XVIII (1920–22), p. 170.

between sexual desire and gender identity.[43] Thus, the "homosexual" can be a man desiring another man who is masculine in character or a woman desiring another woman who is feminine in character. The very blandness and neutrality of the term "homosexuality" supports this separation of sexual desire from gender characteristics. To be sure, medical experts of the time made the theoretical separation of sexual desire from gender later for women than for men, a difference reflected in Freud's greater modification of this claim in respect to women.[44] And also, in popular thinking, the older association between gender and sexual desire lingered on so that even today many perceive the male homosexual as necessarily effeminate and the female homosexual as necessarily masculine. But this understanding, suggested in such slang derogatory labels as "faggot," "fairy," or "butch," represents the legacy of an earlier heritage at odds with newer understandings, particularly with those coming to be dominant in social scientific/psychological discourse.

This detachment of sexuality from gender was liberating. It suggested that the homosexual is different from the heterosexual only in one respect: his or her sexual desire. Therefore, he or she is not a radically different kind of human being. It will not be until much later in the century that these implications of the detachment of sexuality from gender made themselves felt in popular culture when the normalization of homosexual desire began.[45] But the isolation of sexual desire from other aspects of character that this acceptance rests upon was being made in the early part of the century by theorists such as Freud.

This separation of character from inherited nature is also, of course, a feature of some of Freud's claims about the male/female distinction. In earlier discussions I have pointed to the commonality of desire between heterosexuals and homosexuals in Freud's writings. But also, as Freud

---

[43] This feature of "homosexuality" and its distinctiveness from inversion is pointed out by George Chauncey, Jr., in his essay, "From Sexual Inversion to Homosexuality: Medicine and the Changing Conceptualization of Female Deviance," in *Salmagundi*, nos. 58–59 (Fall 1982–Winter 1983), pp. 114–46. David Halperin also elaborates on it in "One Hundred Years of Homosexuality," in David Halperin, ed., *One Hundred Years of Homosexuality* (New York and London: Routledge, 1990), pp. 15–40.

[44] Chauncey, Jr., discusses this difference in "From Sexual Inversion to Homosexuality," pp. 124–27. Freud's greater linkage of gender and sexuality in the case of women is expressed in *Three Essays on the Theory of Sexuality*: "The position in the case of women is less ambiguous; for among them the active inverts exhibit masculine characteristics, both physical and mental, with peculiar frequency and look for femininity in their sexual objects – though here again a closer knowledge of the facts might reveal greater variety" (p. 145).

[45] For a discussion of this process of normalization see Steven Seidman, *Beyond the Closet: The Transformation of Gay and Lesbian Life* (New York and London: Routledge, 2002).

consistently argued, the libido is neither male nor female. But if the libido is neither male nor female, then the traits that we associate with "maleness" and "femaleness" cannot be *direct* products of it. Consider again the chart where Freud is considering the causes of homosexuality:

> It [the mystery of homosexuality] is instead a question of three sets of characteristics, namely –
>
> Physical sexual characters
> (physical hermaphroditism)
> Mental sexual characters
> (masculine or feminine attitude)
> Kind of object-choice
>
> which, up to a certain point, vary independently of one another, and are met with in different individuals in manifold permutations.[46]

As Freud is distinguishing the character of the homosexual from his or her body and desire, so also is Freud distinguishing here the character of the male or female from body type and desire. The distinction that Freud makes in this chart between physicality and "mental sexual characters" replicates the distinction feminists in the 1960s began to make between "sex" and "gender." These feminists recognized that an important obstacle standing in the way of the expansion of women's roles was the widespread belief that women's biology suited women only for certain activities. They recognized that the reduction of social role to biology was made possible by the collapse of the characterological and the biological in the phrase "sex differences," and they sought to prevent this collapse in the use of the word "gender." We can see that Freud in this chart is making a similar theoretical move.

But, while Freud, in some aspects of his writing, moved towards undermining the bases for the kinds of distinctions between heterosexuals and homosexuals and between men and women that were associated with late nineteenth-century, somatically based theories, Freud, as is well known, also produced analyses that maintained some of those distinctions. For example, Freud's doctrine of penis envy states that because of the smaller size of the female clitoris in comparison to the male penis, little girls and little boys develop their sexual desire and other aspects of their character in different ways. Freud interprets the smaller size of the girl's clitoris as an obvious cause of alarm for both girls and boys, leading little boys in one direction and little girls in another. Among the consequences of these different turns are that girls develop weaker superegos, a stronger sense of

---

[46] Freud, "The Psychogenesis of a Case of Homosexuality in a Woman," p. 170.

jealousy, vanity, etc.[47] Indeed, it is upon the basis of this doctrine that Freud justified many of his most sexist claims.

To recognize this aspect of Freudian theory is to recognize that while Freudian theory did move an understanding of human differences in new directions, it did not consistently do so. Elements within his writings point to the existing legacy of late nineteenth-century views. One place where the transitionality of his own thinking is particularly obvious is in his own self-conscious reflections on the relation between hereditary versus environmental influences, reflections which continue throughout his life. Thus, even in his last book, *An Outline of Psychoanalysis*, Freud adopts a "compromise" position:

The determining causes of all the forms taken by human life, is, indeed, to be sought in the reciprocal action between innate dispositions and accidental experiences.[48]

In the *Three Essays on the Theory of Sexuality*, Freud makes the following comments:

It is not easy to estimate the relative efficacy of the constitutional and accidental factors. In theory one is always inclined to overestimate the former; therapeutic practice emphasizes the importance of the latter. It should, however, on no account be forgotten that the relation between the two is a co-operative and not a mutually exclusive one. The constitutional factor must await experiences before it can make itself felt; the accidental factor must have a constitutional basis in order to come into operation.[49]

From the above we can conclude, therefore, that while Freud was inaugurating significant changes in how human character was to be understood, there remained the legacies of late nineteenth-century somatic perspectives even in his own writings, and these legacies enabled him to stress differences between women and men that other aspects of his theory would otherwise have precluded. Moreover, these legacies cannot simply be written off as understandable reflections of his time. Not only from the perspective of contemporary vantage points, but even from the

---

[47] Sigmund Freud, Lecture XXXIII, "Femininity" (1933 [1932]), in *New Introductory Lectures*, *The Standard Edition*, Vol. XXII, pp. 124–30. For Freud's discussion in his later years of the role of penis envy in differentiating the developmental histories of boys and girls, see, in addition to his discussion in the *New Introductory Lectures*, "Female Sexuality" (1931), *The Standard Edition*, Vol. XXI, pp. 223–43; "Some Psychical Consequences of the Anatomical Distinction Between the Sexes" (1925), *The Standard Edition*, Vol. XIX, pp. 248–58; "The Psychogenesis of a Case of Homosexuality in a Woman," pp. 147–72; and his discussion in *An Outline of Psychoanalysis*, p. 155.

[48] Freud, *An Outline of Psychoanalysis*, p. 183.

[49] Freud, *Three Essays on the Theory of Sexuality*, p. 239.

perspective of some of his colleagues, Freud's thoughts on these issues reveal decidedly Victorian biases.[50]

It is not simply Freud's continued invocation of bodily differences that reveals the legacy of Victorian perspectives in his writings. There are other ways in which these perspectives surface that cannot merely be explained as a function of Freud's only partial commitment to dynamic psychology. Dynamic psychology challenges the idea that human character is a function of inborn, physiological factors, replacing such factors with common structures and diverse environmental influences. But dynamic psychology has nothing to say about the values that attach to the diverse outcomes of human character development. And, because it does not, it leaves the question of values unaddressed, providing no conceptual impetus for questioning the legitimacy of whatever values already attach to such outcomes.

This limitation of dynamic psychology surfaces in Freud's writings in a variety of places. Take, for example, Freud's claims about the greater maturity of vaginal over clitoral stimulation. Such claims can only be explained through an implicit understanding that women's desire ought to be geared towards procreation.[51] That Freud endorsed such an understanding is further revealed in his claims that "normal femininity" means heterosexuality, marriage, and the production of babies.[52] Thus, that a little girl resolves her "penis envy" by deciding to become heterosexual, marry, and to have babies, was for Freud a more normal and desirable resolution than other possible resolutions. And Freud's arguments that women are more narcissistic, vain, jealous, and possess less of a sense of justice than men, reflected a value system not only where women and men are expected to be different from one another, but one which depicted

---

[50] For an excellent discussion of Freud's struggles with some of his colleagues around the "woman question," see Mari Jo Buhle, *Feminism and Its Discontents: A Century of Struggle with Psychoanalysis* (Cambridge, Mass.: Harvard University Press, 1998), pp. 53–84. For useful analyses about how Freud's biases are biases and exist in contradiction with other aspects of his theory and method, see Nancy J. Chodorow, "Feminism, Femininity and Freud," in Nancy J. Chodorow, *Feminism and Psychoanalytic Theory* (New Haven and London: Yale University Press, 1989), pp. 165–77 and Roy Schafer, "Problems in Freud's Psychology of Women," in *Journal of the American Psychoanalytic Association 22*, no. 3 (1974), pp. 459–85.

[51] See Freud, "Female Sexuality," p. 225. See also Freud, "Femininity," p. 118. The remarks he makes in this latter work are the following: "With the change to femininity the clitoris should wholly or in part hand over its sensitivity, and at the same time its importance to the vagina. This would be one of the two tasks that a woman has to perform in the course of her development, whereas the more fortunate man has only to continue at the time of his sexual maturity the activity that he has previously carried out at the period of the early efflorescence of his sexuality."

[52] Freud, "Femininity," pp. 124–30.

women as less serious and more self-involved beings than men when they fulfill such expectations.[53]

This surfacing of the values of his time is also apparent in some of Freud's claims about homosexuality. The language Freud used to explain the occurrence of homosexuality is the language of things "gone wrong" – overly attached mothers or disattached fathers. Freud assumed that "normal" human beings are heterosexual and resolve their Oedipal complexes in certain commonly accepted ways. These kinds of claims about homosexuality – that it reflects an aberration caused by the failure of a child to successfully resolve his or her relationships with parents – appear more reminiscent of a nineteenth-century linkage of homosexuality with sin than they do with a more late twentieth-century attitude of acceptance.[54]

The conceptual problem here is that to the extent that both gender and sexuality are separated from physiology, that is, to the extent that neither follow *directly* from physiology, then the claim that certain outcomes are "successes" and others are "failures" requires justification outside of the theory; the "success" or "failure" status of such outcomes no longer simply follows from biology. Freud knew that to construe the libido as "naturally" neither heterosexual nor homosexual made heterosexuality itself a phenomenon in need of explanation. He states the following:

On the contrary, psycho-analysis considers that a choice of an object independently of its sex – freedom to range equally over male and female objects – as it is found in childhood, in primitive states of society and early periods of history, is the original basis from which, as a result of restriction in one direction or the other, both the normal and the inverted types develop. Thus from the point of view of psycho-analysis the exclusive sexual interest felt by men for women is also a problem that needs elucidating and is not a self-evident fact based upon an attraction that is ultimately of a chemical nature.[55]

But Freud did not explore the question of why, given that different possible resolutions of the Oedipal complex are developmental possibilities, homosexuality and some but not other versions of gender are developmental "failures." For that kind of questioning to arise, different kinds of challenges were necessary to late nineteenth-century modes of thought.

---

[53] *Ibid.* pp. 132; Freud, "Some Psychical Consequences," pp. 254, 257–58.

[54] As example see the footnotes added by Freud in 1910 and 1915 to his discussion of inversion in *Three Essays on the Theory of Sexuality*, pp. 144–45, 145–46.

[55] *Ibid.* pp. 145–46. This quote is from a footnote added in 1915.

Conclusion

In the above I have attempted to concentrate on those aspects of Freud's theory that were representative of changes made by dynamic psychology in general. The point was not to claim that Freud was alone, or was even the first, to challenge aspects of late nineteenth-century somatically based models of identity. Rather, I have used Freudian theory as a case study, as an example of the kinds of theoretical moves that were necessary to make this challenge. Freud is especially useful as a case study both because of the timing and context of his intellectual development and also because he combined in one powerful and comprehensive body of work many of the moves that were involved in this challenge.

The kinds of challenges that dynamic psychology made to the somatically based theories of the late nineteenth century are revealed in Freud's theory in both its "strong" environmentalism and in its significant focus on the physiological as what we share rather than what differentiates us. In Freud's focus on thoughts and memories as the causes of behavioral disturbances, he opened a space for attention to be given to complex human interactions as formative of character. By combining a strong environmentalism with a view of physiology as mostly what we have in common, Freud makes character more loosely attached to the body and less coherently constructed than it had been.

These points remind us of some of the liberatory consequences of the introduction of dynamic psychology into popular discourse. As noted earlier, when cultural critics have reflected upon the introduction of psychological talk into twentieth-century culture, they have often emphasized the negative aspects of such talk, for example, the self-involvement that has often seemed to accompany popularizations of this discourse. But while such criticisms point to real aspects of this new discourse, they do not tell the whole story. As the above discussion suggests, this new talk also made possible the theorization of human behavior in new kinds of ways, ways that were particularly liberating for women, the racially stigmatized, and those who experienced same-sex desire. Types of behaviors that had been seen as naturally linked to the bodies of members of these groups could now be explained as only accidently associated with such bodies. And the bodies of members of such groups could no longer be as easily employed as reasons for excluding such individuals from activities previously denied them. In short, it is difficult imagining many of the social changes that took place in the course of the twentieth century occurring apart from the creation of these new ways of theorizing human identity. As Virginia Woolf asserted, something importantly beneficial occurred to human character, on or about 1910.

To be sure, this introduction of psychological talk constituted only part of the intellectual resources that contributed to such changes. As we have seen from the preceding discussion, while dynamic psychology undermined the idea that character followed from biology, it left unchallenged the idea that certain character traits and behaviors were inherently superior to others. While dynamic psychology undermined the rationale for thinking that such superiority was grounded "in nature," it left unexamined the question: What then *did* ground such claims of superiority? Other disciplinary innovations and cultural shifts were necessary to make this question a significant part of public debate. Let us now turn to one particularly important such innovation in the discipline of anthropology.

3   The culture concept and social identity

"Culture," in its anthropological sense, provided a functionally equivalent substitute for the older idea of "race temperament." It explained all
the same phenomena, but it did so in strictly non biological terms ...
(George W. Stocking, Jr.)[1]

In the previous chapter I described one type of challenge to the late
nineteenth-century use of nature to sort social groups, that made by
dynamic psychology. This new turn in psychology, and its growing appeal
outside of the academy, contributed to an increased sense within popular
thought that individual character is the unique outcome of a variety of
environmental interactions rather than a "bundled" set of attributes
emanating from inherited, natural givens. Thus, the emphasis in
dynamic psychology on the environmental causes of character expressed
a new appreciation that, for all, character is more individual than group
based.

In this chapter I want to look at another means by which the employment of identity labels to differentially rank human beings began to
unravel in the early and mid part of the twentieth century. I want to look
at changes in the use of a particular concept, "culture," as playing a
particularly important role in this unraveling. In this case, the move did
not suggest a greater individuality of identity, but rather a greater equivalence in the value of the practices of different social groups. "Culture"
described many of the practices previously associated with racial identity
as less naturally acquired. It also described many of the practices associated with national identity as less rationally acquired than national identification had done. Thus, it leveled some of the differences associated
with the differential deployment of these two forms of identity. In connection with leveling such differences, "culture" described many of the

---

[1] George W. Stocking, Jr., *Race, Culture, and Evolution: Essays in the History of Anthropology*
(New York: Free Press, 1968), p. 265.

practices associated with all social groups as more arbitrarily acquired and more arbitrary in value.

I want to begin this examination of changes in the use of "culture" by focusing on certain transformations in American anthropology inaugurated by Franz Boas. As many commentators have pointed out, Franz Boas is a singularly important figure in the history of the "culture" concept. Boaz, more extensively than any of his predecessors in American anthropology, displaced the idea of race through use of the concept of "culture," and this achievement has been well documented. But I want to focus on a particular aspect of this achievement that is more controversial: how his use of "culture" can be associated with the advancement of moral relativism, at least in regard to a wide variety of social practices that had otherwise been understood in less relativistic ways.

This claim is controversial because scholarship on the issue of Boas' moral relativism displays a curious disparity. On the one hand, there are scholars who argue against a description of Boas as a moral relativist, distinguishing Boas' position from that of some of his students and from other interpreters. An example of such a scholar is the philosopher, John Cook, who argues that Boas' elaboration of the "culture" concept cannot be interpreted as an endorsement of moral relativism. Cook responds to those who link Boas with such relativism by making a distinction between "cultural relativism," whose goal is to make sure that social group practices are described within the terms by which their practitioners understand them, and "moral relativism," which has to do with how social group practices are judged. Cook claims that one finds in Boas only "cultural relativism" – a position that states that practices found in societies different from the observer's own may possess different meanings from apparently similar practices in the observer's. "Cultural relativism" cautions the observer to be open to such differences. Consequently, "cultural relativism" represents only an admonition concerning the first steps in moral judgment. It advises the outsider to make certain he or she has the moral facts right before moving to moral assessment. Cook states that what Boas is warning us against is mistaken description of moral facts, descriptions made faulty by the outsider's act of projection. Cook quotes the following passage from Boas where Boas warns against a faulty description of an act as murder, that is, as undertaken for those motives westerners associate with murder:

From an ethnological point of view murder cannot be considered as a single phenomenon ... [A] father who kills his child as a sacrifice for the welfare of his people, acts from such entirely different motives [i.e. motives so different from jealousy, greed, and rage], that psychologically a comparison of their actions does not seem permissible. It would seem much more proper to compare ... the sacrifice of a child on behalf of the tribe with any other action performed on account of strong altruistic motives, than to base our comparison on the common concept of murder.[2]

Thus, according to Cook, "cultural relativism" for Boas is really about getting such facts right, that is, describing acts with the motives and under the descriptions held by those who perform them. But that Boas emphasizes the need to get the facts right does not entail that he finds moral judgment about such facts problematic. In the above passage, Boas certainly appears to be allowing for comparison once the description is done right. Cook distinguishes between the kind of "cultural relativism" present in Boas, a relativism that only insists on getting the facts right, from the moral relativism present in some of Boas' students.[3] Cook's argument about Boas' position is replicated in Carl Degler's claim that it would be a mistake to view Boas as a relativist if we mean by that "someone who saw all cultures as equal, or who refused to recognize a hierarchy among societies."[4]

On the other hand, there are many, including the renowned historian of anthropology, George Stocking, Jr., who argue that Boas' elaboration of "culture" is associated with a move to understand social group practices in more relativistic terms. Thus, in an essay titled "Franz Boas and the Culture Concept in Historical Perspective," Stocking argues that Boas inaugurated the modern concept of culture, a concept Stocking describes as decidedly "relativistic."[5] While recognizing that Boas remained "enough of a Victorian liberal-positivist to retain a limited belief in the progress of civilization,"[6] Stocking also claims that Boas' idea of culture entailed rejection of belief in any single, external standard of evaluation that could be used to rank a society as a whole:

Beyond this, the general effect of Boas' critique of evolutionism was to show that various elements of human culture did not march together in any sort of lock step

[2] John W. Cook, *Morality and Cultural Differences* (New York and Oxford: Oxford University Press, 1999), p. 69. The citation from Franz Boas is from *The Mind of Primitive Man* (New York: Free Press, 1963), p. 203.
[3] Cook, *Morality and Cultural Differences*, pp. 51–75. The distinction Cook makes between "cultural relativism" and "moral relativism" parallels a distinction David Hollinger makes between methodological and ideological relativism in "Cultural Relativism," pp. 708–20 in *Cambridge History of Science*, Vol. VII, *Social Sciences*, ed. Theodore Porter and Dorothy Ross (Cambridge University Press, 2003), p. 710.
[4] Carl Degler, *In Search of Human Nature* (New York and Oxford: Oxford University Press, 1991), p. 80.
[5] George Stocking, Jr., "Franz Boas and the Culture Concept in Historical Perspective," in Stocking, *Race, Culture, and Evolution*, pp. 195–233. Stocking does not distinguish between forms of relativism in this essay.
[6] *Ibid.* p. 222.

or regular sequence. Once the "one grand scheme" of evolutionism was rejected, the multiplicity of *cultures* which took the place of the cultural *stages* of savagery, barbarism, and civilization were no more easily brought within one standard of evaluation than they were within one system of explanation.[7]

Susan Hegeman also claims that relativism is central to the thesis of Boas' important work, *The Mind of Primitive Man*. In referring to a letter Boas wrote to the editor of *The New York Times* in 1916, Hegeman makes the following comment:

Here, Boas applied to contemporary problems the fundamental tenet of his 1911 *The Mind of Primitive Man*, the morally relativist view that societies should not be judged by standards external to their own contexts.[8]

In this chapter I want to argue against Cook and Degler and claim that Boas' elaboration of the culture concept took Boas beyond raising admonitions about social description. Rather, this elaboration led him to challenge the grounds upon which many social practices had been judged inferior or superior within prior evolutionary frameworks. In particular, it led him to discount the tendency, common to social evolutionary frameworks, to rank social practices as "backward" or "advanced" merely because of their placement in societies themselves labeled in such terms. For Boas, there was no judgment by association; individual practices had to be individually assessed as to whether they were amenable to cross-cultural judgment. While he did believe that certain practices, such as those of science and democratic politics, were so amenable, he also believed that many social practices, previously understood by many in moralistic terms, were not. At minimum, then, Boas restricted the arena of what might count as open to cross-cultural judgmental evaluation.

But I emphasize the association between Boas' use of "culture" and a restriction of the arena of what might be cross-culturally judged not to make some point about Boas or his students alone. Rather, as I used Freud in the previous chapter as a means to highlight changes in ways of thought taking place in the wider society in the early part of the twentieth century, so also am I using Boas to highlight other changes in ways of thought taking place in the wider US society in this period. The use of "culture" that Boas and his students began to employ in the 1920s became widely used in US public discourse during the 1930s and 1940s. And here it also was associated with the tendency to view many differences among social groups in less judgmental terms, i.e. more as merely "differences"

---

[7] *Ibid.* pp. 228–29.
[8] Susan Hegeman, *Patterns for America: Modernism and the Concept of Culture* (Princeton University Press, 1999), p. 53.

and less as signs of inferiority or superiority. The growth of such forms of acceptance enabled members of some groups the means to proudly assert differences while still claiming identification as American citizens. This proud proclamation of difference could be used as a political tool for challenging discrimination. In short, "cultural" identity became an important political tool in twentieth-century America. As we shall explore in later chapters, the question only became, to whom, and at what point, it did become available. But for now, let us focus only on the nature of the tool itself: how it was developed and what attachments came with it.

The evolution of the attack on social evolution

The use of the concept of "culture" undercuts the differential evaluation of social group practices in one obvious way. Insofar as "culture" relies on environmental explanations to explain differences among social groups, it undercuts the differential naturalization of such group practices that the use of "race" supports. But while this replacement is part of the story, it is not the whole story. To understand in a fuller way how Boas' use of "culture" undermines such differential evaluation, it is useful to focus on the school of thought that Boas developed his ideas against, that of evolutionary anthropology. This school of thought was dominant in England and the United States in the late nineteenth and early twentieth century.

On the one hand, much of evolutionary anthropology was grounded in naturalistic explanations. "Race" was an important concept within this school and was heavily employed to explain the differential social progress of social groups. Thus, even one of the more enlightened theorists in this school, E. B. Tylor, who most often stressed learning and environmental factors as the motor force of human history, occasionally resorted to "race" to explain differential social progress.[9] Marvin Harris points to

---

[9] One question is how Tylor could hold on to these biological views in the context of his otherwise very environmentalist views. From the vantage point of contemporary perspectives, holding both sets of positions seems highly contradictory. But one point that needs to be kept in mind in thinking about Tylor's position is the continuing presence in Tylor's time of the belief in the inheritance of acquired characteristics. This belief enabled Tylor, like others, to admit environmental causes of social differences while also subscribing to biological or racial causes. One could state that people were products of their environments, while also claiming that some of the ways that people's diversely experienced environments affected them was in their physiologies. And these environmentally caused differences in physiology could in turn be invoked to explain other differences. As Stocking points out, building on some thoughts of Alfred Kroeber, Lamarckianism importantly functioned to support prevalent racial assumptions. Stocking makes this point eloquently in the following:

the following passage from Tylor's *Anthropology: An Introduction to the Study of Man and Civilization*, as illustrating this use:

There seems to be in mankind inbred temperament and inbred capacity of mind. History points the great lesson that some races have marched on in civilization while others have stood still or fallen back, and we should partly look for an explanation of this in differences of intellectual and moral powers between such tribes as the native Americans and Africans, and the Old World nations who overmatch and subdue them.[10]

But if even Tylor sometimes fell back on natural differences to account for the "advanced" nature of some groups' practices in distinction from the "backward" nature of others, social evolutionary theory did not require recourse to race to support such judgments. As noted, Tylor himself most often explained the differential social progress of social groups as a consequence of learning:

In the first place, the facts collected seem to favour the view that the wide differences in the civilization and mental state of the various races of mankind are rather differences of development than of origin, rather of degree than of kind.[11]

And the possible independence of social evolutionary theory from racial premises is indicated even more strongly by another famous late nineteenth-century social evolutionist, Karl Marx. In the case of Marx, it is a society's stage of economic activity that accounts for its stage of development. Marx could speak about "stages" of economic activity because he assumed that different forms of economic activity could be evaluated in relationship to each other through reference to a type of rationality. Marx believed that humans become increasingly better in developing the means of satisfying their material needs. Because for him, diverse economic practices reflect the progressive development of that rationality, some economic practices can be judged as superior to

But standing almost unnoticed at the periphery of social theory, it [Lamarckianism] provided the last important link between social and biological theory. The problem facing the social sciences in the early twentieth century was not their domination by notions of biological or racial determinism, but rather their obfuscation by a vague sociological indeterminism, a "blind and bland shuttling" between race and civilization. As Kroeber suggested, the Lamarckian notion of the inheritance of acquired characteristics was the bridge over which this shuttling took place. As long as this bridge remained standing, the fully independent study of society and culture was difficult if not impossible. (Stocking, *Race, Culture, and Evolution*, p. 265)

[10] Marvin Harris, *The Rise of Anthropological Theory: A History of Theories of Culture* (New York: Thomas Y. Crowell Company, 1968), p. 140. The references Harris cites are E. B. Tylor, *Primitive Culture* (New York: Harper Torchbooks, 1958 [1871]), Vol. I, p. 7 and E. B. Tylor, *Anthropology: An Introduction to the Study of Man and Civilization* (New York: D. Appleton, 1899 [1881]), p. 74. In the 1904 edition this quote is found on p. 57.

[11] E. B. Tylor, *Researches into the Early History of Mankind and the Development of Civilization* (Chicago and London: University of Chicago Press, 1964 [1865]), p. 232.

others. Since for Marx the type of economic practice found in a given society affects all other social practices of that society, societies as a whole can be situated on a stage of human development.

In light of the above discussion, we can understand the importance of two aspects of Boas' challenge to evolutionary anthropology: (1) Boas' elaborated attack on the idea of "race" and thus on physiological differences as the source of difference in social practices, and (2) Boas' attack on the idea of rationality as the source of difference in many social practices. While Boas admitted that differences in the exercise of rationality account for differences in *some* social practices – for example the practices of science from other ways of dealing with nature – he did not believe that such differences in rationality were encompassing across societies as a whole. The former attack undermined the idea that natural differences link levels of social progress with different groups. The latter attack undermined the idea that differences in rationality link social progress with different groups. Both attacks together undermined the idea that there is *any* one factor that links social progress with social groups as a whole. Boas' attack on both ideas constituted a thorough challenge to the idea that social progress is encompassing across societies. Let me examine Boas' attacks on each idea in turn.

Boas' attack on the idea of race became gradually more powerful during the course of his life. In his early writings, even including *The Mind of Primitive Man*, Boas occasionally attributed some importance to race as determinant of human behavior. Thus he claimed in this work that the physiological differences among the races probably entail some mental differences as well.[12] But such claims, even here, are surrounded by qualifications. He states that the physiological differences among races appear only as statistical variations, with some individuals in each race being more similar to individuals of other races than they are to the average of their own race.[13] By 1928, Boas has elaborated this argument about physiology so as even to suggest suspicions about the concept of race. In *Anthropology and Modern Life*, he argues that there are no pure racial types if we mean by "racial types" distinguishable groups where all individuals share common characteristics not shared by those

[12] Franz Boas, *The Mind of Primitive Man* (New York: Macmillan Co., 1911), p. 115; Franz Boas, "Human Faculty as Determined by Race" (1894), in *The Shaping of American Anthropology 1883–1911: A Franz Boas Reader*, ed. George W. Stocking, Jr. (New York: Basic Books, 1974), p. 234.
[13] Boas, "Human Faculty as Determined by Race," p. 227; Boas, *The Mind of Primitive Man* (1911), pp. 94, 269.

outside of the group.[14] In his later writings, this questioning of the concept of race was coupled with his insistence that heredity is better understood as operating at the individual rather than group level.[15]

Boas not only questioned the idea of race as a physiologically useful concept, but he also discredited its role in effecting social practice. Large sections of *The Mind of Primitive Man* are devoted to denying connections among racial types, languages, and cultures. In this work, he notes the ways each varies independently of the other. Thus he points to the primitive culture of the ancestors of contemporary Europeans and the advanced culture of the ancestors of contemporary "primitives."[16] He also points to the many ways language is independent of both race and culture. He sums up his position as follows:

These considerations make it fairly clear that, at least at the present time, anatomical type, language, and culture have not necessarily the same fates; that a people may remain constant in type and language, and change in culture; that it may remain constant in type, but change in language; or that it may remain constant in language, and change in type and culture.[17]

Appeals to "nature" and to "natural development" were an important resource in late nineteenth-century social theory for weaving together practices and physique in assumed "natural" types, types that were thought to represent distinct stages of development. But, as my earlier reference to Marx indicated, an appeal to natural differences was not the only means by which the idea of social hierarchy could be sustained. This idea could also be sustained by the claim that different social groups were governed by different levels of rationality. Boas moved away from this position by limiting the sphere of rationality to certain circumscribed arenas.

---

[14] Franz Boas, *Anthropology and Modern Life* (New York: W. W. Norton & Company, 1928), p. 35. On p. 62 of this work Boas also states: "We have seen that from a purely biological point of view the concept of race unity breaks down. The multitude of genealogical lines, the diversity of individual and family types contained in each race is so great that no race can be considered as a unit. Furthermore, similarities between neighboring races and, in regard to function, even between distant races are so great that individuals cannot be assigned with certainty to one group or another."

[15] Boas, "The Aims of Anthropological Research," in Franz Boas, *Race, Language, and Culture* (University of Chicago Press, 1940), p. 255 (originally, "Address of the President of the American Association for the Advancement of Science, Atlantic City, December, 1932," *Science* N.S., 76 [1932], pp. 605–13). This point is also made in "Some Problems of Methodology in the Social Sciences," in *Race, Language and Culture*, p. 265 (originally in *The New Social Sciences*, ed. Leonard D. White [University of Chicago Press, 1930], pp. 84–98).

[16] Boas, *The Mind of Primitive Man* (1911), p. 13. This point is also made in Boas, "The Aims of Anthropological Research," p. 249.

[17] Boas, *The Mind of Primitive Man* (1911), p. 133.

This restriction of the scope of rationality followed from his view that many of the practices thought to be the outcomes of rational thought are more the outcomes of the contingent and arbitrary processes of psychology. As an example are those practices Boas describes as "customary." Boas labels many of the practices of western societies as "customs": while justified through local systems of rules, they cannot be justified outside of such rules. But insofar as these practices cannot be justified outside of such local rules, they cannot be described as superior in any absolute sense. He argues that while many in his own society may be tempted to think of such practices in such terms, they are mistaken in doing so. Consider his following discussion of etiquette and modesty:

A good example of what I refer to are breaches of social etiquette. A mode of behavior that does not conform to the customary manners, but differs from them in a striking way, creates, on the whole, unpleasant emotions; and it requires a determined effort on our part to make it clear to ourselves that such behavior does not conflict with moral standards. ... In certain lines of conduct the association between traditional etiquette and ethical feeling is so close, that even a vigorous thinker can hardly emancipate himself from it. This is true, for instance, of acts that may be considered breaches of modesty.[18]

While today one might be tempted to say, but, of course, etiquette and manners are not matters of moral concern, it is worth considering that many have not always understood this to be the case. Moreover, some of the types of conduct that Boas describes as "customary" – such as for example, "breaches of modesty" – are even today considered by many to be matters for moral judgment. And that Boas was intending the category of the customary to include a large class of actions, many surrounded by strong feeling and a belief in their cross-cultural justifiability, is supported in the following:

Besides this, there are a thousand activities and modes of thought that constitute our daily life, – of which we are not conscious at all until we come into contact with other types of life, or until we are prevented from acting according to our custom, – that cannot in any way be claimed to be more reasonable than others, and to which, nevertheless, we cling. These, it would seem, are hardly less numerous in civilized than in primitive culture, because they constitute the whole series of well-established habits according to which the necessary actions of ordinary every-day life are performed, and which are learned less by instruction than by imitation.[19]

Boas emphasizes the strong tendency to give such customary actions rational explanations. However, he claims that such explanations are best described as rationalizations. Rather than being the outcome of a

[18] *Ibid.* pp. 211–12.   [19] *Ibid.* p. 241.

reflective judgment that initiates action, they are created after the fact to justify emotional reactions already in place. He claims that the tendency to so rationalize actions is as true of his own society as it is of more "primitive" ones:

I think, however, that a close introspective analysis shows these reasons to be only attempts to interpret our feelings of displeasure ... I think the existence of such secondary interpretations of customary actions is one of the most important anthropological phenomena, and we have seen that it is hardly less common in our own society than in more primitive societies.[20]

One reason that many social practices fall within the category of the "customary" is because they are rooted in interests that are demanded by the particularities of specific circumstances. One example is language, where some of the interests that govern its content are local, making cross-cultural comparisons about "better" or "worse" irrelevant. Boas argues against an evolutionary approach to linguistic analysis by making the following argument:

It seems fairly evident that the selection of such simple terms must to a certain extent depend upon the chief interests of a people; and where it is necessary to distinguish a certain phenomenon in many aspects, which in the life of a people play each an entirely independent role, many independent words may develop, while in other cases modifications of a single term may suffice.

Thus it happens that each language, from the point of view of another language, may be arbitrary in its classifications; that what appears as a single simple idea in one language may be characterized by a series of distinct word-stems in another.[21]

As noted above, Boas believed that many of the practices not capable of assessment by reference to cross-cultural criteria are nevertheless subject to rules. As the example of language demonstrates, complex rules may govern the use of distinctions that are based only in local needs. Because such practices are subject to rules, it is possible to speak about "right" or "wrong" or "good" and "bad" examples without believing such assessments to be capable of cross-cultural justification. In short, Boas' analysis suggests the need for recognition of two types of assessment: that which is based on local rules or criteria and that which makes claims to cross-cultural justification.

Boas does depict some practices as falling within the latter category, that is, as representing areas where human beings have made progress. In

---

[20] *Ibid.* pp. 218, 226.
[21] *Ibid.* pp. 146–47. In this work and in others Boas claims that the cultural specificity of language in turn affects both our thought and our behavior. See, for example, his discussion of language in *Anthropology and Modern Life*, pp. 146–48 or in *The Mind of Primitive Man* (1911), p. 153.

many of his works, Boas speaks about advances in reasoning processes, claiming that with civilization much reasoning has become more logical and less governed by contingent and emotional associations. Boas also speaks about progress in the degree to which the ethical ideals of human fellowship and freedom are applied in human life, subsuming this progress also to advances in human reasoning.[22] And, at times, he becomes quite explicit in making the connection between these positions with his rejection of a more philosophical type of relativism.[23]

But such claims about human progress do not allow for a stage theory of social development. To speak about progress, for Boas, is to speak about development only in restricted areas:

It seems impossible, if we disregard invention and knowledge, the two elements just referred to, to bring cultures into any kind of continuous series.[24]

It is not easy to define progress in any phase of social life other than in knowledge and control of nature.[25]

This restriction of progress to specific areas follows for Boas from the fact that development in one area does not entail development in another. There is no "progress by association" in Boasian theory.

That Boas did not believe social development to occur across social practices is evidenced in many of his claims. As he points out, some peoples have advanced in many of the arts but have not discovered pottery. Similarly, neither the development of metallurgy, agriculture, nor the domestication of animals is necessarily linked to other forms of development.[26] Boas claims that anthropologists have tended to overlook such disparity in development by depicting as similar what is similar only in very superficial respects:

[22] For his claim that civilization brings with it an advance of reasoning processes see *The Mind of Primitive Man* (1911), pp. 206–08, 219, 220. In this work Boas also talks about civilization bringing with it a broadening concept of fellowship among human beings (p. 207). In *Anthropology and Modern Life*, Boas claims that there is progress in ethical conduct based upon "the recognition of larger groups which participate in the rights enjoyed by members of the closed society, and on an increasing social control" (p. 219). Boas also mentions in this latter work that the advance of civilization has brought about an expansion of the freedom of individuals. This has resulted from the lessening importance given to status considerations (pp. 220–21). In this work he identifies both of these latter types of advance with advances in knowledge (p. 220). Indeed, he claims that: "It is not easy to define progress in any phase of social life other than in knowledge and control of nature" (p. 214).
[23] Franz Boas, "An Anthropologist's Credo," in *The Nation* 147 (1938), p. 202.
[24] Boas, "The Aims of Anthropological Research," p. 254.
[25] Boas, *Anthropology and Modern Life*, p. 214.
[26] Boas, *The Mind of Primitive Man* (1911), pp. 182–83.

The principal obstacle in the way of progress on these lines seems to my mind to be founded on the lack of comparability of the data with which we are dealing. Attention has been directed essentially to the similarity of ethnic phenomena, while the individual variations were disregarded. As soon as we turn our attention in this direction, we notice that the sameness of ethnic phenomena is more superficial than complete, more apparent than real.[27]

Boas' move to disaggregate social group practices, that is, to challenge the idea that practices are associated in distinct "types" of societies, is also apparent in the kinds of explanations he was drawn to. Boas was drawn to those kinds of explanation that stress the contingent and incidental nature of social change. Thus, for example, he often invoked diffusion, that is, the spread of culture through contact among societies, to explain why societies are as they are. He argued that societies differ in terms of their history of exposure to other societies and in terms of the history of the conditions of that exposure. As he claimed, mere contact is not enough. Some types of contact are conducive to much sharing of culture; others are not. He argued that one of the reasons the ancestors of contemporary Europeans were able to develop cultures advanced in many areas was that they had contact with other peoples who had made important innovations. Because these European ancestors were similar in many respects to those of these more advanced societies, such as in physiology, these ancestors were able to gain much from such contact.[28] In the following, he concludes that such arguments mitigate the need for appeals to physiology:

We conclude, therefore, that the conditions for assimilation in ancient Europe were much more favorable than in those countries, where in our times primitive people come into contact with civilization. Therefore we do not need to assume that the ancient Europeans were more gifted than other races which have not become exposed to the influences of civilization until recent times.[29]

Boas did not believe that only diffusion explains social change. He noted other factors, including environmental conditions, economic factors, as well as independent innovation, as similarly contributing to this process.[30] But it is interesting that even when he allowed for such factors,

---

[27] *Ibid.* p. 188.
[28] Boas, "Human Faculty as Determined by Race," pp. 223–27; Boas, *The Mind of Primitive Man* (1911), pp. 8–17.
[29] Boas, "Human Faculty as Determined by Race," p. 225.
[30] This is a point that Harris makes in *The Rise of Anthropological Theory*, p. 260. It is evident in many of Boas' writings, as for example, in "Some Problems of Methodology," pp. 265–67 and in "The Aims of Anthropological Research," pp. 253–56. Indeed, on p. 256 of the latter work, Boas states: "every attempt to deduce cultural forms from a single cause is doomed to failure, for the various expressions of culture are closely interrelated and one cannot be altered without having an effect upon all the others."

he did so only on condition that we do not interpret such factors as making possible generalizations across individual societies. Boas made the following objection to those who would explain an individual society's customs and beliefs by reference to geographical generalizations:

Thus it would seem that [geographical] environment has an important effect upon the customs and beliefs of man, but only in so far as it helps to determine the special forms of customs and beliefs. These are, however, based primarily on cultural conditions, which in themselves are due to historical causes.[31]

Thus most fundamental in Boas' understanding of the constitution of culture is that it is a historically contingent process, defiant against attempts at generalization. This was his argument in his early work when he was arguing against the focus on independent innovation:

Thus we recognize that the fundamental assumption which is so often made by modern anthropologists cannot be accepted as true in all cases. We cannot say that the occurrence of the same phenomenon is always due to the same causes, and that thus it is proved that the human mind obeys the same laws everywhere.[32]

It was also a point he stressed in his later work:

In short, the material of anthropology is such that it needs must be a historical science, one of the sciences the interest of which centers in the attempt to understand the individual phenomena, rather than in the establishment of general laws which, on account of the complexity of the material, will be necessarily vague and, we might almost say, so self-evident that they are of little help to a real understanding.[33]

Boas' emphasis on the non-law-like aspect of social change had radical implications for theorizing social differences. Boas' appeal to contingent historical factors as the primary causes of social change invalidated the legitimacy of situating individual societies within overarching schemas of social change. In the previous chapter I argued that Freud's positing of personal development as the outcome of each individual's accidental encounters with a complex world expressed a new "individualization" of personal identity. But Boas' explanation of societal development as the outcome of each group's particular encounters with a complex world

[31] Boas, *The Mind of Primitive Man* (1911), pp. 162–63. For Boas' more elaborate arguments against this position, see pp. 159–64.
[32] Boas, "The Limitations of the Comparative Method of Anthropology," in *Race, Language, and Culture*, p. 275 (originally from a paper read at the meeting of the American Association for the Advancement of Science, Buffalo, *Science* N.S., 4 [1896], pp. 901–08).
[33] Boas, "The Aims of Anthropological Research," p. 258.

similarly individualized *group* identity. Boas notes this emphasis on individuality:

The phenomena of our science are so individualized, so exposed to outer accident that no set of laws could explain them. It is as in any other science dealing with the actual world surrounding us. For each individual case we can arrive at an understanding of its determination by inner and outer forces, but we cannot explain its individuality in the form of laws.[34]

This individualization of group identity is related to a point George Stocking emphasizes, that Boas was the first to use the term "culture" in the plural, that is, to speak of "cultures." Stocking argues that while Tylor was the first to introduce the modern definition of "culture," his actual usage suggested a singular phenomenon, that is, some one thing that occurs in "stages." Boas, on the other hand, spoke of "culture" in the plural and it is this plural usage, Stocking argues, which was unique to "culture's" twentieth-century anthropological meaning:

Preanthropological culture is singular in connotation, the anthropological is plural. In all of my reading of Tylor, I have noted no instance in which the word *culture* appears in the plural. In extended researches into American social science between 1890 and 1915, I found no instances of the plural form in writers other than Boas prior to 1895. Men referred to "cultural stages" or "forms of culture," as indeed Tylor had before, but they did not speak of "cultures." The plural appears with regularity only in the first generation of Boas' students around 1910.[35]

In the above, I have associated Boas' enlargement of the arena of the socially relative with his tendency to understand the practices of a given society as internally related in arbitrary ways. But that kind of claim raises the question about whether such relativism ought to be found in the writings of those students, such as Ruth Benedict and Margaret Mead, for whom the social practices of a particular society were described as more internally connected than they were for Boas. For example, Benedict's major work, *Patterns of Culture*, distinguishes societies on the basis of their exemplification of distinct psychological orientations. So important for her were these orientations in shaping the societies she described, that such societies became in her writings highly integrated,

---

[34] *Ibid.* p. 257. In "Some Problems of Methodology" Boas states the following about the social sciences in general and anthropology in particular: "It is often claimed as a characteristic of the *Geisteswissenschaften* that the center of investigation must be the individual case, and that the analysis of the many threads that enter into the individual case are the primary aims of research. The existence of generally valid laws can be ascertained only when all the independent series of happenings show common characteristics, and the validity of the law is always confined to the group that shows these common characteristics" (p. 268).

[35] Stocking, Jr., "Franz Boas and the Culture Concept," p. 203.

unified by the power of these underlying orientations. While she claimed that not all societies are as integrated as those she described, she insisted on the general power of such underlying psychological states to give shape to social life. These points are illustrated in the following passage:

What has happened in the great art-styles happens also in cultures as a whole. All the miscellaneous behavior directed toward getting a living, mating, warring, and worshipping the gods, is made over into consistent patterns in accordance with unconscious canons of choice that develop within the culture. Some cultures, like some periods of art, fail of such integration, and about many others we know too little to understand the motives that actuate them. But cultures at every level of complexity, even the simplest, have achieved it. Such cultures are more or less successful attainments of integrated behavior, and the marvel is that there can be so many of these possible configurations.[36]

What is relevant, however, to the issue of social relativism in Benedict is that, for her, social practices were connected by underlying psychological orientations. Since such orientations, unlike physiological differences or rational choices, cannot be situated within overall frameworks of "development," they do not provide the means for comparison that such other connecting frameworks do. Because Benedict viewed the differences among societies as based in "unconscious choices," these differences were for her "incommensurable," that is, rooted in purposes and orientations outside of rational reflection. Benedict elaborated this position, citing Wilhelm Dilthey's emphasis on the relativity of philosophical systems as reflecting a similar theoretical orientation to her own. She thus extended the relativism espoused by Boas to an arena – philosophical inquiry – that he had left exempt:

Especially in *Die Typen der Weltanschauung* he [Dilthey] analyzes part of the history of thought to show the relativity of philosophical systems. He sees them as great expressions of the variety of life, moods, *Lebensstimmungen*, integrated attitudes the fundamental categories of which cannot be resolved one into another. He argues vigorously against the assumption that any one of them can be final.[37]

In Mead, psychological orientations were not as powerfully unifying as they were in Benedict. But they were not less important. The subtitle of her first major work, *Coming of Age in Samoa: A Psychological Study of Primitive Youth for Western Civilization*, provides a clue to their importance.[38] In this work, as also in its two sequels, *Growing Up in New Guinea*, and *Sex and Temperament in Three Primitive Societies*, Mead examines those

---

[36] Ruth Benedict, *Patterns of Culture* (Boston: Houghton Mifflin, 1934), p. 48.
[37] *Ibid.* p. 52.
[38] Margaret Mead, *Coming of Age in Samoa: A Psychological Study of Primitive Youth for Western Civilization* (New York: William Morrow, 1961 [1928]).

differences in psychological attitudes that explain differences in behavior among these societies and with contemporary western ones.[39]

In these works as well as in some of her later ones, Mead focuses on a specific aspect of social life, sex, and the attitudes of one group in particular, young women. Thus Mead is using psychological orientations to give coherence to the sexual practices of specific groups. Like Benedict, and following in the tradition of Freud, Mead is claiming that the practices enacted by such groups are the coherent end result of a particular psychological history. Since such practices are the result of such a history, they cannot be explained merely as a result of biology. But since the history that these practices are the result of *is* psychological, they also cannot be explained by reference to rational reflection.

Because such practices are psychologically caused, rather than by biology or reason, they cease being "natural" or inevitable; instead they become arbitrary, the outcome of contingent factors. And indeed, a large part of Mead's purpose in describing the coming of age of young women in the South Pacific was to show the arbitrariness of adolescent female sexual practices, not only in the South Pacific, but more importantly, in Europe and North America. As in the work of Benedict, Mead presents a mosaic of possibilities where the mosaic itself suggests the contingency of any one pattern within it:

Sometimes one quality has been assigned to one sex, sometimes to the other. Now it is boys who are thought of as infinitely vulnerable and in need of special cherishing care, now it is girls. In some societies it is girls for whom parents must collect a dowry or make husband-catching magic, in others the parental worry is over the difficulty of marrying off the boys. Some people think of women as too weak to work out of doors, others regard women as the appropriate bearers of heavy burdens, "because their heads are stronger than men's."[40]

It is not surprising that when US feminists of the early 1970s also wanted to stress the arbitrariness of modern western norms of male and female behavior, they looked to Mead to generate examples of other possibilities and thus the contingency of their own.[41]

[39] Margaret Mead, *Growing Up in New Guinea* (New York: Blue Ribbon, 1930); Margaret Mead, *Sex and Temperament in Three Primitive Societies* (New York: William Morrow, 1963 [1935]).
[40] Margaret Mead, *Male and Female: The Classic Study of the Sexes* (New York: William Morrow, 1975 [1949]), p. 7.
[41] One of the most important examples of this use of Mead is in the very influential essay by Michelle Zimbalist Rosaldo, "Woman, Culture, and Society: A Theoretical Overview," in Michelle Zimbalist Rosaldo and Louise Lamphere, eds., *Woman, Culture and Society* (Stanford University Press, 1974), p. 18.

While Mead often focused on norms of female and male behavior, her attention was not confined to such issues. She concerned herself with other specific issues of human social life as well as with the general nature of human action. And when she turned her attention to such topics, one sees the same stress on contingency that was present in her discussion of male/female differences:

Each primitive people has selected one set of human gifts, one set of human values, and fashioned for themselves an art, a social organisation, a religion, which is their unique contribution to the history of the human spirit.[42]

Like Benedict, this stress on the contingency of social practice led her at times to make comments that suggested the incomparability of such "choices":

But it is unthinkable that a final recognition of the great number of ways in which man, during the course of history and at the present time, is solving the problems of life, should not bring with it in turn the downfall of our belief in a single standard.[43]

The problem, of course, as many later commentators have pointed out, is that in making such claims, Mead and Benedict then faced the difficulty of justifying the social judgments they did wish to make. And both often made such judgments. Mead used her studies to provide examples of ways of life better than those in the United States. In *Coming of Age in Samoa*, Mead contrasts the lives of adolescents in the United States with their counterparts in Samoa. She claims that the emotional distress common to US adolescents is a consequence of specific features of their society: its emphasis on achievement, the variety of choices it presents to young people, that children grow up in nuclear families, that experiences of sex and death are wrought with tension. Where all of these features are different, as in Samoa, there is less of the stress of adolescence.[44] The implicit premise in her argument is that greater stress is worse than less stress. But how can one justify such a premise if one raises doubts about the possibility of single standards?

Benedict and Mead did not provide convincing answers to this question, indeed did not even spend much time addressing it.[45] As David

---

[42] Mead, *Coming of Age in Samoa*, p. 13.   [43] *Ibid.* pp. 247–48.
[44] Mead elaborates this argument in *ibid.* chapter 13, pp. 195–233.
[45] Mead occasionally made claims that suggest some kind of philosophical position. Sometimes she seemed to suggest that there are general cross-cultural psychological ends such as achieving harmony or being able to enact all of one's naturally given aptitudes that can be used to justify cross-cultural judgments. This seems the premise, for example, of chapter 18 in *Male and Female*, "To Both Their Own." Sometimes her writings suggest a more pragmatic philosophical stance, that all practices have their costs

Hollinger has suggested, the philosophical concerns raised by their claims would only begin to engage the attention of scholars extensively later on in the century.[46] However, that these scholars ran up against such concerns is not, I would argue, a function of their having committed a silly mistake, easily remedied. Benedict and Mead, like Boas before them, took seriously the idea that large spheres of social life are best understood as caused by contingent environmental factors, factors that are reducible neither to nature nor to reason. This focus on the arbitrary nature of at least much of social life raises questions about what, if anything, can be claimed as not so arbitrary and how we justify making such claims. The concept of "culture" that these theorists elaborated did indeed raise concerns about relativism, questions that we are still struggling with today.

"Culture" and its social implications

In the above, I have attempted to draw lines of connection between the development of the twentieth-century, anthropological concept of "culture," and the emergence of a more relativist stance towards many social practices. I have focused on a small group of intellectuals because the work of this group so strikingly and clearly illuminates these connections. But, as I would like to show now, this use of "culture" spread beyond this small group of intellectuals to public discourse outside of the academy and contained here many of the same kinds of implications we saw in the writings of these anthropologists. In public discourse, as in the discussions among the anthropologists, the new use of "culture" led to a view of many practices of daily life as more arbitrarily associated with other social practices – such as politics and technology – than had earlier been assumed. Consequently, it made possible a form of identity, "cultural identity," that was less susceptible to evaluative judgment than were other forms of identity – such as national or racial identity.

and benefits about which there may be no means of resolution. This seems to be the stance she was taking in *Coming of Age in Samoa* when, speaking of the Samoans, she stated: "And however much we may deplore such an attitude and feel that important personalities and great art are not born in so shallow a society, we must recognize that here is a strong factor in the painless development from childhood to womanhood" (p. 200). However, such statements only suggest philosophical positions since the philosophical argument is not made explicit.

[46] As Hollinger argues in "Cultural Relativism": "Benedict and her allies did not find this concern [reconciling political judgment with cultural relativism] nearly as pressing as did discussants of cultural relativism during the 1980s and 1990s. By then, a host of intellectual and political transformations within and beyond the North Atlantic West – to which this article attends below – had given urgency to questions that had struck Benedict, Herskovits, and their associates as nit-picking distractions from the big issues" (p. 716).

As Warren Susman notes, during the 1930s, the term "culture" became widespread in public discourse, replacing the term "civilization" in many of the contexts where the latter had previously been employed.[47] During the 1920s, when commentators referred to America as a society, they often talked about "American civilization." The question of what constituted "civilization" was of great concern, of what made it, of what destroyed it, and, in the case of America, the extent to which its presence was dependent upon a population of a certain racial stock.[48] The term "civilization" was also paired with "western" as educators and others worked to establish the continuity of American history with a particular past.[49] In both cases, "civilization" suggested a level of encompassing societal accomplishment not easily or frequently achieved within human history. Thus, when "civilization" was attached to a country or region, as in "American civilization" or "western civilization," that attachment suggested that that country or region had achieved a certain level of development primarily signaled by the complexity of its political organization or the level of its technological accomplishments:

Civilization meant technology, scientific achievement, institutions and organizations, power and material (financial) success.[50]

The centrality of technological or institutional success to the concept of "civilization" meant that in the 1920s, as in earlier decades, "civilization" was often differentiated from "culture," where the latter referred to the very special artistic accomplishments or mannerisms of a society or of a group within it.[51] But when civilization was attached to a country or region, as in "American civilization" or "western civilization," the assumption often was that the technological, institutional, artistic accomplishments and daily mannerisms of a society were all of one piece, that a country or region which was able to accomplish great technological or political feats had the mental resources to distinguish itself in other arenas as well. The kind of "stage" perspective that was part of evolutionary ways of thought present in this period suggested this integration of technological, political, and other types of achievement.

---

[47] Warren I. Susman, *Culture as History: The Transformation of American Society in the Twentieth Century* (New York: Pantheon, 1984). See particularly Susman's discussion in chapter 7, "Culture and Civilization: The Nineteen Twenties," pp. 105–21 and chapter 9, "The Culture of the Thirties," pp. 150–83.
[48] *Ibid.* p. 118.   [49] *Ibid.* p. 118.   [50] *Ibid.* p. 156.
[51] For a discussion of the relationship between "civilization" and "culture" see *ibid.* pp. 156, 157 and Raymond Williams, *Keywords: A Vocabulary of Culture and Society* (New York: Oxford University Press, 1976), pp. 76–77.

But when a meaning of "culture" emerged that abandoned its association with "special accomplishment," so also did that meaning begin to lose its sense of necessary connection to technological or institutional advance.[52] This newer meaning of "culture" meant "way of life," where "way of life" referred primarily to the private habits and attitudes of a people: their dress, mannerisms, forms of worship, aesthetic tastes, etc.:

It is not too extreme to propose that it was during the Thirties that the idea of culture was domesticated, with important consequences. Americans began thinking in terms of patterns of behavior and belief, values and life-styles, symbols and meanings. It was during this period that we find, for the first time, frequent reference to an "American Way of Life."[53]

We can see this new fascination with different "ways of life" in the growth of a new popularity for social-scientific and fictionalized accounts of foreign customs, where patterns of daily life were the primary focus and where such patterns were described in sympathetic ways. For example, Ruth Benedict's *Patterns of Culture* (1934) became one of the largest selling non-fiction books published in the twentieth century in the United States. Other best-selling, non-fiction books of this period include Margaret Mead's *Coming of Age in Samoa* (1928) and Stuart Chase's *Mexico: A Study of Two Americas* (1931).[54] In terms of fiction, an example is Pearl Buck's *The Good Earth* (1931). This book, with other works of Buck, contained some of the first popular depictions of Chinese life in the United States that portrayed Chinese people in three-dimensional terms.

---

[52] To be sure, the process of disassociating aspects of American "culture" from its politics or technology has been complex, achieved gradually, not necessarily coherently, and differently for different individuals and groups. Thus, even today, some conservative art and literary critics claim a necessary connection between American democratic practices and particular aesthetic and literary values; other conservative politicians claim a necessary connection between such political practices and the practice of Christianity.

[53] Susman, *Culture as History*, p. 154.

[54] For the popularity of Benedict's *Patterns of Culture*, see Margaret M. Caffrey, *Ruth Benedict: Stranger in this Land* (Austin: University of Texas Press, 1989), p. 214. This comment was brought to my attention by Louise Lamphere who also makes the following remarks about Mead: "Margaret Mead became for Americans the voice of anthropology, not only through the sales of her books but also through her columns in *Redbook Magazine* and her public lectures," in "Gendering the Boasian Revolution," unpublished paper, p. 33. The ability of Mead to still generate controversy is illustrated in the publication and attention given in recent years to Derek Freeman's critique of Mead, in his *Margaret Mead and the Heretic: The Making and Unmaking of an Anthropological Myth* (New York: Penguin, 1997) and *The Fateful Hoaxing of Margaret Mead: A Historical Analysis of Her Samoan Research* (Boulder, Colo.: Westview Press, 1999). Hollinger also points out that Benedict's *Patterns of Culture* "was recognized, at the end of the twentieth century, as one of the most widely read books ever produced by a social scientist in any discipline" (Hollinger, "Cultural Relativism," p. 714).

The Good Earth was chosen as a Book of the Month Club selection in 1931 and became the best-selling book of both 1931 and 1932.[55]

The 1930s witnessed the rise of a similar type of fascination with the daily habits and social values of Americans. In 1935, George Gallup established the American Institute of Public Opinion and so made "polling" a feature of American life:[56]

If there was an increased awareness of the concept of culture and its implications as well as a growing self-consciousness of an American Way or a native culture of value, there were also forces operating to shape that culture into a heightened sensitivity of itself as a culture. The development of systematic and supposedly scientific methods of measuring the way "the people" thought and believed is certainly one important example.[57]

This fascination with daily habits – and differences among human beings' daily habits – extended to a new focus on subgroups within American society, and about individuals depicted as representative of such subgroups. This focus is evident in the popularity of such books as Van Wyck Brooks' *The Flowering of New England* (1936) and Robert S. Lynd and Helen Merrell Lynd's *Middletown* (1929).[58] It is also evident in the popularity of James Agee and Walker Evans' *Let Us Now Praise Famous Men* (1941), a sympathetic portrayal of members of three sharecropping families in the south.[59] As Susan Hegeman elaborates, this latter book, like the new film form of documentary, joined ethnography to such other ends as journalistic education, entertainment, and social reform:

Most obviously, however, the efflorescence of the documentary form itself, that strange hybrid of ethnography, social realism, and the Movietone News, is the most ubiquitous sign of this convergence, turning a remarkable range of people – writers, photographers, social crusaders, bureaucrats – into ethnographers, all working on the premise that there were "cultures" out there to be revealed.[60]

The new popular use of "culture" reflected not only an attitude of tolerance towards those practices which differentiated communities within the United States, but also a sense of appreciation for these differentiating practices. Those practices associated with "culture" – such as dress, mannerisms, forms of worship, etc. – were seen as "private" matters. This

[55] Peter Conn, *Pearl S. Buck: A Cultural Biography* (Cambridge and New York: Cambridge University Press, 1996), pp. 122–23.
[56] Susman, *Culture as History*, p. 158.   [57] *Ibid.* p. 158.
[58] *Ibid.* pp. 155–57; Hegeman, *Patterns for America*, pp. 135–38.
[59] Susman notes the importance of *Let Us Now Praise Famous Men* for this period and points out that while this book was not published until 1941, it was begun in 1936 (*Culture as History*, p. 182).
[60] Hegeman, *Patterns for America*, p. 128.

enabled many Americans to view such aspects more in aesthetic rather than moral terms. It contributed to the sense that diversity in such aspects of life made the United States more "interesting," more aesthetically complex. This appreciation of cultural diversity was not new. In the earlier part of the twentieth century it had been articulated by such scholars as Randolph Bourne and Horace Kallen. In the decades beginning in the 1930s, however, this perspective became the position not only of a few intellectuals but a significant thread within public discourse.

Contributing to this move to disassociate "private" ways of life from the political structure which united America, or from the technological accomplishments many viewed with pride, were changes in American demographics. During the late 1920s and 1930s, there emerged in America a new political and cultural power base composed of second generation European immigrants. This was a population of those who had achieved a degree of integration into American society – who could speak English, had gone through high school or beyond, and had at least enough means to purchase magazines and books – but for whom that integration was recent and partial enough to sustain a sense of allegiance to the ways of life of their parents and grandparents. These children of European immigrants were, with their parents, sufficient in numbers and political organization to make possible the nomination of Alfred Smith for president in 1928, and to form a significant component of the coalition that put Franklin Delano Roosevelt into power and that constituted a newly aligned Democratic Party. But they were also numerous enough to initiate certain changes within popular discourse. As Carl Degler points out, "the coming into power of a new racial and ethnic pluralism" created "in the process a cultural as well as political atmosphere within which a recourse to biology or heredity in accounting for human differences would be increasingly difficult to condone."[61]

This population helped to create and consume books, magazines, radio, music, and film that broke the boundaries between an older "high culture" that had been the province of a moneyed white Protestant establishment and a "low culture" that had been associated with rural life, first generation immigrant society, and poor rural and urban blacks. In the early part of the twentieth century, the forms of entertainment enjoyed by these two different kinds of groups had existed, as Michael Denning claims, in different worlds:

The popular arts – dime novels, melodramas and vaudeville acts, blues singers and string bands, traveling circuses, minstrel shows, and tent shows, as well as the

[61] Degler, *In Search of Human Nature*, p. 202.

foreign-language cultures of immigrant neighborhoods – inhabited a different universe from the budding metropolitan high culture – "legitimate" theater, symphony orchestras, universities, art museums, the publishers and magazines like Charles Scribners and the Atlantic Monthly that published the novels and stories of Howells, James, and Wharton.[62]

But during the 1920s and 1930s, as these children of immigrants, and also some émigré African Americans in the north, were becoming more integrated into mainstream US society, so also was the music industry beginning to reach a mass audience through the public phonograph and the jukebox, the motion picture industry was expanding with the development of sound, and the radio industry was coming to reach millions through the development of national networks.[63] A base for the creation of a "middlebrow" reading public had begun with the creation of such magazines as *Time*, *Life*, and *Fortune*.[64] It was expanded through the creation of such institutions as the Book of the Month Club.[65] Unlike the forms of entertainment discussed above, these were media that aimed for a mass audience and that blurred the boundaries between "art" and "entertainment."

Many of those who were involved in creating this new "middlebrow" culture were from this new second generation immigrant population or were northern urban African Americans.[66] Changes in the publishing industry illustrate this point. George Hutchinson describes a dramatic transformation in the US publishing industry during the late teens and early 1920s, with New York replacing Boston as a center for book publishing. The founders of many of the new, New York publishing houses, including Alfred A. Knopf, Harcourt & Brace, Boni & Liveright, and Ben Huebsch (who merged with Viking in the mid 1920s) were Jewish, and were ideologically committed to creating a non "Anglo-Saxon" American literature.[67] As Hutchinson notes, these houses:

concentrated initially in critical realism and regionalism, left-wing political theory, modernist anthropology (Boasian and Malinowskian), American cultural nationalist and ethnic writing, modern continental European fiction, and new studies of sexuality and gender ... They published virtually all the books concerned with the new ideology of cultural pluralism ...[68]

[62] Michael Denning, *The Cultural Front: The Laboring of American Culture in the Twentieth Century* (London and New York: Verso, 1996), p. 40.
[63] *Ibid.* p. 42.   [64] *Ibid.* p. 43.
[65] Peter Conn points out that the Book of the Month Club was founded in 1926 and by the end of the 1930s had reached a membership of 350,000. See Conn, *Pearl S. Buck*, p. 122.
[66] Denning, *The Cultural Front*, p. xvii.
[67] George Hutchinson, *The Harlem Renaissance in Black and White* (Cambridge, Mass. and London: The Belknap Press of Harvard University, 1995), p. 344.
[68] *Ibid.* p. 343.

The increasing presence of Jewish Americans in the publishing industry was accompanied by a similar growth of Jewish Americans, Italian Americans, and African Americans in such other developing industries as film and music. In these latter industries, forms of expression emerged which conveyed the intertwined contributions of such groups:

When Louis Armstrong first recorded a Tin Pan Alley song in 1928, "I Must Have That Man," he embodied the dialectic that was to dominate American music for a generation, a dialectic between the blues and the Tin Pan Alley "standard," between the neighboring urban communities of working-class African Americans and working-class Jews, Italians, and Poles, between the blues scales of African American music, the *frigish* scales of Yiddish popular music, and the pentatonic scales of Eastern European folk music.[69]

Thus, in the new "middlebrow" media that combined entertainment and art, and aimed to reach a mass audience, there existed a significant representation of those who would be sympathetic to the perspective reflected in the new use of "culture."

Other phenomena of the 1930s also contributed to the spread of this new perspective. The depression intensified sympathetic attitudes towards poverty and social outsiders. It was less easy to identify economic success with inherited intelligence and racial "stock" when so many of supposedly "good stock" became poor. And the rise of Hitler and fascism made talk of inherited racial differences more suspect.[70] But also, the children of European immigrants, though not the children of African American northern émigrés, were, in the 1930s, beginning the process of becoming "white."[71] These new "Caucasians" adopted the category of "ethnic" to label who they were in non-racial terms and employed the concept of "culture" to describe their differences. It was to their advantage to separate out aspects of what made them different – religion in the case of Catholics and Jews, food preferences, styles of dress, and humor – from the political structure which made Americans proud. "Culture," with its implication of tolerance towards these non-political differences, became an important tool for societal acceptance.

---

[69] Denning, *The Cultural Front*, p. 41.

[70] Degler discusses these factors as causes of shifts in the academic community away from racial frameworks (*In Search of Human Nature*, pp. 202–04).

[71] As Matthew Jacobson has pointed out, in the decades following passage of the 1924 restrictive immigrant act, US racial categorization underwent a significant change. Immigrants from Ireland and from southern and eastern Europe, who previously had been classified in racial terms, became categorized with other whites under the newly popular category of "Caucasian." Matthew Frye Jacobson, *Whiteness of a Different Color: European Immigrants and the Alchemy of Race* (Cambridge, Mass. and London: Harvard University Press, 1998).

To be sure, this tolerance was only a thread within American society, and coexisted uneasily with both continuing views that the political and technological advances of a society were linked with its "culture" and also with uncertainties about how such tolerance was to be reconciled with other moral claims. As the Second World War approached, some intellectuals argued for a connection between the rise of fascism and the failure of intellectuals to defend the values of "the west." Others became more insistent on disassociating themselves from moral relativism.[72] In the middle period of the twentieth century, there existed no simple consensus on how "culture" was to be employed politically:

First, there was in the discovery of the idea of culture and its wide-scale application a critical tool that could shape a critical ideal ... Yet often it was developed in such ways as to provide significant devices for conserving much of the existing structure ... The reliance on basic culture patterns, stressed by further development of public opinion, studies of myth, symbol, folklore, the new techniques of the mass media, even the games of the period could and did have results more conservative than radical ...[73]

These debates about the relationship between cultural diversity and absolute values, and between tolerance towards such diversity and the maintenance of "core" American values have persisted until the present day. I noted earlier that the new use of "culture" instigated some philosophical dilemmas we are still struggling with today. These debates have not been limited to academic or intellectual circles.

But another qualification needs to be made about how much this new use of "culture" transformed American society. As we will see in a later chapter, in the 1930s, 1940s, and 1950s, the new concept of "culture" did not apply to the "ways of life" of African Americans. Rather the specific forms of speech, styles of dress, modes of religious practice, and other

---

[72] Thus, as Hegeman points out, in 1940 Archibald MacLeish published an essay titled "The Irresponsibles" which "connected the 'cultural crisis' of fascism, which he saw as a kind of anticulture, to the failure of intellectuals to actively defend the eternal principles of the 'culture of the West.'" See Hegeman, *Patterns for America*, p. 160. Hegeman references this essay in Constance Rourke, *The Roots of American Culture and Other Essays*, ed., with a preface by Van Wyck Brooks (Port Washington, N.Y.: Kennikat, 1965). But the rise of the Second World War caused even many liberals to become more explicit in their rejection of moral relativism. At this time Boas, Mead, and Benedict all made efforts to distance their use of "culture" from any simple assertion of cultural relativity. Not only did all of these theorists take strong stands in favor of democracy against fascism, but all made concerted efforts to elaborate the difference between the kinds of positions they did hold on "cultural differences" from other forms of relativism. That these scholars felt particularly compelled to distance themselves from all forms of cultural relativism with the onset of the Second World War is discussed by Hegeman, *Patterns for America*, pp. 158–92.
[73] Susman, *Culture as History*, p. 164.

distinctive characteristics associated with African Americans continued to be looked down upon or perceived as a "problem" by much of white America. While the children of immigrants from Ireland and Eastern and southern Europe were becoming "white" in the 1930s, 1940s, and 1950s, those with African ancestry remained racialized. Indeed, as Matthew Jacobsen argues, it was in part because relationships between blacks and whites came to occupy such a central role in discussions about "race" in America, that these other groups were able to escape racialization themselves.[74] For the children of European immigrants, the process of becoming "white" – in distinction from those who remained "black" – was linked with the success of these children in having their distinctive practices and preferences depicted as "culture."

Conclusion

Beginning in the second and third decades of the twentieth century, the word "culture" began a metamorphosis in meaning. Whereas earlier it had referred to the specific, mostly artistic or daily life habits of elite groups, it now became employed in more egalitarian ways. It came to be synonymous with "way of life" and applicable to many regions and communities.

The new meaning of "culture" was first elaborated within the academy by a group of academics, primarily American anthropologists. But it soon became a part of public discourse outside of the academy. As this new meaning generated among anthropologists a more relativistic stance towards many social practices, so also did it generate a similar stance within the general public. It enabled many social groups to differentiate some aspects of who they were – their religious practices, food preferences, aesthetic tastes – from their identity as "Americans." It made possible the proud celebration of "the hyphenated American." Whereas during the First World War, this hyphenization referred mostly to a concern about divided political loyalties, in later decades, it could more centrally refer to the possibility of combining loyal citizenry with diverse private practices.[75]

This new meaning of "culture" became an important political tool in the 1930s, 1940s, and 1950s for the children of European immigrants. It enabled these children to claim proud identification as "Americans" while

---

[74] See Jacobson, *Whiteness of a Different Color*, pp. 246–73.
[75] See Hegeman, *Patterns for America*, pp. 53–54 for a discussion of the negative associations of the term "hyphenate" in the First World War.

also retaining allegiances to others of similar backgrounds. These allegiances enabled these children to mobilize as political groups and thus exert political pressure on American political life. But while "culture" became an important political tool for the children and grandchildren of European immigrants during the middle third of the twentieth century, it was not yet a tool that a large segment of the African American population could mobilize behind. Why this was so and how and when it ceased being so, shall be important questions in the following chapter.

Introduction to chapters 4 and 5

The discussions of the previous chapters help us to understand some of the complexity in beliefs about identity operating in the United States in the twentieth century. As the century opens, the identities of women and African Americans are more naturalized than they are for men and whites. But, during the first half of the twentieth century, new ways of thinking about identity are beginning to undermine the naturalization of racial and sexual identity for everyone, and, in the process, making more similar the identities of men and women and blacks and whites. Firstly, this new stress on the environmental causes of character led, as it did in Freud's work, to a growing appreciation for the individuality of identity. Secondly, it generated, first in the academy, and then within wider public discussions, a new concept of "culture." This concept lent support to an increased tolerance for diversity in the practices of different social groups.

But while popular acceptance of the individualization of identity grew in general over the course of the first half of the twentieth century, the idea of tolerance was more selectively applied. It was not applied to those aspects of African American life that differentiated African Americans from European Americans. These ways of life were still mostly understood as a function of natural factors or as the problematic outcome of environmental conditions. And the practices that distinguished women from men, while more ambiguously seen as less worthy, were also not understood as "cultural" differences. Consequently, in the first half of the twentieth century, both women and African Americans were much more able to use environmental arguments that stressed the individualization of identity than to claim that the practices that distinguished them from whites and men were "cultural." Those from both groups who were best able to use arguments about the individualization of identity to counter social exclusion were those whose differences were least challenging to prevailing norms and values.

In the following two chapters I focus on the question of which subgroups among women and blacks were most able to employ this strategy, and how their abilities to do so affected the politics of the social movements identified with women and African Americans in the first half of the twentieth century. I then focus on changes among the populations of both groups in the course of the twentieth century and on how these changes brought about the need for different strategies and different politics. As I will argue, various demographic changes led to the involvement of new subgroups in these movements and to the search for new strategies not hampered by the limitations of the older ones. Understanding these demographic changes and the changes in thinking that accompanied them will help us understand why identity politics emerged when it did and what problems it was created to address.

4 Before Black Power: constructing an African American identity

In the mid 1960s, the slogan "Black Power" burst forth upon the US political stage, expressing an important transformation in African American politics. That politics, previously focused on the elimination of legalized segregation and discrimination, became something more. African Americans were no longer only demanding rights to work, eat, go to school, and reside where they wished; now black people were also expressing a pride in being black and a demand for greater control over black life. The phenomena associated with "Black Power" were complex: Black Panthers organizing breakfast programs for children; middle-class African Americans wearing African-style clothing and Afro haircuts; college students asking for the creation of African American Studies programs; residents of inner city neighborhoods calling for community control of school districts. But all of these phenomena seemed to possess at least certain elements in common: a pride in being black and a belief that this pride should organize African American political, institutional, and personal life.

The identity this pride expressed was new. While it shared features with forms of identity that had existed within African American communities prior to the 1960s, it was not quite identical to these earlier forms of identity. From the middle of the nineteenth to the middle of the twentieth century, two forms of identity were most open to African Americans. On the one hand, there existed a racialized identity that portrayed blacks as a distinct natural type, a type whose natural characteristics entailed greater similarities with others of African ancestry than with those of different racial "stock." On the other hand, in the late nineteenth and early twentieth century, some African Americans, later joined by some white liberals, also began to describe African Americans as Americans, differing from other Americans only in terms of superficial characteristics. In the opening years of the twentieth century, these two forms of identity existed in uneasy coexistence, as two possibilities, conceptually and politically in tension. The uneasy coexistence of these two types of identity is eloquently remarked upon by W. E. B. Du Bois, both in his "The Conservation of the

Races," first given as a talk in 1897, and in his book *The Souls of Black Folk* published in 1903. In "The Conservation of the Races," Du Bois describes this unease:

Here, it seems to me, is the reading of the riddle that puzzles so many of us. We are Americans, not only by birth and by citizenship, but by our political ideals, our language, our religion. Farther than that, our Americanism does not go. At that point, we are Negroes, members of a vast historic race that from the very dawn of creation has slept, but half awakening in the dark forests of its African fatherland.[1]

Du Bois makes a similar point in *The Souls of Black Folk*:

One ever feels his two-ness, – an American, a Negro; two souls, two thoughts, two unreconciled strivings; two warring ideals in one dark body, whose dogged strength alone keeps it from being torn asunder.

The history of the American Negro is the history of this strife – this longing to attain self-conscious manhood, to merge his double self into a better and truer self. In this merging he wishes neither of the older selves to be lost. He would not Africanize America, for America has too much to teach the world and Africa. He would not bleach his Negro soul in a flood of white Americanism, for he knows that Negro blood has a message for the world.[2]

For much of the first half of the twentieth century, African Americans found difficult the merger of this double self, and were often pulled to emphasize one or the other of these two forms of identity. Those who saw little hope of advancement for those of African descent in the United States tended to emphasize the racial distinctiveness of African Americans and to be drawn to a politics of geographical separation. Others, more optimistic about such advancement, tended to be drawn to those accounts which emphasized the similarities between those of African descent in the United States and other Americans. These latter accounts drew on the new stress on the individuality of human character that was gaining increased credibility in the first half of the century. They also fit best with the politics that many middle- and working-class African Americans saw as necessary in this period: the fight against lynching, Jim Crow legislation in the south, and pervasive discrimination in the north.

To be sure, in the first half of the twentieth century, there were emerging intellectual and political phenomena that suggested a new type of identity, one which emphasized the distinctiveness of African Americans *as* Americans. The Harlem Renaissance expressed a move on the part of some artists and intellectuals to describe a distinctively African American

[1] W. E. B. Du Bois, "The Conservation of Races," pp. 20–27 in David Levering Lewis, ed., *W. E. B. Du Bois: A Reader* (New York: Henry Holt & Co., 1995), p. 24.
[2] W. E. B. Du Bois, *The Souls of Black Folk* (New York: Penguin, 1989 [Chicago: A. C. McClurg & Company, 1903]), p. 5.

cultural identity. And in the 1930s, 1940s, and 1950s, some political activists and organizations were beginning to argue for a type of separatist politics aimed not at geographical separation but at establishing economic and political bases of power for African Americans within the existing United States. However, as long as the fight against segregation and discrimination was the most pressing struggle from the perspective of most African Americans, these kinds of cultural and political claims remained marginal.

This situation changed in the middle of the 1960s. Black Power came into existence. Black Power was a heterogeneous phenomenon, in part drawing on older, naturalized understandings of identity. However, it also drew on the new concept of culture that had become part of public discourse by the 1960s and used this concept to describe a type of identity that was both American and distinctive. It employed this concept to ground a politics that was neither focused on geographical separation nor on integration, at least as integration had previously been understood. Rather, Black Power argued for the creation of separate institutions within the existing United States. And, unlike previous attempts by intellectuals and activists in earlier decades to argue for such an identity or for such a politics, this time such calls were taken up by a mass constituency.

In this chapter, I elaborate on this prehistory and then deal with the question as to why this movement surfaced in the United States at this moment in time. Black Power, I argue, was the outcome of a variety of political, intellectual, and economic factors. As the movement on behalf of African Americans began to focus less on the issue of segregation of African Americans in the south, and more on the issue of the political and economic alienation of African Americans in the north, a politics based more on group power and less on universal rights came to be seen by many as necessary. A concept of group identity, lent more appeal by the new concept of "culture," provided the ideological basis for such a politics. And, economic changes occurring in the post-Second World War period – changes that generated a new amount of class fluidity – made the idea of black unity suggested by this idea of group identity appealing to a wide audience.

Black power, while praised by many, has also been widely attacked. In the epilogue I examine some of these criticisms, attempting to separate out those criticisms that have merit from those that do not. In this chapter, however, my goal is less to assess the value of Black Power than to place it within an historical context and to help us understand better the political, intellectual, and social forces that caused it to come into being. Such a goal tends to possess a sympathetic bias. However, it also counters the negative bias implicit in accounts which describe this movement as a kind of historical wrong turn, a simple mistake. Black Power contained many problems, but as I hope the following will show, it was not a simple mistake.

Mainstream perspectives on the idea of black identity in the early twentieth century

I'd like to begin this account by turning first to the early twentieth century and to the identity options available to African Americans at this time. These options were affected by the strongly held beliefs of European Americans in the naturalization of African American identity. In the period between the early part of the century and the mid 1960s, many whites in the population strongly naturalized African American identity, that is, they regarded black people as possessing certain shared psychological and behavioral characteristics that were thought to be as much rooted in "nature" as were an alleged common skin color and other physiological characteristics. The acceptance of legalized segregation and explicit forms of discrimination throughout much of the country attests to the continued power of this model of identity up until the 1960s.

To be sure, as I've claimed in previous chapters, the naturalization of African American identity became subject to various kinds of pressure during the first half of the twentieth century. One such pressure came from the spread of the idea of a new, more egalitarian meaning of "culture." But, in mainstream European American writing, this new use of "culture" was rarely applied to the ways of life of African Americans, neither during the 1930s nor even up to the early 1960s. From the 1930s through the early 1960s, and particularly after the Second World War, immigrants from Ireland, Italy, and Eastern Europe became increasingly understood as "ethnic" groups.[3] The new concept of "ethnicity" allowed for the idea of differences that were culturally constructed and thus not reflective of inner character. "Ethnicity" encompassed differences in behaviors that were either relatively minor, such as food preferences, or in a country committed to freedom of religion, acceptable if limited to private life. But African Americans were not considered an "ethnic" group. Instead, African Americans remained racialized, that is, distinguished in terms of biological rather than cultural characteristics,

---

[3] Among many books that trace this process are Karen Brodkin's, *How Jews Became White Folks: And What That Says About Race in America* (New Brunswick, N.J.: Rutgers University Press, 1998); Theodore Allen, *The Invention of the White Race* (London: Verso, 1994); and Matthew Jacobson, *Whiteness of a Different Color: European Immigrants and the Alchemy of Race* (Cambridge, Mass. and London: Harvard University Press, 1998).

and perceived by white Americans as different from themselves in deep ways. In short, in the period from the 1930s to the 1960s, as Jews, Italians, and the Irish became deracialized, race became predominantly a question of black and white.

The belief that race was most significantly about black and white affected even the thinking of those who saw themselves as most enlightened. In the period from the 1920s to the early 1960s, as many liberal scholars began to stress the non-racial nature of the differences between newer and older European immigrant groups, so did they continue to accept the idea that the distinction between black and white was a racial one. They expressed their liberal political stance through the claim that race, however, was about "skin color only"; it had no meaning in terms of psychological or behavioral characteristics.

That liberal scholars felt compelled to attack racism through this kind of rhetorical move attests to the strength of the idea that the division between blacks and whites was truly biological, i.e. reflected a real division within nature. "Race" might be *only* about skin color, but it was still *really* about skin color. To argue that the totality of the distinction might be socially constructed would have entailed a complete rejection of the idea of "race," a move few liberal scholars yet knew how to make. But if "race" was real and truly captured the black/white distinction, then the only apparent way to attack racism was to deny the importance of race. The irony, however, as Matthew Jacobson points out, is that this kind of attack on racism sometimes reinforced the idea of race even as it explicitly denied the significance of race as a determinant of behavior. As an example of this point, Jacobson points to the public exhibit "Races of Mankind," developed by the Cranbrook Institute of Science in 1943. The exhibit opened with a panel stressing the common origins of all human beings as a consequence of our common parentage in Adam and Eve. But the way this commonality was presented was through pictures of Adam and Eve assembled with children whose skin tones were portrayed as either white, yellow, or brown. Jacobson notes that a similar "enlightened" presentation of race, Ruth Benedict's *Races of Mankind* (1943), included a map that divided the world into three racial regions, labeled "Caucasian," "Mongoloid," and "Negroid."[4] In short, even for those arguing that "race does not matter," race was a reality manifesting itself in three major colors.

Thus white liberals tended to share with the rest of the white population the idea that race was real, based in biology, and clearly present in the distinction between black and white. But they also shared with the rest of

---

[4] Jacobson, *Whiteness of a Different Color*, pp. 103, 106–07.

the white population, and also with some in the black population, the idea that the ways in which blacks were behaviorally different from whites was a problem. The argument that "race does not matter" had to contend with the fact that many African Americans lived lives that deviated in various respects from ideals of "normal" American life. The poverty, and closeness to southern, rural, and segregated communities that marked the lives of many African Americans, resulted in styles of speech and other practices that, to many European Americans, seemed incompatible with such hegemonic ideals. Such differences, combined with physical differences, stretched farther the idea of what it meant to be a real American than was stretched by European immigrants. The liberal solution was to describe the behavioral differences as a problem. White and black liberals, of course, identified the problem as a consequence of slavery, racism, and other environmental factors, factors that could be changed. They vehemently opposed those who identified the causes of behavioral differences in biology. But because they also identified the behavioral differences only as a problem, they could also identify only problematic causes. Slavery could figure into the explanation; cultural legacies from Africa could not. Black people had problems; they did not have "culture."

This position has to be seen as at least partly affected by complexities still prevalent in what was understood as "culture." In the period from the 1920s through the 1960s, as "culture" was coming to be understood as referring to the adaptations all people make to the specificities of their lives, it still retained some of its elitist connotations, that is, as representing a group's special accomplishments. This tendency to equate "culture" with "special accomplishment" is illustrated in the following passage from Ruth Benedict's *Race: Science and Politics* (1940):

Their patterns of political, economic, and artistic behavior were forgotten – even the languages they had spoken in Africa. Like the poor whites of the South, they gathered together instead for fervent Christian revivalist camp meetings: they sang them better and invented countless variations of great poignancy; nevertheless the old forms which they had achieved in Africa were forgotten. Conditions of slavery in America were so drastic that this loss is not to be wondered at... The Negro race has proud cultural achievements, but for very good reasons they were not spread before our eyes in America.[5]

If "culture" means special achievement, and if African Americans were deprived of the opportunities to develop such, then African Americans, through no fault of their own, have "no culture." This kind of position is also expressed by the African American sociologist E. Franklin Frazier in

---

[5] Ruth Benedict, *Race: Science and Politics* (New York: Viking Press, 1945), pp. 86–87.

his essay "Traditions and Patterns of Negro Family Life in the United States" (1934):

To be sure, when one undertakes the study of the Negro he discovers a great poverty of traditions and patterns of behavior that exercise any real influence on the formation of the Negro's personality and conduct. If, as Keyserling remarks, the most striking thing about the Chinese is their deep culture, the most conspicuous thing about the Negro is his lack of a culture.[6]

As Frazier elaborates this point, African Americans are a people who have had a culture "stripped from them" and who have come to adopt behaviors imposed by the conditions of their history in North America. These conditions have been complex, resulting in a variety of patterns of behavior. When Frazier speaks about family patterns of the American "Negro," he distinguishes four different types. Three of those types are the consequence of African Americans being influenced by the family patterns of whites or of "Indians." One type, however, described by Frazier as "the maternal family pattern" emerges partly as a consequence of the dominant role African American women played under slavery, and partly as a consequence of circumstances African Americans faced upon emigration to urban areas. Frazier describes this type in the following terms:

The maternal family pattern may be considered then, as a prominent feature of Negro family life. It represents in its purest and most primitive manifestation a natural family group similar to what Briffault has described as the original or earliest form of the human family. (3) It also indicates the absence or the ineffectiveness of institutional control of sex behavior or the lack of the moralization of Negro life. The effect of urbanization is demoralizing in that it destroys the sympathetic basis of the harmless folkways of the peasant Negro.[7]

This family type is thus for Frazier clearly a problem. But if one situates this family type in relation to the others Frazier describes, one is left to conclude that African Americans either possess a family type adopted from some other group, or exhibit a family type that is a problem. In short, what African Americans do that is distinctive from other groups does not constitute a culture, but a problem. A similar position was argued

[6] E. Franklin Frazier, "Traditions and Patterns of Negro Family Life in the United States," pp. 191–207 in E. B. Reuter, ed., *Race and Culture Contacts* (New York: McGraw-Hill, 1934), p. 194. Frazier cites Count Hermann Keyserling, *The Travel Diary of a Philosopher*, Vol. II, p. 28. For an excellent discussion of the positions of Benedict, Frazier, and other intellectuals of this period, see John F. Szwed, "The Politics of Afro-American Culture," pp. 153–81 in Dell Hymes, ed., *Reinventing Anthropology* (New York: Random House, 1969), pp. 157–62. It was Szwed who alerted me to these passages from Benedict and Frazier.
[7] Frazier, "Traditions and Patterns of Negro Family Life," p. 198.

as late as 1963 by Nathan Glazer and Daniel Moynihan in *Beyond the Melting Pot*:

[I]t is not possible for Negroes to view themselves as other ethnic groups viewed themselves because – and this is the key to much in the Negro world – the Negro is only an American, and nothing else. He has no values and culture to guard and protect. He insists that the white world deal with his problems because, since he is so much the product of America, they are not *his* problems, but everyone's. Once they become everyone's, perhaps he will see that they are his own too.[8]

Within scholarly and intellectual communities there were some others who did not share this perspective and who began to describe such differences in neutral or positive terms. Shortly I will focus on African Americans who began developing this point of view in the pre-1960s period. For the moment, however, I would like to briefly focus on one white liberal whose views differed from the above, Melville Herskovits. While Herskovits advanced a position similar to Benedict's in his 1925 essay, " The Negro's Americanism," during the late 1920s he began to change his mind.[9] After researching the descendants of a group of runaway slaves in Surinam, he became impressed by the correspondence between many traits of this society with those found in West African societies. After doing fieldwork in Dahomey and Haiti in the 1930s, Herskovits became even more strongly convinced of the importance of African influences on New World African American communities. His new position was expressed in his 1941 book, *The Myth of the Negro Past*.[10]

From the perspective of understanding dominant views of the time, what is most interesting, however, about the book is less its content and more the way it was received. This reception was not very favorable. While a few African American scholars praised it – specifically W. E. B. Du Bois and Carter Woodson – other African American scholars such as E. Franklin Frazier and Alain Locke were critical.[11] The critical response from Locke

[8] Nathan Glazer and Daniel Patrick Moynihan, *Beyond the Melting Pot* (Cambridge, Mass.: MIT Press, 1963), p. 53.
[9] This essay was Herskovits' contribution to the special edition of the magazine *Survey Graphic* that later became the famous collection, *The New Negro*. See Melville Herskovits, "The Negro's Americanism," pp. 353–60 in Alain Locke, ed., *The New Negro: Voices of the Harlem Renaissance* (New York: Simon & Schuster, 1997). The original version of *The New Negro* was published in 1925 by Albert & Charles Boni, Inc.
[10] Melville Herskovits, *The Myth of the Negro Past* (New York and London: Harper and Brothers, 1941). The story of Herskovits' change in thinking is related in Walter Jackson, "Herskovits and the Search for Afro-American Culture," pp. 95–126 in George W. Stocking, Jr., ed., *Malinowski, Rivers, Benedict and Others: Essays on Culture and Personality, History of Anthropology*, Vol. IV (Madison, Wis.: University of Wisconsin Press, 1986). See particularly Jackson's discussion pp. 107–14.
[11] Jackson, "Herskovits," pp. 120–23.

is a bit surprising since, as we shall see, Locke was a theorist who was central in the development of the idea of a distinctive African American culture and pointed to African influences in shaping this culture. But even Locke worried that Herskovits' emphasis on African survivals was "obsessive." The worry that Locke expressed was that this overemphasis would "lead to the very opposite of Dr. Herskovits' liberal conclusions, and damn the Negro as more basically peculiar and unassimilable than he actually is or has proved himself to be."[12] Guy Johnson expressed a similar point of view when he worried that this book might become "the handmaiden of those who are looking for new justifications for the segregation and differential treatment of Negroes."[13]

These reactions tell us that, in addition to deviations of black behaviors and appearance from dominant ideals, and ambiguities in the meaning of culture, there was another factor influencing liberal denial of "culture" to black people. There were also real political concerns about how claims about difference would be interpreted. These liberals knew that many in the population believed firmly in the biological basis of black/white differences. Such conservative beliefs were often put forth to undermine liberal reform efforts. Consequently, liberals worried that any emphasis on African legacies could easily reinforce such a conservative politics. Those who were arguing for civil rights for black people needed to convince white America of the plasticity of the African American psyche; a stress on African legacies could easily undermine that argument.

Thus, from the perspective of most of white and some of black America, African Americans did not possess a distinctive cultural identity. According to conservative whites, black people possessed only a biological identity: they were people of the African race who merely happened to be in the United States. According to many liberals, both white and black, black people had no distinctive cultural identity because they did not have a distinct culture: they were Americans who merely happened to have dark skin. This meant that their behaviors were either identical to those of white people or were the problematic consequences of slavery and discrimination. Neither position allowed for the idea that African Americans had created behaviors that were different from those of a certain American ideal and also positive.

[12] Alain Locke, "Who and What Is 'Negro?'," in *Opportunity* 20 (March–April, 1942), pp. 83–84. This reaction is cited in Jackson, "Herskovits," p. 121, as part of a larger discussion by Jackson of the reception given to *The Myth of the Negro Past* by many intellectuals (see pp. 120–23).
[13] Jackson, "Herskovits," p. 121. The original is from Guy Johnson, "Review of Herskovits 1941," in *American Sociology Review* 7 (1942), pp. 289–90.

Constructing an African American identity: Part I

While the above two positions represented powerful perspectives in mainstream thought, they did not reflect the thinking of everyone in the population. A position different from both of the above began to develop from within African American communities in the early part of the twentieth century. To understand the emergence of a distinctive African American cultural identity requires focusing on the historical context out of which it grew.

In the United States in the late nineteenth century, African Americans saw themselves as a people in need of political organizations devoted to fighting common obstacles. This understanding is, for example, clearly expressed in Frederick Douglass' claim in his newspaper *The North Star* "that we are one, that our cause is one, and that we must help each other, if we would succeed."[14] There existed differences among leaders as to what the nature of those organizations should be and what political goals should inform them. One major source of difference existed between those who argued for emigration from the United States out of a more pessimistic view of the possibilities for African Americans in white America, and those who stressed the existing American identities of African Americans and argued for political struggle based on that identity.[15] The extent of support for these two different positions had much to do with changes in American politics, with the passage of virulent anti-black measures resulting in the growth of support for the former position.[16]

---

[14] These claims and quotes of Douglass were pointed out to me by Wilson Jeremiah Moses, *The Golden Age of Black Nationalism 1850–1925* (New York: Archon, 1978), pp. 85–86. Moses references *The North Star* (December 3, 1847), reprinted in Philip Foner, ed., *The Life and Writings of Frederick Douglass* (New York: International Publishers, 1955), Vol. I, p. 283.

[15] The growing use of labels like "Afro-American" in the last two decades of the nineteenth century attest to this claim of American identity. Sterling Stuckey points out: "From the late 1880s down to the opening years of the new century, the term Afro-American, frequently used, easily competed with Negro as the most popular designation for black people. Especially then, Afro-American began appearing in the titles of black organizations." Sterling Stuckey, *Slave Culture: Nationalist Theory and the Foundations of Black America* (New York and Oxford: Oxford University Press, 1987), p. 239. Stuckey observes in a footnote to the above that the most prominent organization bearing that title was the Afro-American League founded in 1890. Stuckey in turn references Herbert Aptheker, ed., *A Documentary History of the Negro People in the United States* (New York: Citadel Press, 1964 [1951]), Vol. II, p. 679.

[16] For discussions about how such support for emigration rose and fell particularly in the rural south in the period from slavery until the early twentieth century, see Steven Hahn, *A Nation Under Our Feet: Black Political Struggles in the Rural South from Slavery to the Great Migration* (Cambridge, Mass. and London: The Belknap Press of Harvard University, 2003).

But this sense of a unified African American political identity did not include the idea of a distinctive African American cultural identity. Scholars and political leaders sometimes made reference to the uniquely positive traits of African Americans, applauding, for example, the more feminine virtues of the freedmen in contrast to the more masculine traits of white men.[17] But such references were made in the context of widely held beliefs about the need for the freedmen to attain those masculine traits that made the white man economically and politically powerful. In the late nineteenth century, the idea of social evolution was not only held by many European American intellectuals; it was also held by many African American intellectuals and political leaders. Unlike many European American intellectuals who used social Darwinism to argue for the inherent inferiority of African Americans, most African American intellectuals argued for the abilities of the freedmen to acquire necessary skills if provided with the right opportunities. But, while debating much among themselves as to what exactly was needed and how such needs were to be satisfied, most assumed that some form of transformation was necessary if African Americans were to successfully compete with whites and to advance to the state of social evolution that whites had attained.[18]

That most intellectuals held such views can also be explained by the sharp differences in skills and life practices generated by slavery versus freedom, by rural versus urban life, and by southern and northern culture. A college-educated northern African American existed in a very different world than that of a southern tenant sharecropper who had spent his childhood as a slave. While the lives and family connections of some intellectuals and political leaders tied them to rural, southern life, the lives and family connections of others were more separated.

This distance was particularly marked among the late nineteenth-century black elite. During the latter part of the nineteenth century, the black elite in the north, very small in number, most often lived in racially mixed residential areas. As William Julius Wilson points out, "in Chicago prior to 1900, one would rarely find a solidly black block, and a significant number of Negroes lived in white neighborhoods."[19] The lack of residential race separation in the north is understandable given that in the last several decades of the nineteenth century, African Americans made up a miniscule part of the populations of northern cities. Thus in Chicago in

---

[17] William Toll, *The Resurgence of Race: Black Social Theory from Reconstruction to the Pan-African Conferences* (Philadelphia, Pa.: Temple University Press, 1979), p. 13.

[18] See Toll's arguments about the pervasiveness of such beliefs in *ibid.* pp. 13–46.

[19] William Julius Wilson, *The Declining Significance of Race: Blacks and Changing American Institutions*, second edition (Chicago and London: University of Chicago Press, 1980), p. 66.

1880, while 40.7% of the population was foreign born, only 1.3% of the population was African American. In Philadelphia, 24.1% were foreign born and 3.7% were African American.[20] Even in southern cities, where blacks constituted a larger percentage of the population, the members of the small black elite were residentially separated from the poor.[21] Only in very small cities in the south was this not the case.[22]

This residential separation of the late nineteenth-century black elite from the rest of the African American population was matched by a familial separation. Family ancestry was an important criterion establishing membership in this elite. As Willard B. Gatewood notes, the late nineteenth-century "aristocrats of color" were intensely focused on family background, with membership in the "right kind of family" serving as an important criterion for social acceptance:

Much depended upon one's answer to the question: "Who are your people?" An answer likely to gain one admission into the colored aristocracy would almost certainly convey information about respectability, manners and deportment, education, ancestry and color, family achievement, and perhaps wealth.[23]

Not only did members of this elite often live closer to whites than they did to blacks, but their social status depended in part upon special relationships to white people. Members of this elite were often of partial white ancestry, and their ability or that of their parents to gain special opportunities often rested on the fact of this white ancestry.[24] The jobs they were able to gain frequently involved being of service to whites. Many members of this elite were barbers, tailors, headwaiters in white restaurants, railroad porters, cooks, and blacksmiths.[25] The service nature of these jobs both kept members of this group in close contact with wealthy whites and also gave these jobs high status within the black community.[26] Not surprisingly, the kind of urban politics that members of this social class came to develop in the early part of the twentieth century has been described as a "clientage" or "patron-client" politics, that is, a politics marked by "a small group of blacks who fashioned personalized links with influential whites."[27]

[20] Ibid. p. 63.
[21] Willard B. Gatewood, Aristocrats of Color: The Black Elite, 1880–1920 (Bloomington and Indianapolis: Indiana University Press, 1990), pp. 69–95.
[22] Ibid. p. 72.   [23] Ibid. p. 18.
[24] Bart Landry, The New Black Middle Class (Berkeley, Los Angeles and London: University of California Press, 1987), pp. 23–24.
[25] Ibid. pp. 28–33.   [26] Ibid. p. 33.
[27] Martin Kilson, "Political Change in the Negro Ghetto, 1900–1940s," pp. 167–92 in Nathan I. Huggins, Martin Kilson, and Daniel Fox, eds., Key Issues in the Afro-American Experience (New York, Chicago, San Francisco and Atlanta: Harcourt Brace Jovanovich, Inc., 1971), p. 171.

As I've noted, this extreme form of social separation did not apply to all intellectuals and political leaders. And, even in the context of differentiated lives, most African Americans in political and educational leadership positions recognized the obligations such privilege brought. However patronizing or condescending such phrases as "racial uplift" may sound to us today, the phrase does suggest that those who were privileged had heavy work to perform.[28] But even in the context of such qualifications, such phrases – like the idea that a "talented tenth" would lead the rest of the race in racial "uplift" – can be interpreted as a combination of political obligation with a certain degree of cultural distance.[29]

This cultural distance became lessened in the 1920s following the emigration of large numbers of African Americans to the north and to cities in the south. Even before the second decade of the twentieth century, African Americans had been migrating, though most of the migration took place from rural to urban areas in the south.[30] The move to the cities intensified after the First World War, though now it was also accompanied by large movements north. From 1900 to 1910, the number of African Americans migrating north was 170,000. During 1910–1920 this figure increased to 454,000. During 1920–1930 the figure rose to 749,000.[31] Many social scientists describe this increased northern migration in terms of both "push" and "pull" factors. In the south, increasing mechanization in agriculture, followed in the period between 1914 and 1917 by a boll-weevil cotton infestation and a series of storms and floods, constituted

---

[28] Howard Brick has pointed out to me in conversation how such phrases as "lift as we climb" suggest the idea that it is not light work that is required.

[29] The phrase "the talented tenth" was penned by Du Bois. It surfaces first in Du Bois' essay "On the Training of Black Men," in *The Souls of Black Folk*, p. 87. However, the phrase is elaborated by Du Bois in his essay "The Talented Tenth," in *The Negro Problem: A Series of Articles by Representative American Negroes of Today* (New York: James Pott & Co., 1903), pp. 33–75.

Kevin K. Gaines elaborates the meaning of uplift ideology in the United States in the twentieth century in his book, *Uplifting the Race: Black Leadership, Politics, and Culture in the Twentieth Century* (Chapel Hill and London: University of North Carolina Press, 1996). Gaines notes the importance of understanding the racial context of this ideology. Thus, in the early twentieth century, many African Americans believed with good reason that they had to show the existence of a "better" class of black people in order to undermine falsely biological and generalizing understandings of race (p. xiv). Gaines also points out that the ideology of racial uplift was based on feelings of real racial solidarity that were an understandable consequence of racism (p. 31). But again, this last point does not contradict the point I am making here – that the ideology of racial uplift was based on a complex combination of belief in political solidarity and cultural difference.

[30] Daniel M. Johnson and Rex R. Campbell, *Black Migration in America* (Durham, N.C.: Duke University Press, 1981), p. 73.

[31] Manning Marable, *Race, Reform, and Rebellion*, second edition (Jackson and London: University Press of Mississippi, 1991), p. 10.

part of the "push."[32] Meanwhile in the north, the First World War brought with it a rapid decline in European immigration. This meant the opening of certain opportunities for wage employment previously unavailable to African Americans. The postwar prosperity of the 1920s combined with new restrictive immigration law expanded those opportunities and encouraged further migration.[33] Between 1890 and 1930, there was a significant movement of African Americans from agricultural employment into industry, commerce, and transportation.[34]

Urbanization brought with it a certain change in class dynamics within African American communities. It created, as it typically does, a new middle class: "The number of black public and private schoolteachers more than doubled from 1910 to 1940. The number of black-owned businesses between 1904 and 1929 grew from 20,000 to over 70,000."[35] Between 1890 and 1930, the number of African Americans identified as in the professions increased from 34,184 to 107,833.[36]

This new urban "bourgeoisie" was a different kind of bourgeoisie than had predominated in the late nineteenth century, one which was more extensively tied, both in terms of residence and family connections, to those of more marginal economic status. The northern migrations produced large numbers of African Americans in cities such as New York and Chicago and these new arrivals were now shuttled to distinct and separated neighborhoods.[37] Out of such neighborhoods emerged those whose relative prosperity was only made possible by the creation of such neighborhoods, but whose neighbors and family members may not have benefitted from such prosperity:

Throughout most of the industrial period of race relations, the growth of the black middle class occurred because of the expansion of institutions created to serve the needs of a growing urbanized black population. The black doctor, lawyer, teacher, minister, businessman, mortician, excluded from the white community, was able to create a niche in the segregated black community.[38]

Not surprisingly, the ties that the black doctor, lawyer, teacher, minister, businessman, and mortician had to poorer segments of the population made possible a sensibility that was somewhat different from that found in the older black elite: more cognizant of African American unity and distinctiveness. Again, it is not that members of the older elite were not

[32] Wilson, *The Declining Significance of Race*, p. 62.
[33] Johnson and Campbell, *Black Migration in America*, pp. 74–83.
[34] Kilson, "Political Change in the Negro Ghetto," p. 176.
[35] Marable, *Race, Reform and Rebellion*, p. 10.
[36] Kilson, "Political Change in the Negro Ghetto," p. 176.
[37] Wilson, *The Declining Significance of Race*, pp. 63–64.   [38] *Ibid.* p. 20.

race conscious and did not feel political obligations to poorer African Americans. But to reiterate, this sense of obligation – reflected in a phrase such as "racial uplift" – was geared towards assisting poorer segments of the African American population achieve the kind of integration into white society that they themselves sought. Whereas the older black aristocracy had "nurtured ties with whites and advocated assimilation into white society," some among the newer black bourgeoisie began to move closer to "an emphasis on black culture and a closer identity with the masses."[39]

To be sure, the "some" of those who began to make such a move in the 1920s represented a small segment of the black middle class. And those most likely to put this view into public forms of expression represented an even smaller grouping, that of intellectuals and artists. In the 1920s, the place where these intellectuals and artists were best able to come together and make public this new view was in Harlem, New York.

Harlem in the 1920s was an exciting place. Many segments of the African American population were politically and intellectually energized by the conditions found here at this time. For artists and intellectuals it offered some particularly exciting possibilities. As George Hutchinson points out, certain concrete conditions came together in 1920s New York in a unique way: the growth of new publishing houses, magazines, and theaters in a city where cultural diversity was greatest and where traditional elites were less able to monopolize culture; where a large and dynamic African American population existed; and where new ideas about culture were being discussed by academics of various disciplines.[40] Such conditions made it possible for a relatively small and privileged group to begin an extensive and self-conscious public discussion about the meaning of being African American. This discussion brought to light a belief about African American cultural identity that stood somewhere between the two ideological perspectives dominant among whites and significantly, though less exhaustively present among blacks: that there was such an identity which was race based and thus shared by all those of African ancestry, and that there was no African American cultural identity distinguishable from American identity.

This is not to say that the intellectuals and artists who came together in Harlem in the 1920s, and who constituted the movement known as the Harlem Renaissance, held to a single position on the meaning of African

---

[39] Gatewood, *Aristocrats of Color*, pp. 335, 336. Gatewood also points out that the eclipse of the power of the old aristocracy was much more gradual in the older cities of the east.

[40] George Hutchinson, *The Harlem Renaissance in Black and White* (Cambridge, Mass. and London: The Belknap Press of Harvard University, 1995), pp. 5–6.

American cultural identity. Even a casual reading of a limited selection of such figures would reveal that to be not the case. Instead, what this movement first began to manifest was a range of positions between the above two alternatives.[41] Some of those who contributed to this movement held positions closer than others to one or the other of these two alternatives. But collectively, and in some writers more clearly and explicitly than others, a new ideological space was opened.

Since I am speaking of a range of positions, I'd like to elaborate a bit more on the boundaries of this range. As I've mentioned, on the one hand was the belief that what distinguished African Americans as a group were race-based characteristics. This belief grounded the view that the affinities between Africans in Africa and those with African ancestry in the United States transcended any differences that diversity in historical experience might have created. This latter view was dominant not only in conservative white circles in the nineteenth and twentieth centuries but was also present in some nineteenth-century black nationalism and in certain strands of twentieth-century black nationalism.

As we will see later, the idea of a transnational identity of blood tended to exert more pull upon the imaginations of poor and working-class African Americans in the 1920s than it did upon middle-class African Americans. The greater pull among middle-class African Americans lay in the opposite position: that blood had nothing to do with African American identity. This position, reflecting the increasing pull of environmentalism, denied the power of blood altogether. But, even in the denial of blood, the presence of blood-based interpretations loomed large. Thus, many of those who argued for the power of environmentalism felt that they had to articulate this position in a way that made no reference to anything common or distinctive about African American life. It was as if reference to any such commonality or distinctiveness could only be explained by recourse to blood. To avoid such a reading meant denying that there was anything distinctive about African American identity. African Americans, therefore, could only be identified as Americans.

This idea that African Americans could only be identified as Americans is clearly articulated in George Schuyler's 1926 essay, "The Negro-Art

---

[41] Hutchinson also depicts "the New Negro" as representative not of a single position but of a range. He describes what he sees as unique in this range, like I do, as therefore best represented by the term "field." Thus, in describing the range of positions put forth in Locke's collection, *The New Negro*, Hutchinson states, "*The New Negro* is less significant for presenting a particular position than for framing a field of commerce and conflict" (p. 397). However, while Hutchinson and I both use the phrase "field" to describe our descriptions, the "fields" we are respectively describing differ in terms of their content.

Hokum."[42] In this essay, Schuyler argues a position similar to the one described in the above as associated with liberal whites and blacks: that there is no distinguishing aspect of African American culture. According to Schuyler, African Americans are merely Americans who have been subject to certain distinctive environmental conditions shared with other Americans. In explaining what might be seen as distinctive about "the dark-skinned sources" of spirituals, the blues, jazz, and the Charleston, Schuyler makes the following argument:

They [these forms of music] are no more expressive or characteristic of the Negro race than the music and dancing of the Appalachian highlanders or the Dalmation peasantry are expressive or characteristic of the Caucasian race. If one wishes to speak of the musical contributions of the peasantry of the South, very well. Any group under similar circumstances would have produced something similar. It is merely a coincidence that this peasant class happens to be of a darker hue than the other inhabitants of the land.[43]

For Schuyler, there were only two ways of defining African American identity. On the one hand, one could emphasize the Negro aspects. But this meant talking about "the Negro race." And here, according to Schuyler, one would be giving credibility to natural factors that ought not to be given weight. On the other hand, one could emphasize environmental factors; but this made the African American no different from other Americans. Because Schuyler could not yet formulate an environmental position that would explain a distinctive African American identity, he opted for the latter position in the choice presented by these two alternatives. From his perspective, to do otherwise, was to align oneself with the ideology of the Ku Klux Klan. Thus, in the following, Schuyler argues that to make any claims about the distinctiveness of Negro art

is probably the last stand of the old myth palmed off by Negrophobists for all these many years, and recently rehashed by the sainted Harding, that there are "fundamental, eternal, and inescapable differences" between white and black Americans. That there are Negroes who will lend this myth a helping hand need occasion no surprise. It has been broadcast all over the world by the vociferous scions of slaveholders, "scientists" like Madison Grant and Lothrop Stoddard, and the patriots who flood the treasury of the Ku Klux Klan; and is believed, even today, by the majority of free, white citizens.[44]

Schuyler's essay makes apparent an important historical point: the very power of appeals to nature during this period made especially attractive to

---

[42] George S. Schuyler, "The Negro-Art Hokum," in Winston Napier, ed., *African American Literary Theory* (New York and London: New York University Press, 2000), pp. 24–26. This essay was originally published in *The Nation* (June 16, 1926), pp. 662–63.

[43] Schuyler, "The Negro-Art Hokum," p. 24.   [44] *Ibid.* p. 26.

some the denial of any claims of group distinctiveness. The idea that African Americans are merely Americans gained much of its credibility from the fear that African Americans would be denied this status altogether.

But if ideas of a transnational identity of blood and the denial of any specificity to African American identity represented significant forces in the cultural landscape of 1920s African American intellectuals and artists, there was also emerging in this period among this group a third alternative: the idea of African American identity as its own form of identity. This idea of identity undermined the claims of a transnational identity of blood by emphasizing the American aspect of identity for those of African heritage in the United States. It undermined the claims to simple American identity by emphasizing the commonalities in historical circumstances that the African heritage caused.

The intellectual who most explicitly and elaborately articulated this third possibility during the 1920s was Alain Locke. As early as 1915, Locke had begun to formulate the theoretical grounds for constructing an African American identity. In a series of lectures delivered in 1915 and again in 1916, Locke formulates the idea of race as a social construct.[45] Like Franz Boas in *The Mind of Primitive Man*, written a few years before,[46] Locke here attacks the concept of race as a meaningful scientific concept. But Locke takes the argument further than Boas did. Locke argues in these lectures that the idea of race is not just a scientific mistake but is a social construct created and furthered for sociological reasons. As he claims, "Consequently, any true history of race must be a sociological theory of race."[47] He argues that the modern concept of race was initially created to justify modern practices of imperialism.[48] While those practices were the cause of its generation, once created, the concept of "race" took on a historical life of its own, generating for different people differences in their "social inheritance":

Race is [,] at present then in a paradoxical stage. It amounts practically to social inheritance [,] and yet it parades itself as biological or anthropological inheritance. It really is either favorable or unfavorable social inheritance, which has been ascribed to anthropological differences. To the extent, therefore, that any man has race, he has inherited either a favorable or an unfavorable social heredity, which unfortunately is [typically] ascribed to factors which have not produced [it,]

---

[45] Alain Leroy Locke, *Race Contacts and Interracial Relations: Lectures on the Theory and Practice of Race*, ed. and with an introduction by Jeffrey C. Stewart (Washington, D.C.: Howard University Press, 1992).

[46] Franz Boas, *The Mind of Primitive Man* (New York: Macmillan Co., 1911).

[47] Locke, *Race Contacts and Interracial Relations*, p. 11.   [48] *Ibid.* pp. 20–35.

factors which will in no way determine either the period of those inequalities or their eradication.[49]

The idea of "race" is therefore a scientific fiction, describing, however, a sociological reality with political and economic implications. That the group designations labeled as racial are not based in biology does not mean they are based in nothing; they are based in common patterns in the ways individuals see themselves and are seen by others, and by the social consequences that have followed from these forms of categorization. Like other group designations, such as ethnicity, these labels sort real differences: "of language, customs, habits, social adaptability, [and] social survival – historical factors of what may have been the actual fate of groups of people."[50] The only difference is that the category of race attributes to such real differences a false naturalistic ground.

Locke's idea that all forms of social categorization are sociological and historical helps explain the identity he is portraying in his important 1925 collection, *The New Negro*. Because Locke thinks of all identities in sociological terms, he has no difficulty in thinking of African American identity as a distinctive phenomenon. Locke rejects any simple equation of African American culture with that of African culture. In Locke's essay on "The Legacy of the Ancestral Arts," he describes the characteristic art expressions of Africa as "rigid, controlled, disciplined, abstract, heavily conventionalized"; and thus different from "those of the AfraAmerican, – free, exuberant, emotional, sentimental and human."[51] The art forms of the American Negro are the product of the specific conditions of life of the American Negro:

What we have thought primitive in the American Negro – his naïveté, his sentimentalism, his exuberance and his improvising spontaneity are then neither characteristically African nor to be explained as an ancestral heritage. They are the result of his peculiar experience in America and the emotional upheavals of its trials and ordeals ... but they represent essentially the working of environmental forces rather than the outcropping of a race psychology; they are really the acquired and not the original artistic temperament.[52]

As we have seen, for other scholars of this period, such as Schuyler, this kind of stress on environmentalism entailed a denial of any common and distinctive patterns among American Negroes. Locke, however, rejects

---

[49] *Ibid.* p. 12. The brackets are Stewart's additions to the previously unpublished transcriptions.
[50] *Ibid.* p. 10.
[51] Alain Locke, "The Legacy of the Ancestral Arts," in Locke, ed., *The New Negro*, p. 254.
[52] *Ibid.* pp. 254–55. That Locke emphasizes the differences between African and African American art is a point also stressed by Hutchinson, *The Harlem Renaissance*, p. 426.

such a conclusion. Locke believes that there is something common and distinctive, indeed "essential" about "the Negro in America," an essence capable of being revealed through self-representation:

Whoever wishes to see the Negro in his essential traits, in the full perspective of his achievement and possibilities, must seek the enlightenment of that self-portraiture which the present developments of Negro culture are offering.[53]

Locke recognizes that it is only at certain moments in time that such commonalities of experience can be expressed. But it is his belief that the 1920s represent such a time:

Yet the New Negro must be seen in the perspective of a New World, and especially of a New America. Europe seething in a dozen centers with emergent nationalities, Palestine full of a renascent Judaism – these are no more alive with the progressive forces of our era than the quickened centers of the lives of black folk. America seeking a new spiritual expansion and artistic maturity, trying to found an American literature, a national art, and national music implies a Negro-American culture seeking the same satisfactions and objectives.[54]

Thus, for Locke, the "New Negro" is not only an American Negro, but a race conscious one, that is, one who has been provided with the right historical conditions to understand and articulate the commonalities in experience that constitute African Americans as a distinct group. Locke views the portrayal of African America identity in the writings of various sociologists and artists in the early twentieth century as representing – to borrow the language of political theory – the transformation of a group "in-itself" into a group "for-itself." This appears to be Locke's point in the following:

Hitherto, it must be admitted that American Negroes have been a race more in name than in fact, or to be exact, more in sentiment than in experience. The chief bond between them has been that of a common condition rather than a common consciousness; a problem in common rather than a life in common.[55]

Because for Locke, "race consciousness" could be a consciousness of commonality of experience rather than a consciousness of commonality of biology, it could go beyond stereotypical representations of what the Negro is thought to be and become the expression of individual experiences, experiences that by their very nature are both idiosyncratic and also expressive of shared patterns.[56] And it is this vision of what is newly possible in the expression of the American Negro that shaped Locke's

[53] Locke, "Foreword," in Locke, ed., *The New Negro*, p. xxv.
[54] *Ibid.* pp. xxv–xxvi.   [55] Locke, ed., *The New Negro*, p. 7.
[56] Locke, "Negro Youth Speaks," in Locke, ed., *The New Negro*, p. 50.

compilation and editing of *The New Negro*. For him, the volume provided the context for a diverse group of writers, essayists, and poets to express what is distinctive about African American life. Through the use of their artistic and scholarly abilities, this group could powerfully describe the lives they lived and the people they knew, and thus bring to the consciousness of whites and to the self-consciousness of blacks a portrait of African American life.

One may question the degree to which Locke was correct in identifying his vision with that of a large group of others in the mid 1920s. The answer to this question must depend upon how one describes Locke's vision. Among many artists and intellectuals there was a sense that something "new" was being expressed. The widespread use of the phrase "New Negro" among artists and intellectuals of this period attests to this shared sentiment of feeling. And also, the content of the fiction and poetry depicts a distinctive identity. On the other hand, few were able to self-consciously articulate the meaning of this identity with the degree of clarity that Locke achieved. If one looks at some of the other theoretical contributions to *The New Negro*, one finds many remnants from older understandings. In the theoretical essays, one finds, in addition to Locke's claims, an argument by Melville Herskovits that denies anything distinctive about African American culture as well as a statement by Albert Barnes that claims that "The Negro is a poet by birth."[57] One of the contributors to the volume, Countee Cullen, said in 1924 that if he were to be poet at all, "I am going to be POET and not NEGRO POET."[58]

As the comment by Countee Cullen indicates, the pull against explicitly endorsing the idea of African American distinctiveness was still strong. The tendencies for even African American artists and intellectuals of this period to identify primarily as Americans and to link their self-identity more with European Americans than with poorer African Americans remained powerful. For this reason, some contemporary critics view the artistic contributions of the Harlem Renaissance writers as less worthy than they might have been if such ways of thought had been less strong. Henry Louis Gates, Jr., provides a forceful example of this position.[59]

[57] See Herskovits, "The Negro's Americanism," pp. 353–54 and Albert C. Barnes, "Negro Art and America," in Locke, ed., *The New Negro*, p. 19. On this point of the diversity of positions expressed in *The New Negro*, again, also see Hutchinson, *The Harlem Renaissance*, pp. 397, 387.

[58] Gerald Early, *My Soul's High Song: The Collected Writings of Countee Cullen, Voice of the Harlem Renaissance* (New York: Anchor Books, 1991), p. 23.

[59] In addition to Gates, other writers have advanced versions of this thesis though in the context of different overall arguments. A short list of such writers would include: Harold Cruse, *The Crisis of the Negro Intellectual* (New York: William Morrow, 1967); Nathan

Gates points to the ironclad "Instructions for Contributors" that were widely circulated in the journals of the period. Among other demands, these rules warn against material that "is likely to engender ill feelings between blacks and whites."[60] Gates makes a more elaborate argument in showing how the writers of the 1920s turned away from the use of African American dialect in their poetry and fiction. As Gates argues, this rejection of dialect was broken only in poetry by the publication of the first edition of Sterling Brown's *Southern Road*, printed in 1932, and in fiction by Zora Neale Hurston's *Their Eyes Were Watching God*, published in 1937.[61] As Gates argues, that it took so long for this break to occur tells us much about the politics of the New Negro Movement of the 1920s:

Despite its stated premises, the New Negro movement was indeed quite polemical and propagandistic, both within the black community and outside of it. Claiming to be above and beyond protest and politics, it sought nothing less than to reconstruct the very *idea* of who and what a Negro was or could be. Claiming that the isolated, cultured, upper-class part stood for the potential of the larger black whole, it sought to imitate forms of Western poetry, "translating," as it was put, the art of the untutored folk into a "higher," standard English mode of expression, more compatible with the Western tradition. Claiming that it had realized an unprecedented level of Negro self-expression, it created a body of literature that even the most optimistic among us find wanting when compared to the blues and jazz compositions epitomized by Bessie Smith and the young Duke Ellington, two brilliant artists who were not often invited to the New Negro salons. It was *not* the literature of this period that realized a profound contribution to art; rather, it was the black creators of the classic blues and jazz whose creative works, subsidized by the black working class, defined a new era in the history of Western music.[62]

But lest one interpret Gates' analysis as disputing the overall argument I am developing here – i.e., that the Harlem Renaissance represents the early expression of a new type of African American identity – let me reiterate my point that this movement represents only an opening moment in the expression and self-conscious elaboration of this new identity. As David Lewis argues, the 1920s was a period of transition. As the decade progressed, black identification with a white audience decreased.[63] Others

Huggins, *Harlem Renaissance* (New York: Oxford University Press, 1971); David Levering Lewis, *When Harlem Was in Vogue* (New York: Knopf, 1981); and Houston A. Baker, Jr., *Modernism and the Harlem Renaissance* (University of Chicago Press, 1987).

[60] Henry Louis Gates, Jr., *The Signifying Monkey: A Theory of Afro-American Literary Criticism* (New York and Oxford: Oxford University Press, 1988), pp. 179–80.

[61] *Ibid.* pp. 177–81. See also, Henry Louis Gates, Jr., "Dis and Dat: Dialect and the Descent," in Henry Louis Gates, Jr., *Figures in Black* (New York and Oxford: Oxford University Press, 1986), pp. 167–95 and in the same volume, "Black Structures of Feeling," pp. 178–87.

[62] Henry Louis Gates, Jr., "The Trope of a New Negro and the Reconstruction of the Image of the Black," pp. 122–55 in *Representations* 24 (Fall 1988), p. 148.

[63] Lewis, *When Harlem Was in Vogue* (1996 preface, in 1997 edition), p. xxiv.

have also pointed to the gradualness of the transition between the older, more adamantly American form of self-identification and one which was more race identified.[64]

One place where we can see the tensions existing between the older and newer perspectives in this decade is in Langston Hughes' famous 1926 essay, "The Negro Artist and the Racial Mountain." In this essay, Hughes describes a mountain standing in the way of the Negro artist: the desire to be white and American:

> But this is the mountain standing in the way of any true Negro art in America – this urge within the race toward whiteness, the desire to pour racial individuality into the mold of American standardization, and to be as little Negro and as much American as possible.[65]

Hughes argues that the pull of the desire to be white and American is of particular power for those who are most privileged. It is members of this group whose churches, jobs, and neighborhoods place them in the closest proximity to the world of white people and for whom the world of white people is most enticing. For poor black people, for those Hughes describes as living on Seventh Street in Washington D.C. or on State Street in Chicago, the world of white people is far away. But, Hughes argues, it is in these latter neighborhoods that the richness and distinctiveness of Negro life resides:

> These common people are not afraid of spirituals, as for a long time their more intellectual brethren were, and jazz is their child. They furnish a wealth of colorful, distinctive material for any artist because they still hold their own individuality in the face of American standardizations. And perhaps these common people will give to the world its truly great Negro artist, the one who is not afraid to be himself.[66]

Thus Hughes is making the following argument: for a great African American art to be created, the Negro artist must shift his or her visionary alliance away from the white middle and upper classes and towards the

---

[64] Gatewood not only points to the gradualness of the transition but also points to regional differences as affecting the extent of the adoption of the new point of view. He notes that the eclipse of the power of the old aristocracy was much more gradual in the older cities of the east in distinction from the newer cities of the midwest and west. See Gatewood, *Aristocrats of Color*, p. 337.

[65] Langston Hughes, "The Negro Artist and the Racial Mountain," in Winston Napier, ed., *African American Literary Theory: A Reader* (New York University Press, 2000), pp. 27–30. This essay was first published in *The Nation* (June 23, 1926), pp. 692–94.

[66] Hughes, "The Negro Artist," p. 28. For a good discussion of the importance of class in Hughes' discussion see p. 300, Rafia Zafar, "Fictions of the Harlem Renaissance," in Sacvan Bercovitch, ed., *The Cambridge History of American Literature*, Vol. VI, *Prose Writing 1910–1950* (Cambridge University Press, 2003), pp. 283–352. This lengthy essay provides a very thoughtful summary and analysis of many of the major contributors to this movement.

black poor and working classes. The vision of an alliance with the white middle and upper classes stands in the way of the Negro artist producing anything great; what is powerful and what is distinctive in what the Negro artist can contribute can only emerge when that artist identifies with ordinary African American life.

While these claims appear mostly about the conditions for good art, there are broader ideas about African American identity that are also here. When Hughes argues that inspiration from the ordinary Negro will make possible the Negro artist "who is not afraid to be himself," Hughes seems to be stating that the "true" identity of the African American artist, the identity that expresses who that artist *really* is, is racial in a way that supercedes class. Noteworthy is that Hughes is making a case for such a cross-class African American identity without appealing to nature. Instead Hughes points to the ability of poor and working-class blacks to exist outside of the narrowness of white, standardized culture. As such, the experiences they have, and the values that they possess, contain a realness, an energy, and a creativity lacking in white middle-class life. The implicit message here is that buried within the middle-class African American artist are also such experiences and values and that these can be summoned forth by the artist when that artist identifies not with the white middle classes but with poor and working-class blacks.

Thus, I view the 1920s as a period where new kinds of cultural identification are just starting to be formed, where a few members of the black middle class are beginning to switch their sense of emotional identification with a white middle class to poorer, black communities. Partly what is making this possible are changes beginning in the nature of the African American middle class itself: from a population sharply differentiated, both geographically and in family terms, from a largely poor, southern, rural community to a population more class hybrid in its family and geographic locations. It is the latter kind of population that makes possible the beginning expression of a distinctive African American cultural identity.

But to again emphasize the point, if the idea of a distinctively African American identity was beginning to emerge as a possible perspective during the 1920s, those who were giving voice to this perspective were a small group of artists and intellectuals. Many scholars point to the social composition of the Harlem Renaissance as an important cause of its limited influence.[67] As Nathan Huggins notes, the Harlem Renaissance

---

[67] As with the question of artistic success, this is a question around which there has been much scholarly debate. Hutchinson provides an interesting summary of this debate, though it is highly structured around the question of how one ought to interpret interracial dynamics in the Renaissance. See Hutchinson, *The Harlem Renaissance*, pp. 16–26.

"had no grass-roots attachments. Its success depended on its strategic placement, not its power."[68] David Lewis makes a similar point when he describes the Renaissance as "a cultural nationalism of the parlor."[69]

These critics are correct in noting the limited appeal of cultural nationalism at this time. And yet, one also must recognize the importance of the Harlem Renaissance in initiating a perspective among intellectuals and artists that would last beyond the 1920s. George Hutchinson points to a line of connection between ideas developed by writers and artists of the Harlem Renaissance and ideas being articulated by some intellectuals and political activists during the 1930s. Against the claims of others that the Renaissance was a failure, Hutchinson claims that "much of the movement's cultural legacy was amplified throughout the late 1930s and institutionalized in programs such as the Federal Writers' Arts and Theatre Projects, which incubated the next generation of African American artists."[70]

One can amplify Hutchinson's point by focusing on other intellectual developments of the 1930s. The 1930s was a period in the US when many intellectuals were radicalized. For many – black and white – this meant the adoption of socialist and communist politics. But for some black intellectuals, "radicalism" also came to mean – in varying types of combination with socialist and communist views – adopting more nationalistic perspectives on race. In chapter 3, I noted how the idea of "culture" was becoming more a part of general consciousness in the 1930s. For growing numbers of artists and intellectuals, adopting a more radical stance on race came to mean applying this concept to African American ways of life. Moreover, some of these artists and intellectuals also began to associate this cultural identity with more of a separatist politics.

What this separatism meant varied for different individuals. On the one hand, there were those, such as Claude MacKay and Harry Haywood, who were members of the US Communist Party and who were involved in that party's development of the Black Belt nation position. This position, originating in a 1917 call by Cyril Biggs, was officially adopted at the 1928 Sixth Congress of the Comintern.[71] The position claimed that black people in the south fulfilled all the criteria of nationhood in that they made up *"a historically evolved, stable community of language, territory, economic life, and psychological make-up manifested in a community of*

[68] Huggins, *Harlem Renaissance*, p. 48.
[69] Lewis, *When Harlem Was in Vogue* (1988 preface, in 1997 edition), p. xxviii.
[70] Hutchinson, *The Harlem Renaissance*, p. 22.
[71] William J. Maxwell, *New Negro, Old Left: African American Writing and Communism Between the Wars* (New York: Columbia University Press, 1999), pp. 91–92.

culture."[72] Since such criteria of nationhood were fulfilled, the legitimate political solution to racism in the United States was the establishment of a black nation in the Black Belt of the United States.

This idea of establishing a separate nation-state for African Americans was not new. Newer – particularly among intellectuals and members of the black middle class – was a kind of nationalism being expressed by other radicals. These radicals began arguing for a distinct kind of nationalism, one where blacks did not create a separate nation-state but instead created separate institutions within the United States as a means to increase the power of blacks within the United States. The position of Du Bois during this period is exemplary of this kind of stance. Du Bois became both more socialist and more nationalist in the 1930s. Du Bois' growing commitment in this period to a long-range socialist vision and an interim separatist strategy is evidenced in the following important 1935 essay, "A Negro Nation Within the Nation":

On this point a new school of Negro thought is arising. It believes in the ultimate uniting of mankind and in a unified American nation, with economic classes and racial barriers leveled, but it believes this is an ideal and is to be realized only by such intensified class and race consciousness as will bring irresistible force rather than mere humanitarian appeals to bear on the motives and actions of men.[73]

Du Bois associates this intensified race consciousness with concrete political strategies:

With the use of their political power, their power as consumers, and their brain power, added to that chance of personal appeal which proximity and neighborhood always give to human beings, Negroes can develop in the United States an economic nation within a nation, able to work through inner cooperation, to found its own institutions, to educate its genius, and at the same time, without mob violence or extremes of race hatred, to keep in helpful touch and cooperate with the mass of the nation. This has happened more often than most people realize, in the case of groups not so obviously separated from the mass of people as are American Negroes. It must happen in our case, or there is no hope for the Negro in America.[74]

Du Bois was not alone in developing this kind of nationalist position at this time. Carter Woodson was another intellectual whose politics became

---

[72] This quote is taken from *ibid.* p. 162. Maxwell's reference is to Joseph Stalin, "Marxism and the National Question," pp. 7–68 in Joseph Stalin, *Marxism and the National Question: Selected Writings and Speeches* (New York: International Publishers, 1942), p. 12. Maxwell notes that the emphasis in the quote was in the original.

[73] W. E. B. Du Bois, "A Negro Nation Within the Nation," pp. 563–70 in Lewis, ed., *W. E. B. Du Bois.* These lines are quoted on p. 567.

[74] *Ibid.* p. 568.

both more socialist and more separatist from the 1930s onward.[75] Woodson
had been a strong supporter of African American pride early on, founding
in 1915 the Association for the Study of Negro Life and History.[76]
However, from the 1930s onwards, this racial pride became more associated with a specific form of segregationist politics – a politics which
argued for temporary black self-segregation within the context of the
existing United States.[77] And during the period from the 1930s to the
1960s, others such as Adam Clayton Powell and those who became
advocates of "Buy Black" began to articulate similar types of positions.[78]

But still, the positions of such figures did not reflect widespread perspectives among the black middle class. Du Bois' separation from the
National Association for the Advancement of Colored People (NAACP)
following his advocacy of a more segregationist position underlines this
point. But it is useful to note the thinking of these figures because they
illustrate that at least some powerful African American thinkers were
beginning to associate the idea of a distinctive African American cultural
identity with a new kind of politics – a politics that might be called "quasi-
separatist." It was "quasi-separatist" because its ultimate aim was not the

[75] Jacqueline Goggin, *Carter G. Woodson: A Life in Black History* (Baton Rouge and London: Louisiana State University Press, 1993), pp. 141–42, 155.

[76] *Ibid.* p. xiv.

[77] I use the phrase "form of self-segregation" because segregation for Woodson is a complicated position. This complexity is illustrated in many of the positions he articulates in
his famous 1933 book, *The Mis-Education of the Negro*. Thus, arguing that theoretically a
white person could be as good, if not better, than a Negro as a teacher in a Negro school,
he still argues for the general desirability of Negroes in these positions. He claims that "the
emphasis is not upon the necessity for separate systems but upon the need for common
sense schools and teachers who understand and continue in sympathy with those whom
they instruct." A similar complex position is illustrated in his arguments in this work on
the idea of a white man as the head of a Negro college. As he states, "It is all right to have a
white man as the head of a Negro college or to have a red man at the head of a yellow one, if
in each case the incumbent has taken out his naturalization papers and has identified
himself as one of the group which he is trying to serve ... The real servant of the people
must live among them, think with them, feel for them, and die for them." As this passage
makes clear, Woodson's idea of African American identity is not based on a simple
biological essentialism but on the idea of a unity of experience and emotional affiliation.
Carter G. Woodson, *The Mis-Education of the Negro* (Washington, D.C.: Associated
Publishers, Inc., 1973 [reprinted from the first edition of 1933]), pp. 28, 129–30.
    That for Woodson, like Du Bois, black self-segregation was only a means towards the
ultimate goals of racial integration is pointed out by Goggin, *Carter G. Woodson*, p. 162.
Goggin also notes that by the end of the 1930s, Woodson was arguing that blacks needed
to remain independent of coalitions with whites (pp. 172–79).

[78] Clayborne Carson, *In Struggle: SNCC and the Black Awakening of the 1960s* (Cambridge,
Mass. and London: Harvard University Press, 1981), p. 209. Carson points also to Paul
Robeson and Jesse Gray as using the phrase "black power" long before the 1960s. Kilson
also notes how Powell's Greater New York Coordinating Committee "made explicit use
of black nationalist ideology" in the late 1930s. See Kilson, "Political Change in the Negro
Ghetto," p. 179.

departure of African Americans from the United States to a separate homeland. Rather its separatism was about unifying African Americans into a separate force to gain full integration into the United States. Its goal was not exodus but power.[79]

Constructing an African American identity: Part II

In the above I've suggested that beginning in the 1920s and further developing during the 1930s, some intellectuals and artists began to call on middle-class African Americans to become more culturally identified with poor and working-class African Americans and to adopt a "quasi-nationalist" kind of politics. I want to claim now that this move on the part of some from this segment of the African American population was being matched in the period between the late 1920s and the 1960s by a subtle turn coming from different parts of the African American population. While some middle-class intellectuals and political figures were beginning to culturally identify with poor and working-class African Americans and, even for some, to promote the idea of a form of quasi-separation, parts of other segments of the African American population were moving towards a form of racial identification that was more US based than was the case with earlier forms of racial identification.

As I have previously noted, in the early part of the twentieth century, two forms of identification exerted varying strengths in defining African American identity. On the one hand, there was the pull towards defining African Americans as Americans, similar to other Americans in many or all respects. On the other hand was the pull towards defining African Americans as members of the African race. As I suggested in the previous section, the pressure on many upper- and middle-class African Americans in the early and middle part of the twentieth century was from the "American" side of this equation. On the other hand, the pull from the opposite direction, that is, the pull to emphasize the racial side of this equation, appears to manifest itself more powerfully among those from less affluent communities.

To gain a sense of changes in the nature of this pull among those from this part of the population, let us go back to the New Negro Movement of the early twentieth century. Sometimes the phrase "the New Negro" has

[79] For an extended discussion of Du Bois' turn and his break with the NAACP as a consequence, see David Levering Lewis, *W. E. B. Du Bois: The Fight for Equality and the American Century, 1919–1963* (New York: Henry Holt & Co., 2000), pp. 302–48. Lewis too points out the complexity of Du Bois' turn, noting on p. 345 his rejection of the Communist Party of the USA's "49th State" idea.

been exclusively applied to members of a particular kind of cultural and artistic elite, those who contributed to the Harlem Renaissance. This is not surprising since members of this group often applied the phrase "the New Negro" to themselves.[80] But Gerald Early suggests that we should think of the New Negro Movement as broader than the Harlem Renaissance, as a movement represented as much by the heavyweight boxing champion Jack Johnson as by the writers anthologized in the famous 1925 collection, *The New Negro*.[81] Thus Early is suggesting a wide class referent for the phrase "the New Negro" and I believe that this suggestion is a useful one. Many of those writing from within this period thought of the phrase as pointing to a sensibility found as much among ordinary Harlemites as among the literary elite.[82] That sensibility was one where blacks showed an explicit pride of association with other black people and a refusal to be subservient to whites.

That this kind of sensibility might have crossed class lines is understandable given the new types of communities it was emanating from: the rapidly growing cross-class, all black neighborhoods of such northern cities as Chicago and New York and in such southern cities as Durham, North Carolina.[83] These neighborhoods developed as a consequence of the great migration of black people from the south to the north and from rural to urban areas in the south beginning in the early part of the twentieth century and intensifying after the First World War. As Nathan

---

[80] For example, in the use of the term as title see Locke, ed., *The New Negro*. Henry Louis Gates, Jr., argues in "The Trope of a New Negro" that Locke's use of the term to describe what he and his colleagues were doing "represents a measured coopting of the term from its fairly radical political connotations, as defined in the *Messenger*, the *Crusader*, the *Kansas City Call*, and the *Chicago Whip*, in bold essays and editorials printed during the post–World War I race riots in which Afro-Americans rather ably defended themselves from fascist mob aggression" (p. 131). Gates dates the origins of the phrase "the New Negro" in the late nineteenth century where the phrase was variously associated with different political agendas (see pp. 125–55).

[81] Early, *My Soul's High Song*, p. 25. The reference to *The New Negro* is to Locke, ed., *The New Negro*. The claim that the New Negro Movement is not to be equated with the Harlem Renaissance has also been made by Wilson J. Moses, "The Lost World of the Negro, 1895–1919: Black Literature and Intellectual Life Before the 'Renaissance,'" in *Black American Literature Forum* 21 (1987), pp. 63–75.

[82] For example, as in Gates' references in the above. Another example can be found in Hubert H. Harrison, *When Africa Awakes*, quoted in Early, *My Soul's High Song*, p. 32. In this quote, Harrison uses the term "the New Negro" to refer to Negroes as a group, not to certain parts of the community. This point, that many thinkers of the period themselves used the term "New Negro" in cross-class terms, would not contradict Early's claim that it was mostly those in the middle class who were responsible for formulating it (p. 31).

[83] Leslie Brown, *Upbuilding Black Durham: Gender, Class, and Black Community Development in the Jim Crow South* (Chapel Hill, N.C.: University of North Carolina Press, 2008).

Huggins points out, this demographic shift could not help but have major cultural consequences:

Large numbers of blacks had streamed into the northern cities in the first years of the new century, forced out by the poverty of southern agriculture and the mean brutality of southern racial bigotry. Harlem gained from that migration ... Harlem had thus freshly become a great concentration of blacks – not peasant but urban – within the most urbane of American cities then just feeling its youthful strength and posturing in self-conscious sophistication. No wonder Harlemites felt that they and their community were something special ... And when black soldiers paraded up Lenox Avenue to a jazz step – returning from a war that had ended war and guaranteed to all men the right of self-determination – it is not surprising that black men's dreams would find in Harlem a capital for the race, a platform from which the new black voice would be heard around the world, and an intellectual center of the New Negro.[84]

One place where one might derive a sense of how this consciousness was being felt by many who were not middle-class intellectuals or artists is Marcus Garvey's Universal Negro Improvement Association (UNIA). The UNIA was a mass organization created in the post-First World War period out of such neighborhoods as well as from the rural and small-town south.[85] While many of its leaders came from the lower middle class, its rank and file members were predominantly poor and working class.[86] What is important to focus on, given the concerns of this chapter, is the sense of identity held by members of this organization. Often this movement has been portrayed as a "Back to Africa" movement. But Judith Stein has powerfully argued that this simple characterization leaves much out, indeed much that was central to the organization. As she notes, the political program put forth at the organization's first convention in 1920 covered a range of demands, from protests about discrimination in public hotels to the issue of imperialism in Africa.[87] She argues that a typical injunction to members of local chapters, as, for example, one given to members in Gary, Indiana, was to "work here and help build up the city in which you live ... In the future we will build large and promising Garys

[84] Huggins, *Harlem Renaissance*, p. 14.
[85] Steven Hahn points out the extent of its southern base as well as the fact that much of its northern membership was composed of first generation southern migrants. See Hahn, *A Nation Under Our Feet*, pp. 469, 471.
[86] Judith Stein, *The World of Marcus Garvey: Race and Class in Modern Society* (Baton Rouge and London: Louisiana State University Press, 1986), pp. 246, 274–75. Stein points out that the membership, while poor, was not part of the very poor. As she states on p. 228: "Active Garveyites were marginal, not desperate, men."
[87] *Ibid.* p. 86. For the content of that program, see the "Declaration of Rights of the Negro Peoples of the World," printed in William L. Van Deburg, ed., *Modern Black Nationalism: From Marcus Garvey to Louis Farrakhan* (New York and London: New York University Press, 1997), pp. 24–31.

in our own beloved land of Africa."[88] And that much of the energy of the organization soon became focused around creating a profitable shipping line, the Black Star Line, gives support to her argument that commerce, not emigration, lay at the heart of the organization's mission.[89]

One can agree with Stein that characterizing the UNIA as simply a "Back to Africa" movement ignores much of the complexity of the organization. But, in arguing against this simple characterization, Stein seems not to give enough attention to one aspect of this organization that seems striking to a twenty-first-century observer: its internationalism. However little emigration figured in the actual practice of the organization, the continent of Africa played an extremely important role in the rhetoric of this organization. This rhetoric continued a tradition with an important history in the late nineteenth-century black south.[90] In accord with this rhetoric, members were asked to look at this continent as their true homeland, not just the place from which their ancestors came, but also as the place to which they would eventually return. Indeed, it was on the basis of this vision that members were asked to join an explicitly international organization, an organization led not by a citizen of the United States but by a man born in Jamaica. At the founding convention of the organization, a flag and an anthem were created that expressed this international vision. To be sure, the UNIA was based in Harlem and described within its program the need for black people in the United States to create local institutions to serve their interests.[91] Nevertheless, the underlying vision of the organization, made clear in Garvey's speeches and in the program of the organization, was that of a worldwide movement of black people, united by racial, not national allegiance. The centrality to the organization of the internationalist vision of race and of the idea of Africa as homeland was well expressed by Richard Wright. The following are some observations he offered in 1944, describing some earlier encounters with Garveyites:

The one group I met during those exploring days whose lives enthralled me was the Garveyites, an organization of black men and women who were forlornly seeking to return to Africa. Theirs was a passionate rejection of America, for they sensed with the directness of which only the simple are capable that they had no chance to live a full human life in America ... On the walls of their dingy flats

---

[88] Stein, *The World of Marcus Garvey*, p. 109.   [89] *Ibid.* p. 108 footnote 1.
[90] Hahn, *A Nation Under Our Feet*, points to the connections between the ideology of Garveyism and a sympathy for emigration that had been a strong presence among southern rural blacks in the late nineteenth century. Indeed, as Hahn notes, Garveyism took especially strong hold in those sections of the rural and small-town south where emigrationism had had a history of support (see pp. 469–70, 472–73).
[91] For the full program of the UNIA see Van Deburg, ed., *Modern Black Nationalism*, pp. 24–31.

were maps of Africa and India and Japan, pictures of Japanese generals and admirals, portraits of Marcus Garvey in gaudy regalia, the faces of colored men and women from all parts of the world ... It was when the Garveyites spoke fervently of building their own country, of someday living within the boundaries of a culture of their own making, and I sensed the passionate hunger of their lives, that I caught a glimpse of the potential strength of the American Negro.[92]

I do not want to suggest that a race-based internationalism was the overriding ideology of poor and working-class African Americans in northern cities or in the rural and small-town south in the 1920s. Against that claim could be marshaled evidence about the number of working-class African Americans who joined the NAACP in this period – an organization explicitly devoted to the advancement of African Americans in the United States.[93] But I stress the internationalism of the Garvey movement because it points to one important thread within racial identification in this period. I emphasize this thread because it seems to represent an increasingly diminishing thread. As the twentieth century progresses, poor and working-class African Americans do not abandon a sense of racial consciousness. Indeed, the growing expression of this consciousness in many of those public venues available to working-class African Americans – such as the worlds of music and sport – is testament to the particular strength of this consciousness among poor and working-class African Americans.[94] But what I would argue is that this racial consciousness becomes subtly but steadily more US based over the course of the twentieth century. In other words, it becomes a racial consciousness that increasingly celebrated the specificity and greatness of the African American.

To illustrate this change, I'd like to turn to certain mid-century political phenomena that possess some roughly comparable features with the

[92] Richard Wright, *American Hunger* (New York: Harper and Row, 1944), p. 28. I found this quote in Bernard Makhosezwe Magubane, *The Ties That Bind: African American Consciousness of Africa* (Trenton, N.J.: Africa World Press, Inc., 1987), p. 97.
[93] During 1919, the organization greatly expanded its size and number of branches, reaching a total membership of 88,000 members in 300 branches. See Rod Bush, *We Are Not What We Seem: Black Nationalism and Class Struggles in the American Century* (New York University Press, 1999), p. 81. Stein, *The World of Marcus Garvey*, makes the following point about the rapid growth of the NAACP in 1919: "Prior to 1919 the organization had been composed principally of members of northern black elites, but the new growth drew large numbers of black workers from Deep South towns and cities" (p. 58).
[94] That in the early and middle part of the twentieth century, poor and working-class African Americans are more apt to possess a racial identification than middle-class African Americans is evidenced in many types of phenomena. One example, which Angela Davis points out, is the greater willingness of working-class singers such as Bessie Smith to be associated with non-European religious phenomena, such as voodoo. See Angela Davis, *Blues Legacies and Black Feminism* (New York: Pantheon, 1998), pp. 154–55.

UNIA. One such phenomenon is the Nation of Islam under Elijah Muhammad. The 1950s and early-1960s politics of Elijah Muhammad were, like the politics of Garvey, very racialist. Muhammad, like Garvey, thought of the differences between blacks and whites in highly physical terms. He described white people as "devils," with an ancestry rooted in a far distant theological past.[95] Thus, there was no talk of the differences between blacks and whites as located in history and experience alone. Moreover, like Garvey, Muhammad viewed segregation as a desirable end in and of itself.[96]

But yet, there were aspects of the Nation of Islam that moved away from Garveyism. Elijah Muhammad, unlike Marcus Garvey, was a citizen of the United States, and the Nation of Islam, unlike the UNIA, was not an international organization. The Nation of Islam was an organization of African Americans. This focus on African Americans was not just tactical; Muhammad believed African Americans to be God's chosen people, picked to lead the pure of soul in an eventual kingdom of God:

Furthermore, we believe we are the people of God's choice, as it has been written, that God would choose the rejected and the despised. We can find no other persons fitting this description in these last days more than the so-called Negroes in America. ... we believe this first judgment will take place, as God revealed, in America ...[97]

Muhammad often spoke of friendship and association between the Nation of Islam and the emerging nation-states of Africa and Asia. But this talk was of a friendship and alliance among separate entities, not of a unified international organization. Indeed, Muhammad argued that African Americans must first unify themselves before any worthwhile union with such other states can take place.[98]

To be sure, there are many similarities between the political goals of the Nation of Islam and the UNIA. Muhammad, like Garvey, spoke of the necessity for the creation of a separate state. And, as earlier noted, one can

[95] Elijah Muhammad, "The Making of the Devil," pp. 101–02 in Van Deburg, *Modern Black Nationalism*, p. 101.
[96] No argument against integration can be expressed more forcefully than the following: "So remember, your seeking friendship with this race of devils means seeking a place in their hell." From Muhammad, "The Making of the Devil," p. 102.
[97] Elijah Muhammad, "What Do Muslims Want?" pp. 404–07 in John H. Bracey, Jr., August Meier, and Elliott Rudwick, eds., *Black Nationalism in America* (Indianapolis and New York: Bobbs-Merrill Co., 1970), p. 406. Originally from Elijah Muhammad, "The Muslim Program," *Muhammad Speaks* (July 31, 1962).
[98] Elijah Muhammad, "Separation of the So-Called Negroes from their Slavemasters' Children Is a Must," pp. 408–11 in Bracey, Jr., Meier, and Rudwick, eds., *Black Nationalism in America*, p. 410. From Elijah Muhammad, "Message to the Blackman" (Chicago: Muhammad Mosque of Islam no. 2, 1965), pp. 34–37.

question how important actual emigration was to the UNIA, given that much of its energy was devoted to setting up business enterprises in the United States and elsewhere.[99] But even in regard to these shared political goals and practices, there were subtle differences. Both organizations spoke of the need for a separate state. But Muhammad was vaguer than Garvey about where that separate state ought to be, describing its location as "either on this continent or elsewhere."[100] While both organizations were involved in setting up local businesses, for Garvey, local business enterprises were eventually to be connected in an international, Pan-African, economic system.[101] Moreover, even in relation to the political goals that were shared, the role of politics in general was different in the two organizations, leading to differences in emphases in the importance of these goals. The Nation of Islam, unlike the UNIA, has been primarily a religious organization, strongly geared towards preparing African Americans for becoming the kind of people worthy of full citizenship in a kingdom of God. Consequently, much of the energy of the Nation of Islam has gone into preparing African Americans for *this* future. This preparation has meant encouraging African Americans to adhere to certain rules of diet, dress, sexual practice, and overall behavior. Thus, much actual energy has been geared not towards African Americans setting up a government separate from where they are at the moment but in taking control of their lives in the present context.[102] As Garveyites who were contemporaries of Muhammad claimed, "Muhammad's promise of exodus to his followers is spurious and that he has no intention whatsoever of encouraging Negroes to emigrate."[103]

I emphasize these differences between Garveyism and the Nation of Islam because I believe they tell us something important about changes in the implicit assumptions of a certain segment of the African American

---

[99] That setting up a variety of independent businesses in the United States as well as elsewhere was highly important to the UNIA is also pointed out by Tony Martin, *Race First: The Ideological and Organization Struggles of Marcus Garvey and the Universal Negro Improvement Association* (Westport, Conn. and London: Greenwood Press, 1976), pp. 33–37.

[100] Muhammad, "What Do Muslims Want?" p. 404. Essien-Udom also notes that Muhammad's calls to "return to our native land" are vague regarding the precise whereabouts of that land. See E. U. Essien-Udom, *Black Nationalism: A Search for an Identity in America* (Chicago and London: University of Chicago Press, 1971), p. 262.

[101] Martin, *Race First*, p. 35.

[102] Thus it is interesting that in Muhammad's 1965 statement, "From a Program for Self-Development," most of the twelve items listed as specific things "so-called Negroes should do," involve behavioral changes that African Americans could do in their own communities. See Elijah Muhammad, "From a Program for Self-Development," pp. 103–05 in Van Deburg, *Modern Black Nationalism* (the list is on p. 104).

[103] Essien-Udom, *Black Nationalism*, p. 264.

community. This segment was, by the 1950s and early 1960s, still much more alienated from mainstream America than was the case with those who would join the NAACP. Those who made up the majority of the membership of the Nation of Islam during the 1950s and early 1960s viewed organizations such as the NAACP in the same kind of way as did those who supported Marcus Garvey in the 1920s, that is, as composed mainly of middle-class African Americans who identified more with white people than with poorer people of their own race. By the mid 1960s, even among this part of the population, enough roots had been created in the United States to make the idea of a truly international organization, and of actual emigration, much less enticing than it had been in the 1920s. The idea of creating separate communities within the United States was now what actually appealed more.

The idea that talk of African American separatism gradually took on a more US-based form as the twentieth century advanced is illustrated by other phenomena of the 1960s and of the post-1960s period. The primary form which separatist talk took during the 1960s was of "community control," with activists increasingly referring to the "black nation" as comprised of those places where African Americans actually lived.[104] Even within the Nation of Islam, the talk of creating a separate black state eventually became jettisoned. In 1975, when Elijah Muhammad died and the leadership of the organization was taken over by his son, Wallace D. Muhammad, the goal of the creation of a separate black state was abandoned: "Before long, members could salute the American flag, serve in the U.S. armed forces, and engage in electoral politics."[105] And though Louis Farrakhan separated from the organization because of many of the changes instigated by Wallace Muhammad, by 1985, even he was

---

[104] Theodore Draper discusses much of the complexity of the talk about the land issue in the 1960s in *The Rediscovery of Black Nationalism* (New York University Press, 1970), pp. 132–47. Draper suggests that by the 1960s, the talk of what a "black nation" might actually consist of was often confused and contradictory. He cites as one example of this confusion Leroi Jones' position. As described by Draper, Jones argued forcefully for the idea of African Americans as a separate nation and also emphasized that in talking about a separate nation one had to be talking about land. But Draper points to the following response by Jones as to where this land might be: "What the Black Man must do now is look down at the ground upon which he stands, and claim it as his own. It is not abstract. Look down! Pick up the earth or jab your fingernails into the concrete. It is real and it is yours, if you want it" (p. 135). The essay Draper refers to is Leroi Jones, "The Legacy of Malcolm X, and the Coming of the Black Nation," in Leroi Jones, *Home* (New York: William Morrow, 1966), pp. 238–50.

[105] Van Deburg, ed., *Modern Black Nationalism*, p. 315.

stating that the goal of a separate state was not realistic and was not supported by the great majority of African Americans.[106]

Thus, as the kind of separatism some middle-class intellectuals were moving towards by the 1960s can be described as a sort of "quasi-separatism," the type of separatism that those from less affluent parts of the population were endorsing was also taking on more of a "quasi" type nature. To be sure, there were large differences between the ideology of a mid-century W. E. B. Du Bois and of a mid-century Elijah Muhammad. But these differences were not so large that the generation of college students who followed Du Bois were not able to find something importantly in common with a former member of the Nation of Islam. The fact that one individual, Malcolm X, was able to bridge the gap between these two populations tells us that something was happening in the pre-1960s period to make such a coming together possible.

Black Power

Thus, in the first half of the twentieth century, a certain similarity in outlook is emerging from segments of poorer parts of the black population and from some intellectuals and activists. The similarity was around a black nationalism centered in the United States. This kind of nationalism, while celebratory of the African ancestry of American blacks, emphasized the ties that bound African Americans to each other.

But to again reiterate the point, while this similarity in outlook is developing in the period from the 1930s to the mid 1960s, in this period it does not play a major role in public life. Because the central ideal for most working-class and middle-class African Americans of the period was that of eliminating the most egregious harms inflicted upon African Americans, from lynching to Jim Crow laws, to other forms of exclusion in United States life, many African Americans were wary about political movements that stressed the distinctiveness of African American life to that of European Americans. Indeed, because this was a period where one of the greatest supports of those who wished to stop challenges to these oppressive practices was the argument that African Americans were fundamentally different from other Americans, a stress on the similarities between African Americans and European Americans was more obviously advantageous than a more complicated position which stressed cultural differences.

---

[106] Louis Farrakhan, "From P.O.W.E.R. at Last and Forever," pp. 316–27 in Van Deburg, ed., *Modern Black Nationalism*, pp. 317 and 320.

The emphasis on similarities was not just made by a few intellectuals; it shaped a significant aspect of African American political activity in the middle part of the century. As Lee Baker has shown, many of those legal scholars and activists who began focusing on the courts in the period from the late 1930s up until the landmark *Brown* v. *Board of Education* decision in 1954, explicitly rejected any celebration of black difference. These scholars and activists, many of whom were associated with Howard University and the NAACP, eagerly drew on some forms of social science. They drew on those studies that documented the deleterious effects of segregation on African Americans. They employed the arguments of Franz Boas and his followers that challenged the idea of race as a determinant of behavior. But they steered clear of any of the work of Boas and his followers that promoted the idea of a distinctive African American culture. As they understood the political context, the goal of political equality could only be undermined by such an idea.[107]

And this perspective came not only from the black middle class. The most powerful political organization of the period, the NAACP, was not just made up of middle-class members. While the NAACP had grown to include a certain number of working-class members after the First World War, during the late 1930s and 1940s it even more dramatically increased its working-class membership.

By the 1940s, in most cities, the NAACP had ceased to be a purely middle-class organization. To be sure, ministers, businesspeople, and professionals remained influential. But the leadership now included postal workers, Pullman porters, longshoremen, plumbers, printers, truck drivers, shopworkers, and factory workers.[108]

And the 1950s and early 1960s civil rights movement in the south – a movement that argued for integration on the basis of black/white similarities – was a cross-class movement. Beginning in the 1930s and continuing into the 1940s, the south had witnessed the growth of large urban populations. These populations created such institutions as churches, newspapers, unions, and businesses which brought together black workers and members of the black middle class.[109] It was out of such cross-class institutions in the south that the 1950s civil rights movement originated. The NAACP had been weakened in the early 1950s by the intense anti-communism that extended throughout the country and by the backlash

---

[107] Lee D. Baker, *From Savage to Negro: Anthropology and the Construction of Race, 1896–1954* (Berkeley: University of California Press, 1998), pp. 168–87.

[108] Adam Fairclough, *Better Day Coming: Blacks and Equality, 1890–2000*, (New York: Penguin, 2002), pp. 184–85.

[109] *Ibid.* p. 205.

against the organization in the south in the wake of the 1954 Supreme Court *Brown* v. *Board of Education* decision.[110] But by the mid 1950s, these other institutions were strong enough to foster the creation of other political organizations, such as the Montgomery Improvement Association (MIA), in Montgomery, Alabama in December 1955, and in January 1957, the Southern Christian Leadership Conference (SCLC). While many of the leaders of these organizations were educated ministers, working-class individuals constituted the bulk of the active membership.[111]

What is true, of course, is that if a large number of those who made up the membership of organizations such as the NAACP and the SCLC were working class, many of these came from the more economically secure, upwardly mobile parts of the working class. As pointed out in the above, they were postal workers, porters, plumbers, and factory workers – i.e. those who had managed to gain access to secure employment. And the leadership of such organizations as the NAACP and the SCLC was mostly middle class. But the alliance between such middle-class leaders and such working-class members did not occur because these leaders manipulated their working-class members to adopt ideals that were alien. Rather, in the period between the 1930s and the 1960s, the needs of most middle-class and working-class members of the African American population coincided. Both needed the elimination of legalized segregation.

However, in the mid 1960s a different kind of class alignment developed, now between younger, angrier members of the middle class – students, artists, intellectuals – with both working-class and more disaffected urban northern blacks. This different kind of political alliance began to command national attention in the mid 1960s, arguing for different kinds of political goals, justified in different kinds of ways. This very different political alliance constituted Black Power.

Black Power began in the south. It emerged out of the student wing of the civil rights movement, from such organizations as the Atlanta Project, the Congress on Racial Equality, and the Student Nonviolent Coordinating Committee (SNCC). Stokely Carmichael famously popularized the phrase "Black Power" at a rally in Greenwood, Mississippi in 1966. This rally was part of the Memphis to Mississippi march, begun by James Meredith, and

[110] *Ibid.* pp. 213, 220. Fairclough points out that while anti-communism was harmful to the NAACP as an organization, the exact dimensions of its harm to the overall movement for black equality is not clear. See his discussion of this issue, pp. 215–18.
[111] *Ibid.* pp. 228–34. E. D. Nixon, one of the primary organizers of the Montgomery bus boycott, and therefore a contender for the presidency of the MIA, was a Pullman car porter without much in the way of formal education. But when it came time to pick the president of the organization, established leaders in the community turned to Martin Luther King, Jr., with his Ph.D. from Boston University. *Ibid.* p. 230.

continued after Meredith was shot, as a coordinated effort by a coalition of civil rights groups. Carmichael's phrase expressed an antipathy towards non-violence and towards alliances with whites, an antipathy that had been growing among younger black civil rights activists.[112]

While the slogan "Black Power" developed out of civil rights organizing in the south, Black Power soon emerged as a national movement, with much of its energy coming out of the urban ghettos in the north. For several years, beginning in the summer of 1965, the black ghettos of the cities of the north erupted in riots, mostly directed against white police and white businesses. These riots shifted the attention of the nation away from the south to the north. Some of the sentiments that generated these riots soon became elaborated and given substance in the speeches, writings, and organizing calls of a diverse group of African Americans: college students, community leaders, artists, intellectuals, unemployed young black men, and politicians. The phrase that captured these sentiments was "Black Power."

As many commentators have pointed out, the slogan "Black Power" brought together a range of political perspectives: the Marxist/revolutionary nationalist/internationalist position of the Panthers; the culturally nationalist position espoused by many artists and writers; the territorial nationalism ideologically endorsed by the Nation of Islam; and the black capitalist and pluralistic positions that were advocated by some.[113] And Black Power not only brought together a range of political positions. It also brought together a range of political emotions. Debbie Louis expresses this range when she eloquently describes Black Power as bringing together anger and hope, desperation and confidence:

the black community stood as a conglomeration of often contradictory interests and directions, dubiously tied together by a common mood which

---

[112] For discussions of the development of these attitudes within the civil rights movement, see Robert Weisbrot, *Freedom Bound: A History of America's Civil Rights Movement* (New York: Penguin, 1991), pp. 193–221; Howard Sitkoff, *The Struggle for Black Equality 1954–1992*, revised edition (New York: Hill and Wang, 1993), pp. 184–209; and Fairclough, *Better Day Coming*, pp. 282–321.

[113] William L. Van Deburg discusses these diverse ideologies at length in *New Day in Babylon: The Black Power Movement and American Culture, 1965–1979* (University of Chicago Press, 1992), pp. 112–91. Elaborated discussions of these different positions are also provided by John T. McCartney, *Black Power Ideologies: An Essay in African-American Political Thought* (Philadelphia: Temple University Press, 1992) and by Alphonso Pinkney, *Red, Black, and Green: Black Nationalism in the United States* (Cambridge University Press, 1976). But many other commentators, including Marable, *Race, Reform, and Rebellion*, p. 99; Draper, *The Rediscovery of Black Nationalism*, p. 125; and Fairclough, *Better Day Coming*, p. 313, all point to the wide-ranging meaning of Black Power.

combined centuries of anger with new hope, increasing desperation with new confidence.[114]

Poorer segments of the community brought to the movement anger, militancy, and an impulse towards separation from white America.[115] College students, as a consequence of their youth and personal identification with those from working-class backgrounds, added their own anger and their own hope. They also added conceptual resources: the kinds of resources that could be got from reading Frantz Fanon's *The Wretched of the Earth* and from being able to make parallels in the situation of African Americans with the struggles of the colonized nations of Africa and Asia.[116] Older, more established members of African American communities brought their own beliefs about the possibility of progress and the ability to mobilize the anger of many into demands for community control of school districts and for greater government funding of black businesses.

That Black Power brought together such a range of beliefs and emotions was early and eloquently pointed out by Harold Cruse who, in 1968, speaking of "Black Power," made the following observation: "Thus we have a unique American form of black revolutionary anarchism with a social reform economic and political 'program.'"[117] Other political commentators make related points when they distinguish between the "pluralist" tendencies that were an important part of the ideology of Black Power from the more radical and separatist strains which also played a central role.[118]

This alliance between reformist goals and revolutionary rhetoric, while on the face of it strange, makes sense when one considers the context of the middle 1960s and phenomena earlier discussed. In the mid 1960s, most African American leaders believed that political action on behalf of African Americans needed to take a new turn.[119] The riots in the urban

---

[114] Debbie Louis, *And We Are Not Saved: A History of the Movement as People* (Garden City, N.Y.: Anchor Books), pp. 296–97.

[115] The association of militancy with working-class participation is noted by Jack M. Bloom, *Class, Race and the Civil Rights Movement* (Bloomington: Indiana University Press, 1987), p. 173. Bloom argues that as lower-class blacks became increasingly involved in civil rights from the early 1960s to the mid 1960s, the movement became more militant. He claims that it is this change which led to Black Power. Bloom backs up his argument by studies which show that by the mid 1960s there was greater class-mixing in student participation in civil rights activism.

[116] Frantz Fanon, *The Wretched of the Earth* (New York: Grove Press, 1968).

[117] Harold Cruse, *Rebellion or Revolution* (New York: William Morrow, 1968), p. 207.

[118] Two theorists whose work illustrates the distinctions between these two tendencies in Black Power thought are McCartney, *Black Power Ideologies*, p. 118 and Van Deburg, *New Day in Babylon*, p. 25.

[119] Thus Sitkoff, *The Struggle for Black Equality*, notes: "After the Selma campaign, the leading organizations of the movement had floundered in their search for new programs. Everyone agreed on the need to move beyond the traditional civil-rights agenda" (p. 195).

cities of the north forced attention on the plight of poor blacks in the north. By 1965, following the passage of the 1964 Civil Rights Act and the 1965 Voting Rights Act, discrimination on the basis of race had been declared illegal. However, it was apparent that blacks in the cities of the north needed more than even the enforcement of such laws. These were people who were segregated from whites, de facto, if not de jure; who had high rates of unemployment; and who, in terms of styles of speech and other cultural mores, were seen as highly alien by many white Americans. Very different political perspectives than those which motivated the struggles around civil rights were needed.

These different perspectives emerged in part from those who lived in such communities. In earlier discussions I pointed to the greater degree of anger and alienation that motivated those who joined organizations such as the UNIA and the Nation of Islam from those who had joined organizations such as the NAACP. That anger and alienation had not gone away; indeed one could say it had only increased with the growth of larger communities of the very poor in northern cities. This anger and alienation fueled the riots of the mid 1960s. But, as also earlier noted, by this time few African Americans desired to emigrate from the United States. Instead, such anger and alienation was expressed in other ways: for some through threats to use guns and violence; for others, through calls to separate from white America by creating communities controlled only by blacks.

Local leaders who hoped to use the anger of the community to gain resources often adopted this latter, more reformist strategy. In doing so they were employing a path familiar in American history: to establish African Americans as an interest group capable of placing demands upon the nation as a whole. This aspect of Black Power expresses what Kwame Ture (formerly known as Stokely Carmichael) and Charles Hamilton have described as one of the important goals of Black Power.[120] Other scholars have expressed a similar point. For example, Martin Kilson used the phrase "the politicization of ethnicity" to describe the use of "ethnic patterns and prejudices as the primary basis for interest-group and political formations, and to build upon these to integrate a given ethnic community into the wider politics of city and the nation."[121] Kilson has argued that while "the politicization of ethnicity" served as an important means by which other ethnic groups had been able to integrate elite members of their groups into

---

[120] Kwame Ture (formerly known as Stokely Carmichael) and Charles Hamilton, *Black Power: The Politics of Liberation* (New York: Random House, 1992), p. 44.
[121] Martin Kilson, "Black Politics: A New Power," p. 336 in *Dissent* 18, no. 4, (August, 1971), pp. 333–45.

city, state, and national politics, and in the process marshal resources towards the voting blocs that they could mobilize, by and large this had not happened with African Americans prior to Black Power. Robert Smith, looking back at Black Power from the vantage point of fifteen years later, described Black Power in similar ways, noting that it stimulated the formation of a wide range of black interest organizations that have "facilitated entry by blacks into the pluralist political arena."[122] As Smith pointed out, these organizations moved the political agenda of African American organizations beyond the goals of civil rights and towards broader public policy concerns:

The black power symbol, with its emphasis on racial solidarity and independent black organization, has operated over the years to stimulate the formation of black interest organizations and to increase the interest-articulation activities of the older, more established "Negro" organizations. ... These organizations cover a broad range of policy or issue areas and black community concerns ranging from general civil-rights organizations such as the NAACP to broad policy organizations such as the Coalition of Black Trade Unionists, the National Association of Black Manufacturers, or until recently the National Welfare Rights Organization.[123]

There is much that is valid in these accounts. However, they only tell part of the story. They leave out what Ture (Carmichael) and Hamilton identify as another crucial element in Black Power, the move to self-definition.[124] While Black Power did function to mobilize African Americans as a legitimate interest group – with rights to claims for jobs and other resources from politicians – it also did something more. Like previous ethnic groups, African Americans needed many of the resources that politicians could provide. But African Americans also needed something that politicians alone could not provide: acceptance on terms that violated hegemonic cultural ideals. Civil rights laws had struck against legal means of excluding African Americans from political and economic integration. But legal exclusion was only one of the ways in which African Americans were barred from such integration. There was also the widespread belief in African American difference and inferiority. Cultural challenges were required to overcome this barrier.

And here the contributions of students, intellectuals, and artists played an important role. These students, intellectuals, and artists employed the concept of "culture" now available in public discourse to describe the differences exemplified by poor black Americans in positive terms and to

---

[122] Robert C. Smith, "Black Power and the Transformation from Protest to Politics," pp. 431–43 in *Political Science Quarterly* 96, no. 3 (Autumn, 1981), p. 433.
[123] *Ibid.* p. 441.   [124] Ture and Hamilton, *Black Power*, pp. 37–39.

express their own identification with such distinctive aspects of African American life. In earlier sections I have talked about the move, beginning in the 1920s and intensifying in later decades, for some members of the African American middle class to move towards closer identification with those from poorer sections of the community. I noted that this identification was made possible by the growth of mixed-class neighborhoods where those who managed a degree of economic success were not that far apart, either geographically or in family terms, from those who had not.

By the middle of the 1960s, the growth of this kind of middle class was even more extensive than it had ever previously been. The post-Second World War period in the United States was a period of economic expansion. While this expansion benefitted whites to a much greater extent than it benefitted blacks, leaving many in the cities very far behind, a certain number of blacks also benefitted. Some of these moved into the kinds of white-collar jobs that most African Americans had long been denied. Bart Landry discusses the changes that occurred in African American class composition in the 1960s as a result of a combination of overall economic expansion with transformations in the law gained from the civil rights movement.[125] He claims that these changes in class composition are significant enough to constitute what he calls a "new black middle class":

Between 1960 and 1970 the percentage of middle-class blacks suddenly doubled, growing from about 1 in 8 to 1 out of every 4 black workers. While this was far below the 1 out of 2 level of whites in 1970, the gain experienced by the black middle class during the 1960s exceeded their total increase during the previous fifty years. It was a growth shared by both black men and black women in all three strata of the middle class: professionals, managers and small businessmen, and clerical and sales workers.[126]

This kind of class fluidity made possible a cross-class cultural identification among many whose lives themselves crossed class lines. To understand the kind of cross-class fluidity I am talking about, one need only look at the backgrounds of those who first popularized the phrase "Black Power." On the one hand, one might describe these backgrounds as "middle class" insofar as many of those who were involved in this early popularization were college students. Stokely Carmichael, who famously popularized the phrase "Black Power" at a rally in 1966, was a 1964 graduate of Howard University.[127] Most of the members of the Atlanta Project – a group influential in moving SNCC away from its earlier

---

[125] Landry, *The New Black Middle Class*, p. 76.   [126] *Ibid.* p. 70.
[127] Marable, *Race, Reform, and Rebellion*, p. 84.

integrationist stance and towards separatism – had attended college.[128] Bobby Seale and Huey Newton, founders of the Black Panther Party, met while both were students at Merritt Junior College.[129]

But if there are some grounds for describing those who first began to talk about Black Power as "middle class," this description needs much qualification. The black students who had initiated the student phase of the civil rights movement – out of which SNCC had emerged – were not students at Harvard and Yale. They were students at the kinds of institutions of higher education more receptive to those from poorer black families. Thus, the four students who initiated the first sit-in at a lunch counter in Greensboro, North Carolina on February 1, 1960 were friends and roommates from North Carolina Agricultural and Technical College.[130] Huey Newton's parents were high school graduates. Newton himself was a man of the streets, interspersing his studies at Merritt Junior College with house burglaries.[131] And those with whom these college students had worked, in organizations such as SNCC and the Black Panthers, were often from poor and working-class backgrounds. The SNCC associate who first suggested to Carmichael the phrase "Black Power," was Willie Ricks, a high school graduate from Tennessee.[132] Those who were recruited into the Black Panthers were from the poor neighborhoods of East Oakland, California.[133] And if many of those who bought and read *The Autobiography of Malcolm X* came from middle-class households, Malcolm X became a publicly recognized figure because of his rise to prominence in the decidedly non-middle-class Nation of Islam.[134]

I emphasize this particular cross-class fluidity because it helps us understand both the range in perspectives exemplified in Black Power and also some of the elements that gave it unity. As earlier noted, Black Power expressed a variety of perspectives and demands from the revolutionary rhetoric of the Black Panthers to the calls of college students for African American academic departments. The range of groups who stood behind

---

[128] Carson, *In Struggle*, p. 192.
[129] Pinkney, *Red, Black, and Green*, p. 99; Draper, *The Rediscovery of Black Nationalism*, p. 97. Hugh Pearson in *The Shadow of the Panther* (Cambridge, Mass.: Perseus Publishing, 1996) refers to the college as "Oakland City College" (p. 76). This probably is its more generic name. On the founding of the Black Panthers, see particularly pp. 108–13. As Pearson notes on p. 112, the party was officially launched on October 15, 1996 with Seale taking on the title of party chairman and Newton taking on the title of minister of defense.
[130] Carson, *In Struggle*, p. 9.   [131] Pearson, *The Shadow of the Panther*, pp. 45, 47.
[132] Carson, *In Struggle*, pp. 208–09.
[133] Marable, *Race, Reform, and Rebellion*, p. 109. Fairclough, *Better Day Coming* makes a similar point, p. 317.
[134] Marable, *Race, Reform, and Rebellion*, pp. 87–88.

this slogan helps explain this diversity in political outlooks and demands. But Black Power also expressed a unity among blacks – a unity made possible by the cultural identification of some of the more privileged with the ways of life of those less privileged.

The unity expressed by Black Power has been criticized as a false unity and also as one which obfuscated some real differences in class, gender, and sexuality, differences that African Americans have needed to address. In the epilogue I will examine these and other criticisms of Black Power. But, as I hope the above to have shown, whatever criticisms one might legitimately make of Black Power, Black Power was not a simple historical aberration. Rather, it represented a political turn that had deep roots in the history of African Americans in the United States. It expressed in mid-twentieth-century terms the alienation and frustration that had been felt by many in the course of that history, with the growing desire on the part of some to culturally identify with the many. The conditions of the mid 1960s brought these trends together and in so doing generated a new type of identity for African Americans.

5   Women's identity/women's politics

In the previous chapter, I argued that changes in the history of black politics in the twentieth century – including the emergence of Black Power in the mid 1960s – were importantly rooted in changing understandings of black identity as these evolved among different groups of African Americans over the course of that century. Similarly, in this chapter I want to make a related claim about the history of activism around women's issues in the United States in the nineteenth and twentieth centuries. Here too, political changes were importantly based in changing understandings of the meaning of female identity as these developed among different groups of women and men over the course of this period.

Moreover, I believe that a focus on these changing understandings of female identity will necessitate a reconsideration of how we think about the history of those political changes. Since the early years of "women's liberation" in the late 1960s and early 1970s in the US, many scholars, including myself, have talked about that history in terms of "waves." The first "wave" supposedly encompassed the nineteenth-century women's movement leading up to suffrage. The period between 1920 and the early 1960s was then described as a time of relative calm. This period of calm supposedly ended in the early sixties with a resurgence of public attention to women's issues, inaugurating feminism's "second wave." Working within the contours of this basic framework, scholars have raised various questions assumed by it: What caused the period of calm in the middle decades of the twentieth century? Is the "second wave" still in existence? Could we now be in a third wave?

The wave metaphor was created out of the upsurge in feminist scholarship that accompanied the women's rights and women's liberation movements of the 1960s and 1970s. Today, looking back from the vantage point of approximately forty years later, it is easy to understand the political usefulness of the "wave" metaphor. That metaphor reminded people that a political movement focused on women's issues did not emerge de novo in the 1960s. The prehistory of the 1960s women's rights and women's liberation movements had been given little attention in either academic

history or in mainstream thought prior to the emergence of these movements. The "wave" metaphor provided, therefore, a useful corrective in
reminding people that these movements had a venerable past. But it is time
that we rethink this framework, to better understand both the history and
future of activism around gender.

A serious problem with the "wave" metaphor is that it assumes a single
movement differing historically only in terms of degree of activity.
Accompanying this assumption of a single movement is the assumption
of a single ideology unifying the movement, i.e. "feminism." Following
many of the difference debates within women's liberation of the 1970s and
1980s, today many have come to define "feminism" broadly.[1] This broad
meaning has made for a more inclusive understanding of "feminism."
However, even such a broad definition tends to presume a single movement, overlooking or minimizing, for example, the historical differences
that existed between those who previously had understood the word
"feminism" in a more narrow sense and other groups. Within the US
context, it can make it harder for us to understand why some groups and
not others started to use the word "feminism" when they did and why
"feminism" has ebbed and flowed in the twentieth century in the ways in
which it has. In other words, when we apply our contemporary broad
understanding of "feminism" to a historical context where "feminism"
itself was understood more narrowly, we tend to lose sight of some of the
reasons for the changing attractiveness of this movement to diverse
groups. To capture such changes, while also employing a broad lens, I
suggest instead that we focus on issues of identity, on how diverse groups
of women understood who they were and how those understandings did
or did not generate movements for social change.

One historian whose work helps us in this project, in part by emphasizing the historicity of the very word feminism, is Nancy Cott. Cott, focusing on the US, describes the process by which "feminism" emerged as a
political label in the early part of the twentieth century, and the differences
that existed between the perspectives held by those who began to use this
new word from the perspectives of many of those who had fought for
women's suffrage and for other changes in women's status in the late

---

[1] Estelle Freedman provides an example of this broad definition. She defines "feminism" as
follows: "Feminism is a belief that women and men are inherently of equal worth. Because
most societies privilege men as a group, social movements are necessary to achieve equality
between women and men, with the understanding that gender always intersects with other
social hierarchies." Estelle B. Freedman, *No Turning Back: The History of Feminism and the
Future of Women* (New York: Ballantine Books, 2002), p. 7.

nineteenth century.[2] In this chapter, I intend to build on some of Cott's insights. Following Cott, I point to the early twentieth century as the context for the emergence of "feminism" in the United States. But I add that this is because the view of female identity that early twentieth-century "feminism" expressed – specifically a view of women as individuals, similar in most important respects to men – only at that time became the view of enough individuals to necessitate the creation of such a new label. And, I further claim that while "feminism" may have originated in the early part of the twentieth century, it was not until the end of the first half of that century that a political movement based on this understanding of female identity became attractive to enough women to serve as the basis for a large-scale social movement. At least in terms of describing a large-scale social movement based upon a particular view of women's relationship to men, "feminism," then *did* emerge de novo in the 1960s.

To make this argument, I will claim that for much of the first half of the twentieth century, the naturalization of women's identity provided most women, for good reasons, with a way of understanding their differences from men. It was not until the latter part of this first half of the twentieth century that a more individualistic model became attractive to a large enough segment of the population to constitute a social movement.

But "feminism" once constituted as a social movement did not remain static. While a mass movement based on this idea of feminism was growing, a different movement, developing a more expanded idea of feminism, was also emerging. This latter movement drew on a model of identity that emphasized less the individuality of women, and thus their sameness with men, and more women's commonalities with each other, and thus their differences from men. This latter model, while not completely overshadowing the former, emerged out of the changing cultural climate of the times and enabled activists in the latter movement to address problems in their own lives less easily addressed by appeal to the more individualistic model. In the process, participants in this latter movement came to create a more expansive definition of feminism than had earlier existed.

In short, I am arguing that conflicts and shifts in understandings of women's identity are central to the history of nineteenth- and twentieth-century women's movements and provide us with necessary clues for understanding changes within these movements. I believe that this kind of a story provides us with the means to begin answering questions that feminist scholars have not yet sufficiently addressed, such as why feminism as an ideology has been particularly attractive to certain groups of

[2] Nancy Cott, *The Grounding of Modern Feminism* (New Haven and London: Yale University Press, 1987).

women more than others and why it has been particularly visible on the public stage when it has. It will also help us better view the history of activism around gender issues as always in flux and as always taking on different meanings as the lives of different groups of women and men change.

Public life and women's identity in the late nineteenth and early twentieth centuries

As scholars have widely recognized, the nineteenth century was a period of important changes in gender relationships. Older patriarchal models of the family gave way to newer understandings of separate spheres which stressed a more "separate but equal" view of the relationship between husband and wife. The ideology of separate spheres can be viewed as in some respects a transitional ideology – transitional between a view of women as lesser versions of men in a social world highly influenced by patriarchal kinship structures, and a view of women more as individuals in a society increasingly organized through the institutions of civil society, the state, and the market. It suited a society struggling to cope with the increasing power of these latter institutions and the decreasing power of patriarchal kinship rules for organizing social life. This ideology both acknowledged women's greater equivalence with men as patriarchal kinship structures lost power even as it functioned to keep this equivalence limited. In its premise of the separate but equal importance of domestic and non-domestic life, the ideology resulted in some women attaining a new stature while also keeping such women confined to a sphere whose stature itself was gradually diminishing. Overall, while women were still viewed as lesser than men and different from them, the ideology of separate spheres now depicted them as somewhat less "lesser" and more different than had been the case when family and kinship ties possessed greater importance as social organizing principles.

While the ideology of separate spheres can be viewed as a type of transitional ideology, the transitional period where it has flourished can also be described as a long one, lasting as a powerful organizing ideology from the mid nineteenth century up until the latter part of the twentieth century, and even continuing in some measure up until the present time. A reasonable question is why it has been so powerful and has lasted as long as it has. As scholars have noted, even in the second half of the nineteenth century, as this ideology was being consolidated, it was simultaneously being challenged. Industrialization and an expanding economy brought many young women off the farm and into factories or into such newly female identified occupations as schoolteaching. And apart from paid employment, others left the confines of the home to contribute to the making of a newly expanding civil society. Such organizations and move- ments as women's benevolent associations; women's working-class mutual aid societies; black and white women's clubs organized for charity, self, and social improvement purposes; social purity as well as temper- ance, abolition, and suffrage crusades and organizations, all contributed to women's increasing role in this expanding civil society and thus, one would expect, towards undermining the ideology of women as domestic beings. All of these patterns intensified in the first half of the twentieth century, theoretically challenging even further the ideology of separate spheres.

But, throughout the late nineteenth and early twentieth century, a variety of factors worked to maintain this ideology even in the face of such challenging phenomena. Women's expanding involvement in civil society was highly justified by the ideology of separate spheres itself, i.e. that women had separate needs that required their participation in public activity. And women's non-domestic labor force participation was either socially marginalized or organized in ways that did not threaten the idea that women's identity primarily lay in their familial roles – and thus in their differences from men. This is not to say that there was not developing a cohort of women and men who were coming to believe in women's equality with men on the basis of male/female similarity. But up until the mid part of the twentieth century, this cohort represented a small proportion of the population, not large enough to sustain a large-scale political movement supported primarily by such beliefs.

Let me elaborate these points by first focusing on women's late nineteenth- and early twentieth-century engagement in various social and political organ- izations and movements. On one level, many of the organizations and movements that women participated in through the nineteenth century and into the early twentieth century did more obviously engage them with others in ways similar to men's public participation. That similarity seems most apparent in women's involvement in organizations devoted to radically reforming society. Focusing on the cities of Boston and New York in the early part of the nineteenth century, Anne Boylan offers the following observations that have relevance also for later in the century:

It was just such reform activity by white women that sparked major controversy in the 1830s, as new, reform-oriented societies emerged in both cities. Their mem- bers' commitment to destroying important social institutions and practices such as slavery, prostitution, and liquor-dealing differentiated the Boston Female Anti-Slavery Society (1833), the New York Female Moral Reform Society (1834), and the like, from existing organizations. By abandoning or downplaying an emphasis on individual reformation, such groups instead stressed the need for radical changes in society. Antislavery societies in particular, with their demands for an immediate end to slavery, their commitment to racial equality (in principle if not always in practice), their integrated memberships, their claims to sisterly bonds with enslaved women, their adoption of highly visible political tactics, and their championing of white women's right to speak to mixed audiences, appeared so different from women's missionary or orphan societies that opponents reviled participants as "unsexed" or "amazons."[3]

Other scholars have made similar points about the temperance movement, seconding insights such as those of Miriam M. Cole, president in 1873 of the Ohio Woman Suffrage Association, when she remarked: "A woman knocking out the head of a whiskey barrel with an axe, to the tune of Old Hundred, is not the ideal woman sitting on a sofa, dining on strawberries and cream, and sweetly warbling 'The Rose that all are praising.'"[4] Jack Blocker elaborates on this perception:

Other opponents of the Crusade perceived it as the opening shot of a women's revolution. For them, marching on saloons represented an illegitimate means of seeking redress for women's grievances, for such action usurped man's sole right to make all important social and political decisions. Such usurpation, some felt, would inevitably lead to a reversal of power roles, with women dominant and men subordinate.[5]

But while engagement in such activity did raise the specter of an attack on existing notions of male/female differences, this specter was significantly contained by counterarguments that justified this activity by reference to women's "special" needs. Women's "special" needs were obvious in relation to the struggle for temperance legislation. But they were also obvious in relation to the struggle for suffrage. The ideology of natural differences implied that women's interests were different from men's. But if women's interests were different from men's, it was less understandable how women's interests could be represented in the voting decisions of their husbands and fathers. Eighteenth- and nineteenth-century justifications for denying the vote to women were based on the idea of coverture, on the idea that women's needs and interests were "covered" by the political participation of their fathers and husbands. But the ideology of separate spheres challenged the legitimacy of this idea. It suggested that women had different needs and values than did men and therefore may

[3] Anne M. Boylan, *The Origins of Women's Activism: New York and Boston, 1797–1840* (Chapel Hill and London: University of North Carolina Press, 2002), p. 36.

[4] Jack S. Blocker, Jr., "Separate Paths: Suffragists and the Women's Temperance Crusade," pp. 460–76 in *Signs: Journal of Women in Culture and Society* 10, no. 3 (Spring, 1985), pp. 466–67. Blocker references this quote from the suffrage publication *Woman's Journal* (Boston) (February 21, 1874).

[5] Blocker, "Separate Paths," p. 464.

very well need separate representation in Congress. Consequently, much of the justification for suffrage, like the justification for women's involvement in other late nineteenth-century social reform movements such as temperance, revolved around women's "special" natures.

Not all of the justification for women's involvement in these organizations and movements lay in women's differences from men. The language of differences was intermixed with the language of women's similarities with men. The early suffrage movement was quite radical in its talk of women's rights and, in this respect, women's and men's similarities. And throughout the course of the struggle, suffragists in general were more likely than participants in other women's crusades to use language that was secular and universalistic. They more frequently spoke in terms of the language of "rights." Thus, even when many white, native suffragists expressed anger over the fact that immigrant and African American men had rights that white native women did not, these same suffragists argued for the rights to vote as an inalienable right of all.[6] Janet Giele, in analyzing the content of the suffrage newspaper, *Woman's Journal*, and the temperance paper, *Union Signal*, in the period between 1885 and 1915, found that the suffrage paper tended more than the temperance paper to favorably describe women in non-domestic settings, and engaged in instrumental as opposed to expressive or emotional activities.[7] Even when the suffrage and temperance papers argued for the same cause – the vote for women – the articles in the suffrage paper were couched in more secular and universalistic terms than were those in the temperance paper:

In addition, suffragists' reasoning was almost always "universalistic," that is, based on claims of equality and justice as ends in themselves. Temperance women, however, were more likely to give "particular" or expedient reasons for the ballot by depicting it as a means of achieving specific ends, such as raising the moral tone, cleaning up politics, or voting for prohibition.[8]

However, one can question how extensively equal rights talk was endorsed by those in the wider population. The early suffrage movement was a small movement, primarily constituted of a small group of friends, a "Garrisonian circle of Hicksite Quakers, Unitarians and radical abolitionists."[9] In the period immediately following the Civil War, when some of these Garrisonians began to make suffrage for women a priority, this issue

[6] Janet Zollinger Giele, *Two Paths to Women's Equality: Temperance, Suffrage and the Origins of Modern Feminism* (New York: Twayne Publishers, 1995), p. 123.
[7] *Ibid.* pp. 117–18. [8] *Ibid.* p. 122.
[9] Suzanne M. Marilley, *Woman's Suffrage and the Origins of Liberal Feminism in the United States, 1820–1920* (Cambridge, Mass. and London: Harvard University Press, 1996), p. 63.

had very limited public support. It was only towards the end of the 1870s, after Frances Willard put the much more mass-based temperance movement on the side of suffrage, that the base of the suffrage movement began to expand. As Suzanne Marilley points out, Willard's arguments for suffrage – that it was needed to improve women's abilities to function well as wives and mothers – was the kind of argument that had popular appeal.[10]

This expansion in justificatory rationale that began in the late nineteenth century intensified during the first two decades of the twentieth century as the movement grew larger. In the first two decades of the twentieth century, the movement extended its range of support beyond those who supported temperance to a wider range of constituencies. The suffrage movement became more of a mass movement, gaining support from trade unionists, black women's clubs, and socialists, as well as extending its white middle-class base.[11] In the process, the discourse of male/female similarity of rights became intermingled now not only with appeals to women's special natures but also with pragmatic arguments for many kinds of social reform:

At the same time there was declining emphasis on the purely egalitarian arguments for suffrage. In the early period before 1895, 29 per cent of the articles in the *Woman's Journal* called for the ballot as a means to give women equal political status. After 1895, the egalitarian argument appeared in only 16 per cent of the articles calling for suffrage. The broadening of specific reform objectives accompanied a more complex and differentiated image of women. Just as women were being portrayed as more feminine, the reforms that suffrage advocated were increasingly aimed at helping others rather than women themselves.[12]

These points are exemplified in African American women's support for female suffrage. By the second decade of the twentieth century, African American women leaders were highly sympathetic to the passage of the Nineteenth Amendment – and this was in spite of the racist treatment African Americans often experienced at the hands of whites fighting for suffrage. During this decade, the National Federation of Afro-American Women, the National Association of Colored Women (NACW), the Northeastern Federation of Colored Women's Clubs, the Alpha Kappa Alpha Sorority, and the Delta Sigma Theta Sorority – organizations representing thousands of African American women – all came out in support of women's suffrage.[13] But similarly with many European

[10] *Ibid.* pp. 93, 99.   [11] *Ibid.* p. 188.   [12] Giele, *Two Paths*, p. 159.
[13] Rosalyn Terborg-Penn, "Discontented Black Feminists: Prelude and Postscript to the Passage of the Nineteenth Amendment," pp. 487–503 in Darlene Clark Hine, Wilma King, and Linda Reed, eds., *"We Specialize in the Wholly Impossible": A Reader in Black Women's History* (Brooklyn, N.Y.: Carlson Publishing Inc., 1995), pp. 487–88.

American women, African American women's support for suffrage did not necessarily entail a belief in women and men's sameness. Instead, it often followed from beliefs about African American women's distinctive strengths and also from the recognition that African American women's suffrage would contribute to the amelioration of problems faced by both African American men and women. As many commentators have noted, for black women, support for suffrage had at least as much to do with issues of race as it had to do with issues of gender. Much of the support that African American women, and men, gave to women's suffrage was based on recognizing the importance of any increase in the African American vote to the well-being of black people. Louis Michele Newman points out that there was no organized resistance among black men to women's suffrage as there was among white men. The reason is that most blacks saw women's suffrage as a way to increase the political power of black people overall rather than as a means of increasing discord among African Americans. It was assumed, as she points out rightly, that black women would vote with black men rather than in alliance with white women.[14] Rosalyn Terborg-Penn makes a similar point, noting that the support of African American women for suffrage indicated less a commitment to a strong feminist ideology than it did a commitment to the vote as a necessary tool for achieving racial equality:

Since the 1880's, most black women who supported woman suffrage did so because they believed that political equality among the races would raise the status of blacks, both male and female. Increasing the black electorate, they felt, would not only uplift the women of the race, but help the children and the men as well. The majority of the black suffragists were not radical feminists. They were reformers, or what William H. Chafe calls social feminists, who believed that the system could be amended to work for them. Like their white counterparts, these black suffragists assumed that the enfranchised held the key to ameliorating social ills. But unlike white social feminists, many black suffragists called for social and political measures that were specifically tied to race issues.[15]

These generalizations appear validated by events occurring after suffrage was achieved. During the 1920s, African American club women showed little concern for such distinctively "women's issues" as the equal rights amendment, focusing their attention much more on issues of specific concern to African Americans as a group, such as lynching.[16]

---

[14] Louise Michele Newman, *White Women's Rights: The Racial Origins of Feminism in the United States* (New York and Oxford: Oxford University Press, 1999), p. 63.
[15] Terborg-Penn, "Discontented Black Feminists," p. 490.   [16] *Ibid.* pp. 493–98.

That arguments about women's similarities of rights with men became a smaller part of the rationale for suffrage as suffrage became more of a mass movement is not surprising. As Marilley notes, at the time of the adoption of the Nineteenth Amendment, "few people agreed with the radical egalitarian premise that, despite sex differences, women and men were naturally equal and thus required political equality."[17] Most women in the United States defined themselves in terms of their present or future status as wives and mothers. As wives and mothers, many understood themselves as having grounds for participation in non-domestic life – in formal clubs, in reform organizations, and, for many, even in political life. A few – those who became college teachers or other kinds of professionals – could begin to think of themselves as independent individuals in more encompassing ways. But in 1920, these women constituted a very small percentage of the US population. Most other women, defining themselves primarily as wives and mothers, believed they possessed a different but equivalently important role with men in shaping the course of the nation. Following the growth of 1960s women's rights feminism, many tend to think of equivalence as meaning sameness. But those two values do not necessarily go together.

Understanding the very gradual nature of women's endorsement of an identity of sameness with men helps us better understand the lack of a sustained women's movement after suffrage was achieved. Scholars have speculated on the reasons as to why the woman's movement did not survive the passage of the Nineteenth Amendment. Some have argued that this failure was a function of the narrowing focus of the movement on suffrage.[18] But I would like to suggest another possibility: in the period following the attainment of suffrage, a mass constituency demanding greater opportunities for women justified by their similarities with men did not exist. Many women wanted the vote by 1920. But they did not necessarily support the vote because they saw themselves as individuals similar to and thus deserving of equal treatment with men in encompassing ways. By 1920, many understood the role of wife and mother to be compatible with, and for some, even demanding of, female voting. But, for the great majority of women, the similarities with men entailed by this participation were of a limited nature.

[17] Marilley, *Woman's Suffrage*, p. 219.
[18] Those who have made this argument include: William O'Neill, *Everyone Was Brave: A History of Feminism in America* (New York: Quadrangle, 1971), p. 75 and Judith N. Sklar, *American Citizenship: The Quest for Inclusion* (Cambridge, Mass.: Harvard University Press, 1991), p. 60.

The limits of the suffrage movement are particularly revealed by contrasting it with another movement that began to emerge in the second decade of the twentieth century: feminism. Nancy Cott elaborates on the differences between this latter movement and suffrage:

At the very point in the 1910s – the height of the suffrage campaign – when *the woman movement* began to sound archaic, the word *feminism* came into frequent use. Its proponents explicitly distinguished it from suffragism, despite their vital connections with the suffrage movement. The meaning of Feminism (capitalized at first) also differed from the woman movement. It was both broader and narrower: broader in intent, proclaiming revolution in all the relations of the sexes, and narrower in the range of its willing adherents.[19]

As Cott points out, feminism referred not so much to a particular set of political goals as to a new and encompassing way of thinking about who women were. Feminists, unlike many of those who supported suffrage, argued for a general way of thinking about women's relationship to men. They stressed women's similarities with men, or argued that existing differences were a product of social convention. Feminists saw male/female differences as arbitrary and accidental and thus differently present among women and among men. Because they understood identity as varying among individuals, they rebelled against economic and political constraints based upon stereotyped understandings of men and women. If human nature was "individual," social rules based upon generalized expectations should be overthrown.

The emergence of feminism is part of that same reaction against Victorianism that can be found in other, early twentieth-century "modernist" movements. It is easy to see the overlap in perspective between feminism and many of those new ways of thinking about "human nature" that I claimed in chapter 2 were reflected in some of Freud's work. Early twentieth-century feminists, like Freud in some of his writing, stressed the commonality of human nature. They argued that all human beings began with similar natures and the differences that resulted were largely the result of social influence. Because of the accidental and arbitrary nature of social influence, different women, like different men, could be differently affected by social expectations regarding femininity and masculinity, resulting in human beings who displayed the characteristics associated with these social roles to varying extents and in varying ways. Because of the accidental and arbitrary nature of social influence in general, different women, like different men, could combine in their personalities different combinations of all types of traits. Feminists, like Freud in some of his

---

[19] Cott, *The Grounding of Modern Feminism*, p. 1.

work, believed that character was individual. Women, like men, were more idiosyncratic in their personalities than Victorian, naturalized models of identity suggested.

The surfacing of a group of people committed to such a stance had much to do with changes occurring in certain parts of United States society in the beginning part of the century – changes that would intensify as the century progressed. The expansion of higher education for women of a certain social class generated a body of women who could begin to conceptualize the possibility of rewarding lives independent of marriage and motherhood. By the early twentieth century, this group comprised those few women who managed to attain a limited number of positions as college professor, social worker, or other type of professional.[20] The growth of cities created the possibility of communities where some of these women could live independent of marriage. Therefore, it is not surprising that a political ideology which envisioned women as fully independent beings might have drawn at least enough adherents in this period to constitute a political grouping requiring a new name.

The question, though, is how significant such a grouping would be in relation to the wider population and the consequent relation between it and other types of women's advocacy organizations in the immediate decades following suffrage. It seems not surprising that the political organization which was most clearly identified with this new kind of politics – the National Women's Party – stood relatively alone in the period after suffrage was achieved. The National Women's Party explicitly expressed the idea of women's sameness with men in its central political goal: an equal rights amendment to the constitution. But, from the perspective of many other political constituencies of the time, this goal was either irrelevant or harmful. As earlier noted, during the 1920s, African American club women showed little concern for such distinctively "women's issues" as the equal rights amendment, focusing their attention much more on issues of specific concern to African Americans as a group. Women labor leaders; members of white, middle-class women's organizations; social reformers; government officials; and male labor leaders were also not willing to organize on behalf of such an amendment. From the perspective of many participants of such groups – and these were groups who were more likely to support the idea of women's equality than many within the population – women *were* different from men and therefore in need of gender specific protection.[21] They feared that such an amendment would jeopardize the protective labor legislation

---

[20] *Ibid.* p. 22.   [21] *Ibid.* p. 128.

that organized labor had achieved. As they understood the situation facing women in the workforce, the major problem was not women being excluded from jobs they might otherwise attain. A more fundamental problem was that without such protective labor legislation, women would lose some of the few advantages they possessed in the existing labor market.

As many commentators have pointed out, most relevant to the conflict between supporters and opponents of the Equal Rights Amendment in the first half of the twentieth century was the issue of social class.[22] In sex-segregated industries, women were likely to benefit from protective labor legislation. In such industries, where hours were likely to be long and working conditions were likely to be bad, such legislation kept such hours and conditions shorter and better than they might otherwise be. On the other hand, in those occupations where segregation by sex was less an issue, and where working conditions and also wages were generally better, such sex-based protective legislation operated as an impediment to women.[23] During much of the first half of the twentieth century, a small percentage of the female workforce had hopes of obtaining the kinds of jobs which were gender neutral and which also enabled any kind of economic independence. For the great majority of women, the goals of marriage and motherhood offered a much more realistic route to economic and psychological fulfillment than did the possibilities offered through work. Consequently, a self-identity that emphasized female difference made more sense than did one that minimized such differences.

Women's work and women's identity

As suggested in the above, an important factor limiting the appeal of feminism to large numbers of US females was the nature of women's labor force participation. Let me elaborate this point by focusing more extensively on women's labor force participation from the late nineteenth

---

[22] This is a point stressed by Dorothy Sue Cobble, *The Other Women's Movement: Workplace Justice and Social Rights in Modern America* (Princeton and Oxford: Princeton University Press, 2004), pp. 61, 65. Cobble also references Carl Brauer, "Women Activists, Southern Conservatives and the Prohibition of Sex Discrimination in Title VII of the 1964 CRA," in *Journal of Southern History* 49 (February, 1983), p. 40; Kathryn Kish Sklar, "Why Were Most Politically Active Women Opposed to the ERA in the 1920s?" pp. 154–73 in Kathryn Kish Sklar and Thomas Dublin, eds., *Women and Power in American History* (Englewood Cliffs, N.J.: Prentice Hall, 1991), Vol. XII, p. 154; Amy E. Butler, *Two Paths to Equality: Alice Paul and Ethel M. Smith in the Era Debate, 1921–1929* (Albany, N.Y.: State University of New York Press, 2002); and Jane Mansbridge, *Why We Lost the Era* (University of Chicago Press, 1986).

[23] Cott, *The Grounding of Modern Feminism*, p. 135.

through much of the first half of the twentieth century. This was a period when women's labor force participation increased dramatically. But a variety of factors, such as the social marginalization of the work of married women, and the organization and conceptualization of the work itself, kept such growing labor force participation from challenging the ideology of separate spheres. Because these factors operated differently for different segments of the population, it is necessary to focus on the changing labor force participation of different groups. Let me begin with the increasing labor force participation of non-professional white women.

In the late nineteenth century, the large number of young white women who left the farm to gain employment as teachers or factory workers did so with the understanding that this was work they would do prior to marriage. As Julie Matthaei notes, for much of the nineteenth century, the paid labor of such young women was understood as merely an extension of older views of children as contributors to the family economy.[24] Thus, the status of these young women as daughters waiting to get married was reinforced by the patriarchal ways in which they were often housed and by the ways their payment was often given directly to their fathers.[25]

Gradually, in the late nineteenth and early twentieth century, "working girls" began to be paid more on their own and also began to live more on their own.[26] But still, the nature of the work they performed reinforced rather than challenged prevailing views of male/female differences. Throughout the first half of the twentieth century, despite certain disruptions caused by the depression and by the Second World War, some broad changes in the nature of the economy led to an overall expansion of many jobs deemed suitable for this group. An increasing number of white, non-college-educated women found such jobs as telephone operators, saleswomen and office workers. Thus, whereas in 1910, 17.5% of white women workers had jobs which fell under the general category of "technical, sales, and clerical," by 1970 that figure was up to 43.4%.[27]

---

[24] Julie A. Matthaei, *An Economic History of Women in America* (New York: Schocken Books, 1982), pp. 143–44, 146–52.

[25] *Ibid.* pp. 141–52.   [26] *Ibid.* p. 156.

[27] Sharlene Nagy Hesse-Biber and Gregg Lee Carter, *Working Women in America* (New York and Oxford: Oxford University Press, 2005), pp. 54–55, Table 2.3, "Percentage Distribution of Employed Women by Occupation, Race, and Ethnic Origins, 1910–2001." As they note, the 1910 data are for those ages ten and older; the 1940–60 data are for those ages fourteen and over, and the 1970–2001 data are for ages sixteen and over. Their sources are Delores Aldridge, "Black Women in the Economic Marketplace: A Battle Unfinished," in *Journal of Social and Behavioral Sciences* 21 (Winter, 1975), pp. 48–62; Teresa L. Amott and Julie A. Matthaei, *Race, Gender and Work: A Multicultural Economic History of Women in the United States*, revised edition (Boston: South End Press, 1996); and the Bureau of Labor Statistics (1980, p. 74; 1997c; 1997d; 2003b).

It was this category of work which evidenced the most dramatic increase among white women between 1910 and 1970. While the category of "professional" women included 11.6% of the white, female, paid labor force in 1910, by 1970, that percentage had increased to only 15.6%. The category including "managerial and administrative positions" increased from 1.5% in 1910 to 4.8% in 1970. In all other categories, the percentages similarly increased only slightly or declined. The percentages of white women workers employed as "operatives and non farm laborers" went down from 23.7% in 1910 to 14.9% in 1970.[28]

The great expansion of "technical, sales, and clerical" work for non-college-educated white women facilitated the entrance of this group of women into the workforce.[29] But this greater workforce participation did not significantly challenge women's self-understanding as being radically different from men. As the white collar nature of these jobs provided them with a certain legitimacy, so it also kept these jobs feminine. These jobs were "ladylike" both because they were not associated with the physical labor of factory work and also because they made use of many of the characteristics associated with proper femininity. Women in these jobs were expected to reenact those characteristics that defined them as different from and as helpmates to men.

Other aspects of these jobs were similarly supportive of these notions. These jobs were typically low paying and did not represent stepping stones to positions with greater authority and higher wages. The assumption was that these were jobs which most women held for parts of their lives: before marriage or children, or after children were grown-up. They were jobs which functioned as supplements to women's primary roles as wives and mothers.

[28] Hesse-Biber and Carter, *Working Women in America*, pp. 54–55, Table 2.3. See note 27 above for qualifications Hesse-Biber and Carter note about this chart and for their sources.
[29] That it was during the middle part of the century that married women workers in general increasingly entered the workforce is noted by Alice Kessler-Harris, *In Pursuit of Equity: Women, Men and the Quest for Economic Citizenship in 20th Century America* (Oxford and New York: Oxford University Press, 2001), p. 205. Kessler-Harris states the following: "During and following World War II, married women moved into the labor force in startlingly high numbers. While the proportion of single women workers remained approximately stable, the proportion of married women doubled between 1940 and 1960, when nearly a third of married women earned wages. By 1970, three times as many married women earned wages as in 1940." The increase here must lie at least partly in the increase among married white women since the statistics for black women show a more gradual rise. Matthaei, *An Economic History of Women*, points out the following increases in African American married women's labor force participation: "from 27.3% in 1940, to 31.8% in 1950, to 40.5% in 1960, to 50% in 1970" (p. 253).

The situation for professional women, predominantly European American during this period, was different.[30] The jobs these women held were more gender neutral in character. Consequently, gender obstacles to advancement would be more obvious than they would be in gender stereotypical positions. These also would be positions with greater social status and higher pay where women might develop a sense of self more independent of familial relationships. It is among women in this group that one might expect to find a greater attraction to feminism.

And this was the case. As noted earlier, it was among this group of women where there existed the greatest degree of equal rights talk within the suffrage movement and the greatest support for feminism in the early twentieth century. But even the support garnered within this population was not such to generate a social movement capable of attracting widespread attention prior to the middle of the century. A variety of factors explain this failure. Most prominent are the related factors of small numbers and social stigmatization. While professional women constituted a larger proportion of the population in the first half of the twentieth century than had been the case in the latter part of the nineteenth century, this group still remained a small and marginalized part of the population. In 1870 only 5.6% of all employed women fell under the category "professional/technical." By 1900 that percentage had increased to 11.2%. By 1930, it was 14.2% and by 1960, it was 12.8%.[31] Remembering that these percentages are percentages of all employed women, one can see how this group would constitute a relatively small part of the female population.

[30] Thus, as of 1940, only 4.3% of employed African American women fell within this category. This percentage represented an increase from only 1.5% in 1910. Matthaei, *An Economic History of Women*, pp. 54–55. Even by 1960, the percentage of employed African American women who fell under the category of "professional" was only 7.7% compared with 14.1% of white women. Among employed African American women who fell under the category of "managerial and administrative" the percentages are .2% in 1910, .7% in 1940, and 1.1 percent in 1960. These figures compare with 1.5% in 1910, 4.3% in 1940, and 4.2% in 1960 for white women. See Hesse-Biber and Carter, *Working Women in America*, pp. 54–55, Table 2.3, "Percentage Distribution of Employed Women by Occupation, Race, and Ethnic Origins, 1910–2001."

[31] Matthaei, *An Economic History of Women*, Table 12-3: "Percentage of Employed Women in Each Occupational Sector, 1870, 1900, 1930, 1960," p. 284. Matthaei bases the chart these numbers were taken from on the following reports from the US Department of Commerce, Bureau of the Census: *Census of Population: 1870, Population and Social Statistics*, Table 29 (persons ten years and older); *Special Reports: Occupation at the Twelfth Census*, Table 1 (persons ten years and older); *Census of Population: 1930, Occupations; by States*, Table 3 (persons ten years and older); *Census of Population: 1960, Occupational Characteristics*, Table 21 (persons fourteen years and older). Within these groups of women the far greater proportion is European American. See the previous note on the percentages of African American women in the professions compared with the percentages of European American women.

The small numbers tell only part of the story. There was also the issue of social stigma. This was particularly the case for European American women, who in the first half of the twentieth century, operated within the predominant social ideology that women were either wives and mothers *or* "career women." The force of this ideology is partly expressed in the fact that it was not until after the Second World War that significant numbers of white married women were part of the workforce, and that it was not until the 1980s that significant numbers of white women with children at home were employed. The flip side of the ideology that had kept white married women or white women with children out of the paid labor force was the idea that white women of marriageable or childbearing age who were in the workforce were women unable or unwilling to be wives and mothers. Given prevailing views about the desirability of marriage and motherhood for women, those women who chose long-term paid employment over marriage and motherhood were seen by many as at least somewhat deviant. Many women struggled with this ideology, their struggles sometimes used as a means to reinforce this ideology.[32] But the potency of this ideology meant that professional women not only constituted a small part of the population but their social status was also somewhat marginal. Such marginality was not conducive to a proud, collective, assertion of rights.[33]

Moreover, the very professional success achieved by these middle-class women was also at odds with the kind of female identification that feminism demanded. Feminism, as earlier noted, emerged in the early twentieth century as a view of women as individuals, similar to men. As Nancy Cott points out, while feminism depicts women as individuals, it also demands that women identify with other women in order to gain those opportunities their individual accomplishments should merit. As Cott notes, feminism contains at its root an important tension: between, on the one hand, women understanding themselves as individuals, and thus the same as men, and, on the other hand, women understanding themselves as women, and thus socially situated differently from men. Many of those European American women who obtained jobs principally held by European American men needed to forcefully assert their sameness with such men in the context of strong social opinion that

[32] One prominent example is the mid-century Katharine Hepburn and Spencer Tracy movie, *Adam's Rib*. While the character played by Katharine Hepburn attempts to assert her equality with the one played by Spencer Tracy, in the end this character recognizes that the rewards of being a wife matter more.
[33] For a more elaborated discussion of the power of this ideology in this period see Matthaei, *An Economic History of Women*, chapter 11, "The Career Girl and the Second-Career Woman," pp. 256–77.

this could not be the case. The very assertion of this individuality stood in contrast with a collective identification with other women.[34]

The analogy here with similar assertions of African American identity are obvious. As I noted in the previous chapter, in the first half of the twentieth century the pervasiveness of the idea of natural differences meant that assertions of collective African American identity always contained the taint of possible agreement with this idea. Identification with other African Americans might readily be interpreted as meaning one shared an encompassing biology with all other African Americans, a biology that caused limited intellectual capabilities and problematic character traits. Professional women faced similar ideological obstacles in claiming identification with women as a group. To assert their very capabilities in male-dominated professions meant asserting their differences, not similarities, with other women.

Again in parallel with African Americans as a group, what is also relevant here are issues of status and class. For middle-class African Americans to assert a collective identity with other African Americans meant identifying with the lives and culture of poor African Americans. Similarly, professional women identifying with women as a group meant also identifying with the lives and practices of poor and working-class women, both white and black. This meant identifying with women, who as wives and mothers or as employed in sex-stereotyped occupations, seemed to prove all of those claims about women's and men's inevitable differences. To become a professional, however, seemed to demand that one prove oneself as very different from all that.[35] Not surprisingly, one finds many professional women in this period prior to the middle of the century – and many even today – forcefully asserting their identities as "human beings" in opposition to their identities as women.

In the above, I have been focusing on the changing nature of the workforce participation of white women during the late nineteenth and early twentieth centuries and the factors that mitigated this participation from challenging the ideology of separate spheres. The situation of black women both contains many similarities with that of white women and also certain differences. For black women, the lack of a prior history of "coverture" and of patriarchal social organizing principles within slavery meant also a lack of a history which stressed women's inferiority to men.

---

[34] Cott discusses this tension regarding the self-understanding of professional women in the 1920s and 1930s most directly in *The Grounding of Modern Feminism*, pp. 231–39, 271–83.

[35] Cott elaborates on these issues of class difference, noting that for professional women, the choice also was between identification with colleagues versus identification with amateurs and clients. *Ibid.* pp. 237–39.

Black women were more likely than white women to be economic partners with their husbands, thus challenging that idea of "difference" associated with white femininity. Consequently, as Deborah Gray White argues, in general, late nineteenth-century urban African American women were more inclined to see themselves as equals to African American men than were European American women, making the black woman's club movement different from its counterpart among white women.[36] But even equivalence of importance in contributing to household maintenance did not necessarily translate into beliefs about male/female sameness. As White points out, equality between black men and women was associated with what each group could accomplish in the public world. And that black women could be as effective publicly stemmed in part *from* their differences with black men. White elaborates on this point:

The economic successes of individual black men, and/or the positions of power a few held in black and white society, mattered less than the ineffectiveness of black men as a group when it came to the race problem. If club leaders considered anything it was the endurance of black women during slavery, their belief in the more humane sensibilities of women, and their acknowledgment of the debilities of black men in white society.[37]

The differential work opportunities for African American women and men continued into the first half of the twentieth century. Like European American women, the jobs that working-class African American women could obtain in this period were often sex stereotyped; in the middle of the century almost half of all African American female workers were engaged in domestic service.[38] In the post-Second World War period, while there was more movement of African American women into manufacturing and the professions, the numbers of African American women employed in these kinds of jobs represented a small percentage of the paid labor force.[39] Such sex segregation in job opportunities helped maintain ideologies of sex differences.

[36] Deborah Gray White, *Too Heavy a Load: Black Women in Defense of Themselves, 1894–1994* (New York and London: W.W. Norton & Company, 1999), p. 39.
[37] *Ibid.* p. 39.
[38] Jacqueline Jones, *Labor of Love, Labor of Sorrow: Black Women, Work and the Family, from Slavery to the Present* (New York: Random House, 1995), p. 262.
[39] Even by 1960, the percentage of employed African American women who fell under the category of "professional" was only 7.7% compared with 14.1% of European American women. This represented an increase from 4.3% in 1940 and from 1.5% in 1910. Among employed African American women who fell under the category of "managerial and administrative" the percentages are .2% in 1910, .7% in 1940, and 1.1 percent in 1960. These figures compare with 1.5% in 1910, 4.3% in 1940, and 4.2% in 1960 for European American women. The percentages of employed African American women in

For middle-class African American women, similar to middle-class European American women, ideologies of male/female differences were also often supported by ideas of respectability. While African American communities were more supportive of middle-class women's participation in the paid labor force than were European American communities, there still existed a degree of social disapproval:

Professional black women and their families were often as financially burdened as unskilled working-class families (though not always for the same reasons), but by couching their work roles in primarily racial uplift terms, they frequently sought a safe haven from criticism of their presence in the labor force.[40]

But if both working-class and middle-class African American women experienced some of the same kinds of factors that preserved ideologies of sex differences for European American women, there were also some important differences between the two groups. One major difference in the twentieth century has been the rate of African American women's labor force participation compared with that of European American women. The participation of African American women in the paid labor force has been consistently much higher than that of European American women.[41] Such higher overall rates of participation have been replicated in higher rates among married women and among women with children. In 1920, one half of all black wives earned wages compared to less than a quarter of married white women.[42] In 1950, the comparative figures were one-third of black wives compared to one-quarter of all women.[43] A study

the category of "operatives and non farm laborers" increased from 2.3% in 1910 to 7% in 1940 to 15.5% in 1960, compared with a slight decrease among European American women from 23.7% in 1910 to 21.2% in 1940 to 18.1% in 1960. See Hesse-Biber and Carter, *Working Women in America*, pp. 54–55, Table 2.3, "Percentage Distribution of Employed Women by Occupation, Race, and Ethnic Origins, 1910–2001."

[40] Sharon Harley, "When Your Work Is Not Who You Are: The Development of A Working-Class Consciousness Among Afro-American Women," pp. 25–37 in Hine, King, and Reed, eds., *"We Specialize in the Wholly Impossible,"* p. 30.

[41] Over the course of the twentieth century the degree of difference has changed, with the gap becoming narrower. Nevertheless, this narrowing of the gap represents only a change from a vastly different percentage of labor force participation to a still significant percentage difference. As Linda Gordon points out, in 1890, 23% of black married women worked, more than ten times the white rate of 2%. By 1980, the figure for black women was 48%, still 12% more than that of white women. See Linda Gordon, "U.S. Women's History," pp. 257–84 in Eric Foner, *The New American History*, revised and expanded edition (Philadelphia: Temple University Press, 1997), p. 275.

[42] Kessler-Harris, *In Pursuit of Equity*, p. 43.

[43] Jones, *Labor of Love*, p. 269. Jones cites Glen C. Cain, *Married Women in the Labor Force: An Economic Analysis* (University of Chicago Press, 1966) and Leonard A. Ostlund, "Occupational Choice Patterns of Negro College Women," in *Journal of Negro Education* 26 (Winter, 1957), pp. 86–91.

of the period 1940 to 1960 shows that black mothers of school-aged children were more likely to work than their white counterparts.[44]

Not only have African American wives and mothers worked at much higher rates than European American wives and mothers; the nature of their contribution to household income has also been different. For most of the twentieth century, when European American women worked outside of the home, they often either did so as single women, prior to getting married, or, when married, to supplement the larger incomes acquired by husbands. Throughout the twentieth century, African American women have also been important contributors to household income. But one difference is that the households towards which they contributed were more likely to be maintained by women alone than were those of white women. This difference was true even in the early decades of the twentieth century, and it began to intensify during the middle part of the century.[45] Thus, the percentage of such households gradually increased from 22.6% in 1940 to 24% in 1950, to 27% in 1960, to 28% in 1970, and then to 40.3% in 1980.[46]

These differences in the lives of African American women from those of European American women, suggest that earlier, and more extensively than was the case with European American women, African American women saw themselves in the world of work as independent beings.[47] To some extent, this aspect of the lives of African American women began to manifest itself in African American women's politics as early as the 1930s. Deborah Gray White points to a subtle change in the viewpoint of some middle-class African American women beginning in the mid 1930s. White focuses on the politics of the National Council of Negro

[44] Jones, *Labor of Love*, p. 269.
[45] Niara Sudarkasa reports on the steady percentage of African American households headed by women from the mid 1700s through the mid 1920s, staying between 20% and 25%, and how this percentage has also historically been higher than for European American households. See Niara Sudarkasa, "African American Families and Family Values," pp. 9–40 in Harriette Pipes McAdoo, ed., *Black Families*, third edition (Thousand Oaks, London, and New Delhi: Sage Publications, 1997), p. 21.
[46] M. Belinda Tucker and Claudia Mitchell-Kernan, *The Decline in Marriage Among African Americans: Causes, Consequences, and Policy Implications* (New York: Russell Sage Foundation, 1995), Table 1.1, "Family Formation Patterns and Living Arrangements, United States: 1940–1990," p. 11. The sources for this table are National Center for Health Statistics, 1990; US Bureau of the Census, 1950, 1951a, 1951b, 1953, 1955, 1961, 1963a, 1963b, 1964, 1966, 1971, 1973, 1975a, 1975b, 1980, 1982, 1984, 1990a, 1991b, 1991c, 1992a, 1992b. For 1940, 1950, and 1960, the percentages of families maintained by women alone are based on "nonwhite" rather than black populations.
[47] Jones, *Labor of Love*, points to a variety of sociological studies published in the 1970s that showed that black women integrated homemaking and paid roles into their personal ideologies more so than did white women. White women tended more to identify themselves with one or other of these types of roles (pp. 305, 408–09).

Women, an organization established in 1935, and differentiates those
politics from both those of a contemporary, working-class organization,
the International Ladies Auxiliary of the Brotherhood of Sleeping Car
Porters, and from the previously existing middle-class African American
women's organization, the National Association of Colored Women.
White points to the greater emphasis on the politics of gender in distinction
from the politics of race that differentiated the politics of the more middle-
class organization, the National Council of Negro Women (NACW), from
the International Ladies Auxiliary of the Brotherhood of Sleeping Car
Porters:

In contrast, as the "Voice for Negro Womanhood," the Council made black
women, not black families or black communities, the hub of their program.
Although neither organization challenged black patriarchy or black male leadership, the Auxiliary's emphasis on race unity through traditional symbiotic familial
relationships left the least room for advancing the cause of female autonomy...
Some of the legislation the Council supported were Civil Rights measures, like
repeal of the poll tax and passage of a federal antilynching law. Most of the
Council's energy, however, aimed to increase black female employment and
economic opportunity.[48]

The earlier National Association of Colored Women had also emphasized the fact that it spoke for African American *women*. However, the
NACW, like the Ladies Auxiliary, and much less than the National
Council of Negro Women, advanced a view of women as decidedly different from men. White analyzes the viewpoints of the publications put out
by the NACW and the National Council, noting how much more intensively the publication of the NACW emphasized the distinctive moral
superiority of African American women and their unique role in "uplifting
the race." The Council's magazine, on the other hand, was much more
concerned with women's advancement in previously defined male arenas:

This strategy was reflected in the Council's magazine, the *Aframerican Woman's
Journal*. Whereas *National Association Notes* carried an endless number of editorials
on the nature of African-American womanhood and female leadership for the
race, the Council's journal offered more general reporting on the status of black
women in arenas such as national defense, organized labor, and service industry
employment. Instead of stories on virtuous motherhood, the *Aframerican* reported
on prospects for world peace and the international status of women.[49]

To be sure, the National Council of Negro Women represented just one
perspective in African American thought in the pre-Second World War
period. And, during the post-New Deal and post-Second World War

---

[48] White, *Too Heavy a Load*, pp. 167, 150.   [49] *Ibid.* p. 152.

periods, it also represented an increasingly minor perspective.[50] The 1940s, 1950s, and 1960s were decades where African Americans were primarily focused upon ending legalized discrimination based upon race. The extensiveness of this form of discrimination overshadowed other issues. However, that the life conditions of many African American women led them to be supportive of feminist ways of thinking in the middle part of the century is indicated by the extent of explicit support African American women gave to feminism when, during the 1960s and 1970s, the issue of women's rights began to surface as an issue for public discussion. Polls taken in the early 1970s found large numbers of African American women expressing support for efforts to change women's status and for feminism per se. For example, a Louis Harris poll in 1971 found that 60% of African American women supported "efforts to strengthen and change women's status in society." This percentage was in contrast to 37% of European American women who expressed such support. A year later, 67% of African American women said they were sympathetic to "women's liberation" in comparison to 35% of European American women. These kinds of results continued in later years, indicating validity in these initial survey results.[51] The differences in the work and family lives of African American and European American women over the course of the twentieth century help explain these numbers.

The rise of feminism

While black women were, by the early 1970s, extremely supportive of the goals of feminism, black women alone were not responsible for the emergence of feminism in the early 1960s. But given the social marginalization of white professional women and the importance of familial identity to many white, non-professional women, what caused the issue of women's rights to begin to be an issue among white as well as black women in the early 1960s?

Scholars have emphasized two factors when they have explained the emergence of a women's rights movement in the early 1960s: the existence of the civil rights movement and women's increased participation in

---

[50] *Ibid.* p. 173.

[51] Jane Mansbridge and Barbara Smith, "How Did Feminism Get to Be All White?" pp. 1–6 in *American Prospect* 11, no. 9 (March 13, 2000), online edition viewed June 21, 2006, p. 1. Myra Marx Ferree and Beth Hess also point to surveys conducted in the 1980s that continued to show a more favorable attitude towards feminism among black women than among white women. See Myra Marx Ferree and Beth B. Hess, *Controversy and Coalition: The New Feminist Movement Across Four Decades of Change*, third edition (New York and London: Routledge, 2000), p. 89.

the paid labor force in the post-Second World War period.[52] It is easy to understand why the civil rights movement was of particular importance: it provided women who would be concerned with issues of women's rights with a political framework for conceptualizing their concerns. If discrimination against one group on the basis of ascribed characteristics could be seen as unfair and out of line with widely accepted American ideals, then why was that not equally the case with discrimination against another group? Again one needs to remember Cott's point that feminism demands of women both that they see themselves as similar to men and that they also see themselves as similar to other women. The civil rights movement would give to those women who might be inclined to raise questions of gender discrimination a way of identifying with other women without abandoning their claims of similarity to men.

But, the question still remains: Who would these women be? For, it is not immediately clear why the increased participation of women in the paid labor force would necessarily lead to this political stance. Women had been steadily increasing their paid labor force participation throughout the twentieth century. Why was it not until the mid 1960s that this increased participation had such consequences? To answer this question, I believe we need to look at changes in the *ways* many women were entering the paid labor force that began after the Second World War and intensified during the 1950s and 1960s.

In the decade between 1940 and 1950, the overall percentage of women in the paid labor force increased from about 20% to over 30%. This began a steady rise in the rate of women's labor force participation that has continued into the present.[53] But what is particularly interesting about this rising rate of women's labor force participation is how it reflected changes in the racial, marital, and economic status of working women. Working women became increasingly white, married, and also middle class. Thus, during this decade, it is not that African American women increased their rates of labor force participation to any great degree. From the turn of the century to 1960, the labor force rates of African American women remained very stable, staying at about 40%. It was only after 1960 that the labor force participation rates of this group of women began to

[52] On the role of the civil rights movement as a cause of the emergence of feminism see particularly Kessler-Harris, *In Pursuit of Equity*, p. 241.
[53] See Hesse-Biber and Carter, *Working Women in America*, Table 2.1, "Percentage of U.S. Women in the Paid Labor Force, 1890–2002," p. 21. Hesse Biber and Carter note that the pre-1945 data are for ages fourteen and older and the data for the period 1945–2001 are for ages sixteen and older. Their sources are the Bureau of Labor Statistics, 1979, 1980, 1997b; US Bureau of the Census, 2002a (Table 576, p. 372).

increase, to 47.5% in 1970 and to 53.3% in 1970.[54] Similarly, during the decade between 1940 and 1950, the rates of single women as a group did not increase in any significant way. Between 1940 and 1950, the overall rates of this group increased only from 45.5% to 46.3% and then decreased between 1950 and 1960 to 42.9%.[55]

What changed, however, was that a greater proportion of white, married women became part of the labor force. Whereas 15.6% of married women overall were in the labor force in 1940, by 1950 that percentage had increased to 23% and by 1960 to 31.7%.[56] This change had a variety of causes. Whereas the need for such female identified jobs as clerks, secretaries, teachers, and saleswomen was steadily increasing in the postwar period, the availability of young, single, white female workers to fill these jobs was not. A low birthrate during the 1930s, a decline in the age of marriage, a postwar rise in the numbers of young white women having babies, and a postwar rise in the numbers of young white women enrolling in school, all led to a shortage in the availability of single white women.[57] That shortage, in combination with existing prejudices against the hiring of black women, led employers to increasingly hire older, white, married women.

These demographic changes reflect the "pull" that came from employers. Pushing older married white women into the workforce were other factors. Post-Second World War inflation was one of those factors.[58] Also contributing was the growth of a new middle class defined by the possession of certain kinds of material objects: a house in the suburbs, ownership of a car, the possession of a new range of household appliances. This meant that women who were married but who could not be considered poor were also entering the workforce in increasing rates. In 1940, while less than 10% of women with husbands whose income placed them in the top income quartile were in the paid labor force, by 1960, over 25% of such women were working. By 1977, that percentage had increased to about 40%. In 1940, slightly over 20% of women with husbands whose

[54] Amott and Matthaei, *Race, Gender and Work*, Table C-1, "Women's Labor Force Participation Rates, by Racial-Ethnic Group, 1900–1980," p. 403.
[55] Matthaei, *An Economic History of Women*, Table 11-1: "Marital Status of Women in the Urban Labor Force, and Labor-Force Participation Rates of Women by Marital Status, 1890–1980," p. 273. Matthaei notes as her sources: for 1890–1970, US Department of Commerce, Bureau of the Census, *Historical Statistics of the United States: Colonial Times to 1970*, p. 133; for 1980, *Statistical Abstract of the U.S., 1980*, p. 402.
[56] Matthei, *An Economic History of Women*, p. 273.
[57] Leila J. Rupp and Verta Taylor, *Survival in the Doldrums: The American Women's Rights Movement, 1945 to the 1960s* (New York and Oxford: Oxford University Press, 1987), pp. 12–13.
[58] Cynthia Harrison, *On Account of Sex: The Politics of Women's Issues, 1945–1968* (Berkeley, Los Angeles, and London: University of California Press, 1985), p. x.

income placed them in the upper-middle quartile (between the second and third quartile) were in the paid labor force. By 1960, that percentage had increased to over 30%. By 1977, it had increased to over 50%.[59]

In short, beginning in the 1940s and increasing in subsequent decades, the lives of white working-class and middle-class women came to resemble more the lives of black working-class and middle-class women, with paid labor now occupying a large proportion of the lives of all. As Dorothy Cobble points out, for growing numbers of women, this lengthening of the part of their adult lives devoted to non-domestic work had important identity implications:

For a growing number of women in the post war decades, paid work was no longer a temporary or fleeting experience; it was an ongoing phenomenon that they combined with marriage and childrearing. For the first time, the typical working woman was now married and many had children … Working class women expressed a strong allegiance to their family roles as wives, mothers, and daughters in the post-depression decades. But their familial commitment did not preclude the development of a strong identity as a wage earner.[60]

One consequence of this movement of working- and middle-class, married, white women into the paid labor force was a decreased stigmatization of women's labor force participation and a new sense of women as legitimately having identities independent of those as wife and mother. These new views were expressed in the popular media of the post-Second World War period. Joanne Meyerowitz argues that, contrary to widely held perspectives on the late 1940s and 1950s, popular magazines of this period were very accepting of women's labor force participation and of their identities as at least partially autonomous beings. As she points out, while these magazines certainly celebrated women's identities as wives and mothers, they also celebrated women's achievements in non-domestic settings, including work. The result, she argues, was a kind of dual understanding of women's identities. Surveying mass-circulation magazines of the period from 1946 to 1958, she makes the following observation:

---

[59] Matthaei, *An Economic History of Women*, Table 10-4: "Labor Force Participation Rates of Married Women, Husband Present, by Husband's Income Position, 1940, 1960, 1977," p. 252. Matthei cites as her sources: US Department of Labor, Women's Bureau, *Handbook of Facts on Women Workers*, Bulletin 225 (1948), p. 11 (for married women whose husbands had no other means of support in cities of 1,000,000 or more); 1960, 1977: US Department of Labor, Bureau of Labor Statistics, *Monthly Labor Review* 102 (June, 1979), Table 2, p. 41. Matthaei notes that for 1940, estimate is not by quartile, but by averaging the labor force participation rates of eight income groups.

[60] Cobble, *The Other Women's Movement*, p. 12.

All of the magazines sampled advocated both the domestic and the nondomestic, sometimes in the same sentence. In this literature, domestic ideals coexisted in ongoing tension with an ethos of individual achievement that celebrated non-domestic activity, individual striving, public service and public success.[61]

   This sense of a dual identity is different from ideals of female identity more pervasive in the late nineteenth- and early twentieth-century women's movement, including suffrage, and in popular consciousness in the first half of the twentieth century. As I earlier argued, even among those who supported suffrage, the predominant viewpoint was that women were primarily wives and mothers. The argument was mostly that wives and mothers should also be able to vote. Women's increasing movement into the professions in the first half of the twentieth century suggested the idea that some women might possess an identity different from that of wife and mother. However, this new identity was still seen as necessarily alternative to that of wife and mother, available to only some, somewhat deviant women. New about popular ways of thinking in the post-Second World War period was the idea that many women might combine in their individual selves a dual identity, that of both wife/mother and of publicly autonomous self. While this new sense of a dual identity did not challenge the idea that, for most women, at least part of their identity would be that of wife and mother, it relegated this aspect of their identity to a part. And it assumed that at least in regard to that part of their identities that was connected with work, women should be treated the same as men.

   To be sure, there were class differences in the time period and exten-siveness to which women adopted an ideology of workplace male/female sameness. Working-class women, both black and white, because of their greater degree of participation in sex-segregated industries, still tended to advocate later in the twentieth century than did middle-class women the need for sex-based protective labor legislation. Such advocacy, which included demands for maternity leave and childcare facilities, combined with a lesser tendency to question the prevalent sexual division of labor. Such recognition of women's "special needs and natures," however, also increasingly combined in the post-Second World War period with demands for equal pay and for equivalent treatment of women and men in regard to many union negotiated rights, such as seniority rights. As Dorothy Cobble points out, the politics of the post-Second World War women's labor movement were complex, where the goal of equal

[61] Joanne Meyerowitz, "Beyond the Feminine Mystique," pp. 229–62 in Joanne Meyerowitz, ed., *Not June Cleaver: Women and Gender in Postwar America, 1945–1960* (Philadelphia, Pa.: Temple University Press, 1994), p. 231.

treatment did not necessarily translate into the belief that men and women should be treated the same. On the one hand, women in the labor movement in the late 1940s and 1950s fought for greater pay and for the elimination of sex-based discrimination. On the other hand, most also accepted the fact that men and women were different and these differences were legitimately expressed in women and men's different jobs and different needs.[62]

However, while such differences between the politics of working-class and middle-class women's advocates remained important in the several decades following the Second World War, over the course of the period between the end of the Second World War and the early 1970s, they gradually became less important. Following the Second World War, women factory workers had increasingly become employed in non-sex-stereotyped jobs, jobs where gender differences in pay and mobility were more glaring. One consequence was that while protective labor legislation remained an issue for union activists up until the 1970s, its importance had steadily diminished in the post-Second World War period. Concurrent with this decreasing emphasis on such legislation was an increasing emphasis on demands which treated women identically with men, specifically, as noted, demands which called for the elimination of sex-differentiated seniority lists and for equal pay for equal work.[63] Dennis Deslippe describes this change in the priorities of union activists:

> While there was no definitive break with protectionism in the 1950s, there were signs that the new roles of women were already changing the goals and strategies of those who were union activists. Quietly, the Women's Bureau Coalition moved away from advocating time and weight limitations and toward expanding job opportunities for women, especially in newly created occupations that were as yet sex-neutral. The coalition did not exactly abandon protective measures as much as subordinate their importance to a new set of priorities, addressing a group of women who were younger and who identified less with the legislation first passed during the Progressive age. These included women in aircraft, electronics and plastic technologies.[64]

The move towards greater overlap in political goals between working-class and professional women in the post-Second World War period made possible a developing network of working-class women with professional women, all committed to the general idea of women's dual identity. These networks included not only such well-known European

---

[62] Cobble elaborates on these points in *The Other Women's Movement*.

[63] Dorothy Sue Cobble, "Recapturing Working Class Feminism," in Meyerowitz, ed., *Not June Cleaver*, pp. 57–83.

[64] Dennis A. Deslippe, *"Rights, Not Roses," Unions and the Rise of Working-Class Feminism* (Urbana and Chicago: University of Illinois Press, 2000), p. 32.

American women as Esther Peterson and Betty Friedan, but also such African American women as Aileen Hernandez, Pauli Murray, Fannie Lou Hamer, Representative Shirley Chisholm, Addie L. Wyatt, and Anna Arnold Hedgeman. Out of these cross-class and cross-race networks was created the National Organization for Women (NOW), an organization committed to the idea that at least in regard to the workplace, women should be freed from those obstacles that differentiated their opportunities from men.

The politics of this organization, like that of the women's rights movement of the early 1960s in general, while committed to removing obstacles to women's full-scale participation in the labor movement, maintained older naturalized expectations of women's identity within the home and family. Consequently, the politics of this movement were mostly focused on removing obstacles to women's full-scale participation in the labor force. These politics raised questions about family and domestic life mostly insofar as prevailing practices within both constituted such obstacles. Thus, of NOW's 1967 Bill of Rights, three of the eight demands explicitly focused on employment issues (with one of these addressing issues of racial discrimination as well), one focused on educational opportunities, and one on issues of childcare.[65] Of the other three demands, one was aimed at expanding options for poor women, one was for passage of an equal rights amendment, and the last was on expanding women's reproductive choices. While workplace equality demanded a certain attention to non-workplace issues, the emphasis was on women's ability to function the same as men outside of the home.[66]

From women's rights to women's identity

As is well recognized, the women's liberation movement of the late 1960s shifted the balance by more extensively focusing on private life. Those who became initially involved in such organizations as Redstockings or New York Radical Feminists assumed the goals of the women's rights movement. But these, and others who described their ideal as "women's

---

[65] "NOW (National Organization for Women) Bill of Rights (Adopted at NOW's First National Conference, Washington, D.C., 1967)," in Robin Morgan, ed., *Sisterhood is Powerful* (New York: Random House, 1970), pp. 513–14.

[66] I deliberately talk about an "emphasis" since one of the demands, that focused on issues around poverty, does state the following: "The right of women in poverty to secure job training, housing, and family allowances on equal terms with men, but without prejudice to a parent's right to remain at home to care for his or her children; revision of welfare legislation and poverty programs which deny women dignity, privacy, and self-respect." This is, however, the only demand that has the aim of protecting women's abilities to function as mothers.

liberation," were also critical of such goals, seeing them as too limited. From their perspective, demands that sought only increased access of women to Congress or to the workforce sought only minor adjustments to a social order that was disordered in more fundamental ways. They focused more extensively on women's roles within private life and argued for a radical revision of the entire "sex-role system." And, in raising questions about "the sex-role" system, they began to talk extensively about what it meant to be a woman and how this identity relates to other types of identity.

The women's liberation movement that began in the late 1960s was not a single movement. For one, there were differences between the movement as it first emerged out of the New Left in the late 1960s and the movement that developed in the early 1970s. In the early 1970s, the movement became more separatist and more culturally oriented than it had been in the late 1960s.[67] Within the New Left, there were divisions among those who identified more with Marxism, socialism, or neither. And there were also many important differences in strategy, goals, and self-description in the organizations that African American women created from those created by European American women. I will explore some of these differences shortly. But while many have noted and elaborated on these differences, less frequently remarked upon is how, in spite of such differences, certain common threads existed among these differences. These common threads included, most importantly, an increased focus on the social relations of private life and a concern about the very meaning of "womanhood." The commonality of these concerns raises the question as to why these concerns originated when they did. What happened in the late 1960s to cause many young women to designate women not only as subject to oppression in public life, but as also oppressed in private life? What caused these women to make "womanhood" itself a category in need of examination?

To answer these kinds of questions, I would like to focus on two different kinds of explanations: (1) the structural contexts in which these women lived and which generated certain experiential problems, and (2) the ideological contexts which gave these women the resources for addressing these problems. Distinguishing between these two kinds of explanations is useful in accounting for an otherwise peculiar set of

---

[67] Alice Echols, *Daring to Be Bad: Radical Feminism in America 1967–1975* (Minneapolis and London: University of Minnesota Press, 1989). These points are qualified for, as Echols points out, even during this early period, there were strains of these tendencies. For her discussion of the early period and of differences within it see her chapter 4, "Varieties of Radical Feminism," pp. 139–202.

phenomena: the continued presence in contemporary life of attention to many of the issues raised by women's liberation in the context of the sharp decline on the public stage of many of those solutions to these issues proposed by this movement. While the structural contexts in which these women lived continue to be the structural contexts for the lives of large numbers of women, the ideological contexts – while very important in enabling these women to formulate their critique – have had less success in remaining a powerful presence in public life. Let me elaborate these points by first focusing on the structural contexts.

We know that those who formulated the politics of women's liberation were – at least in the late 1960s and early 1970s – mostly young and in college, and had been active in earlier political campaigns of the civil rights movement and of the New Left. I would like to focus on these characteristics for clues about why this new kind of feminism emerged when it did and why its politics took on this new kind of form.

As is well known, the 1960s was a period where there was enormous growth in higher education. A greater percentage of the population was attending college than had ever before been the case in the United States. Many of those young men and women now in college were first generation college students who came from upwardly mobile working- or lower-middle-class families. More than ever before, these young people attending college were women. These college students were part of the baby-boom generation that grew up in the cultural milieu of the post-Second World War period. As earlier noted, this was a cultural milieu in which the idea that a woman could combine the roles of wife and mother and paid worker had become more widely accepted. Thus, while many of those young women in college assumed that they would shape their future work lives to accommodate their responsibilities as wives and mothers, and some, as the joke of the time suggested, entered college primarily to get their Mrs. degree, many also recognized that a large part of their lives would be spent in the paid labor force. A large part of the purpose of college was to insure that the time spent there would lead to rewarding and well-paid work in the future.

In short, we can say that many of these young women began their adult years with the assumption of a dual identity, that of future wife and mother and also that of future participant in the paid labor force, functioning the same way as men. But this meant, particularly for young white women, that their self-understanding was often different from that of their mothers, whose workforce participation as wives and mothers was something relatively new and not an identity that shaped their premarriage years. In other words, this was the first time in the history of the United States when a large group of women began adult life with the assumption of a dual identity: that in their work lives they would participate identically with men but in their private lives they would function differently from men.

The duality so experienced was not abstract, but present in the very fabric of these young women's lives. On the one hand, as students, they were treated, and thought of themselves, as the same as their male colleagues. On the other hand, in their personal lives, older expectations about male and female roles persisted. On college campuses, these professional and personal lives existed in close proximity.

Public and private lives also existed in close proximity in many of those political organizations that constituted the New Left. Many of the explanations that have been put forth to account for the rise of women's liberation have focused on the sexism that young, female activists experienced in the political movements of the New Left. Scholars have pointed to the fact that these women were routinely kept out of leadership positions and were expected to do such housekeeping and secretarial tasks as making coffee or taking minutes at meetings. While these explanations are important, it is only through hindsight that they explain why the women involved took offense. After women's liberation, it is easy to see these requests as offensive. The question, though, is why at the time the young women *did* take offense. The young men were following norms that dominated much of domestic life and some of public life at the time. But they did not always comprehend how these norms collided with the sense of self that their female colleagues were bringing to these organizations. When women entered these organizations, they did so with a sense of self similar to that which they brought to their studies: as full participants able to contribute the same degree of courage and insight as their male comrades. Requests that they make the coffee or take the minutes conflicted with that vision. In sum, this was a group of women who experienced in their immediate lives contradictions between a sense of themselves as the same as men in their school lives and activist organizations and the sense of identity they were expected to adopt in their personal and private lives, a sense that cast them as different from men.

This sense of contradiction was more intense for European American women than for African American women. African American women more frequently came from backgrounds where mothers and grandmothers had been important contributors to household income. Thus, African American women saw themselves as more equal to men than did white women even in private life. This different history often provided younger, black women with a different sense of strength than they perceived available to white women. The complaints that their white female co-activists expressed sometimes seemed to these young black women a function of the weakness of the white women and thus irrelevant to their own lives.[68]

But even among a certain segment of young black women, frictions were developing between expectations that these women had of themselves and expectations others had of them. These tensions became particularly marked following the emergence of Black Power, a political movement which strongly celebrated masculinist attitudes.[69] Responding to such tensions, but finding much in the white women's liberation movement with which to disagree, these women formed their own organizations. Such organizations included the SNCC Black Women's Liberation Committee, the Black Women's Alliance, the Third World Women's Alliance, the National Black Feminist Organization, and the Combahee River Collective. These women also began to create their own writings, from the early collection of Toni Cade Bambara, *The Black Woman* (1970), to the writings of Audre Lorde, Angela Davis, Alice Walker, and others.[70] These books and organizations expressed ideas that differed in many ways from those coming out of the white women's movement, including, most importantly, a much greater recognition of the intersection of sexual categories of identity with racial categories. These organizations and writings also expressed, as did those being created by young white women at the time, not just arguments about the rights of African American women to have access to better jobs or more opportunities for political participation, but also a need for African American women to rethink existing assumptions about the social relations of private life.

In the above, I have focused on the unique nature of the lives of these young women to help us partly understand these transformations in United States feminism. But these personal life experiences tell us only part of the story. We also need to focus on the ideological context in which these women existed. That ideological context included an existing women's rights movement, ideas derived from experience in the New

---

[68] Winifred Breines, *The Trouble Between Us: An Uneasy History of White and Black Women in the Feminist Movement* (Oxford University Press, 2006), pp. 34–38.

[69] For an excellent elaboration of these points see Benita Roth, *Separate Roads to Feminism: Black, Chicana, and White Feminist Movements in America's Second Wave* (Cambridge University Press, 2004), pp. 76–128.

[70] In addition to Roth, *Separate Roads*, see also E. Francis White, *Dark Continents of Our Bodies: Black Feminism and the Politics of Respectability* (Philadelphia, Pa.: Temple University Press, 2001); Kimberly Springer, *Living for the Revolution: Black Feminist Organizations, 1968–1980* (Durham, N.C.: Duke University Press, 2005); Beverly Guy-Sheftall, "Introduction: The Evolution of Feminist Consciousness Among African American Women," in Beverly Guy-Sheftall, ed., *Words of Fire: An Anthology of African-American Feminist Thought* (New York: The New Press, 1995), pp. 14–15; Breines, *The Trouble Between Us*, pp. 117–49.

Left, and the emerging presence of Black Power. These phenomena intersected in a variety of ways to generate this new turn in women's activism.

The emergence of an earlier women's rights movement made the issue of women's political needs an issue of national debate. It constituted women as a political group with distinct needs and interests. But, as noted earlier, to many young, female veterans of the New Left, the women's rights movement was a limited movement. While they recognized the need for laws prohibiting discrimination on the basis of sex, they thought such laws would mostly benefit the already privileged. They saw anti-discrimination measures as primarily helping those who, except for the factor of gender, could otherwise flourish in a capitalist society. And they saw the heavily professional nature of the leadership of the women's rights movement as confirming this vision of the movement.

Black Power, conjoined with their own feelings of frustration in male/female relations, enabled them to think about women not only as a political group with distinct political needs, but as a group oppressed in deeper ways. As elaborated in the previous chapter, Black Power activists took the notion of "culture" that had, by the late 1960s, become part of national discourse, and applied it to the distinct ways of life of African Americans. This application was understood as radical because it meant a celebration of the distinguishing practices and features of African Americans, practices and features most clearly present in poor African American communities and that were highly disparaged by white America. Black Power stood for an identification of middle-class blacks with poor and working-class blacks around such practices and features. Thus it represented a united defiance against such forms of disparagement. At a certain point, some white, female New Left activist coined the slogan, "woman as nigger," and a new way of understanding the oppression of women was created. Women, too, could be understood as constituting something more than a group united by limited political interests. Women could be understood as sharing a "culture" or way of life that was socially constructed and contingent but which caused women to possess less power and privilege in many arenas of social life.

Some of these young women borrowed language and ideas from their experiences in the left to elaborate this new perspective. From the older left of the 1930s and 1940s they borrowed the phrase "male chauvinism" to describe the power and privileges that men assumed to keep women in this less privileged position. From the newer left of the 1960s, they borrowed the idea that injustice existed outside of the relationship between capitalists and workers. The New Left had adopted the phrase "radical" to express a form of critique – one that went to the "roots" of a problem – but that was not just about class. It used terms such as "oppression" to express the harm done by groups that went beyond economic exploitation and "liberation" as the freedom from such harm. It argued that societies could oppress others in ways that Marx did not fully elaborate – such as through imperialism – or through institutions other than the economy – such as the state in institutionalized racism.

Female activists began to use this language and these ideas to explain their new movement. White feminists started calling themselves "radical feminists" and their movement "women's liberation" to distinguish themselves and their movement both from the women's rights movement and from a more traditional Marxism. In opposition to women's rights activists, they started looking for the deep and structural causes of women's oppression and found those causes in the institution of the family. They claimed that the "sex roles" generated and reproduced within the family caused women to be less powerful than men in all arenas of social life, in personal as well as in political and economic arenas. In opposition to Marxism, they argued that the form of the family found in most human societies, "patriarchy," was as old, as deep, and as pervasive in its effects as any social structure that had been identified by Marx. Young, black, female activists rejected some of these ideas – for example, that the concept of "patriarchy" was applicable to the social relationships of black men and women – but elaborated the point that gender was a basic form of social organization, intersecting with such other forms as race and class to oppress in fundamental ways.[71]

Since the early 1970s, the ideas of women's liberation have attracted a range of support throughout the United States, causing institutional changes within educational institutions, the medical industry, the military, the corporate world, etc. Today, nearly forty years after the first emergence of "women's liberation," many of its phrases and ideas, such as that of "date rape" and "marital rape" have become an accepted part of social discourse. Issues of women's personal lives, from childcare to housework, are regularly discussed in public life. The idea that there exist socially constructed differences between women and men is now widespread throughout the society. "Women's liberation" has seeped into the consciousness and structure of American society in deep and important ways.

Yet, today, many are wondering about the life of the movement. Conservative pundits have long proclaimed the death of feminism. But

---

[71] The most powerful early statement of this position was articulated by the Combahee River Collective. See, the Combahee River Collective, "A Black Feminist Statement," pp. 63–70 in Linda Nicholson, ed., *The Second Wave: A Reader in Feminist Theory* (New York: Routledge, 1997).

even scholars sympathetic to feminism have speculated about whether feminism might be in a "third wave," implicitly recognizing the end of the second. The public presence of active feminism seems very different in the early twenty-first century than it did in the period from the 1960s through the 1980s. Where, exactly, is feminism today?

My sense is that while the form of feminism that emerged in the late 1960s – with much of its rhetoric and analyses – is now dead, feminism, in a more quiet, institutionalized form, is still alive. The latter is the case because large numbers of contemporary women still experience many of the tensions that led to the emergence of women's liberation. As women increasingly enter the workforce and are in gender neutral jobs, they still face more pressures than do men about maintaining households and being the primary caretakers of children. They still must attempt to negotiate public worlds where they are expected to function similarly to men and private worlds where norms of male/female difference still exist. While different expectations for women and men in private life are not quite as extreme as they were when women's liberation was developing – contemporary young men spend more time in childcare than did their fathers – they still exist. The problems that women's liberation began to identify in private life have not disappeared.

But the 1970s and 1980s radical feminist solutions to such problems could not continue to generate widespread support. These solutions – such as women's separation from men, or the overthrow of the family – while reasonable to a baby-boom cohort of young women willing to engage in radical experimentation for a certain period of time, could not remain credible for large numbers of women for an extended period. Most young women want to attain the American dream: a stable partner and children, a physical appearance that generates public approval, and those accoutrements of a good life that are pressed by a consumer society. Consequently, while many of the ideas of women's liberation have become part of everyday life, today, lesbians press for marriage more than for all-women's enclaves, women envisage the possibility for daycare more in terms of something they might privately purchase than in terms of something the government should provide for free, and the beauty industry thrives. The concerns that women's liberation raised have seeped into the fabric of our society even as the more radical, encompassing critique it also generated has become a more silent aspect of our public world.

Conclusion

The above represents a simplified summary of a complex history. But, this summary is necessary to highlight an important theoretical point: that in the history of the United States there has not existed a single "women's movement" unified by a single ideology. Rather, that history is better understood as the story of different movements governed by different circumstances. Thus, diverse circumstances have motivated different groups of women at different points in time to understand themselves differently than they had, and to be motivated to make changes to accord with these new understandings.

As noted earlier, following women's liberation, there has been an increased recognition of diversity in the kinds of perspectives that have motivated women to change their lives, and an opening of the meaning of feminism. That broad definition of feminism has helped identify forms of women's activism that narrower understandings have overlooked. But, as I also earlier pointed out, even this broad definition risks maintaining the assumption of a single movement, ultimately governed by one overarching ideology, sometimes more publicly present than others. It risks taking us back to thinking in terms of "waves" and towards limiting us to such questions as: Is feminism today alive or dead? Are we still in the second wave, in possibly a third wave, or maybe in a period between waves?

We can better avoid such dangers by recognizing the historicity of our own definition of feminism and through recognition of the importance of identity issues to all forms of political activism around gender. Instead of asking such questions as whether "feminism" is today alive or dead, we may be better served by asking such questions as: How do women understand the relationship between private and public life today? How do they understand themselves in relation to men? How are these understandings different for different groups of women? And, among which of these understandings does there exist a sense of tension or conflict? By addressing these latter kinds of questions rather than the former, we may be better able to assess the present and possible future state of activism around issues of gender.

Epilogue: identity politics forty years later: assessing their value

Feminist and black politics, as identity politics, celebrated black and female identities. The celebration was to counter negative elements of older naturalized versions of identity and to attain ends judged unreachable by individualistic accounts of identity. From the perspective of proponents of identity politics, while arguments which pointed to the individual nature of human character challenged the legalized discrimination justified by naturalistic accounts, they accomplished little else. For young, college-educated black men and women who identified with the poor and working-class communities from which many had come, and for young, first generation, college-educated black and white women who were trying to resolve tensions between expectations in private and public life, such claims about the individual nature of identity were inadequate to the newly pressing needs of the time. For blacks, claims about the individual nature of human character allowed only for the advancement of those few individual blacks who most resembled whites. For these young women, such claims similarly allowed only for the political and economic advancement of a few and left unchallenged prevailing attitudes about private life. For many in both groups, a more radical assault on the social order was required. Identity politics were born out of the belief in the necessity of such a radical assault.

The above narrative, elaborated in the preceding chapters, explains the context for the emergence of identity politics. Not addressed in the preceding chapters, however, is the question as to how well either form of identity politics solved those problems it was created to solve and/or created others in its wake. Therefore, before concluding, I'd like to briefly assess the consequences of identity politics from the vantage point of forty years later. Today, identity politics is sometimes regarded by aging feminists and Black Power advocates as a lost nirvana whose ongoing accomplishments were limited only by the failure of a younger generation to continue the fight. Others, both on the right and on the left, regard it as a simple wrong turn in American history, a political move that caused innumerable harm and that is best erased from historical memory.

Thus, any assessment of the place of identity politics in United States history requires some analysis of what it has or has not accomplished.

I want to structure this assessment around two, somewhat distinct, issues. Firstly, I want to look at the real-world ways in which United States life has been changed or not as a consequence of identity politics. In other words, I want to look at identity politics from the standpoint of the impact they have had – or failed to have had – on the institutions and structural patterns of United States life. But secondly, I want to look at the more ideological consequences of these movements. How do we think – or fail to think – about social identity as a consequence of these movements, and in what ways are these consequences useful or not? Let me begin this assessment with a look at the real-world consequences.

One criticism that has been leveled against identity politics is that it caused the demise of the left of the 1960s, a left that might have kept issues of class inequalities central to public debate. As this argument is often elaborated, while proponents of identity politics were making issues of social identity central to public debate, no one was focusing on the continuing growth of poverty and economic inequality. And since that poverty has affected black people so profoundly, the principal targets of attack here are those who turned the civil rights movement into Black Power.

One critic who has eloquently elaborated this position is Adolph Reed.[1] Reed argues that the inordinate focus on culture promoted by Black Power worked to hide important social and economic differences between a black managerial elite and the vast majority of the African American population. Reed claims that while the former has benefitted from Black Power, the latter has not. The former has benefitted because it has been able to gain economic and social benefits from its managerial functions in a post-1960s capitalist order committed to the appearance of racial integration. The latter has not only failed to achieve such benefits but the idea of a unified black community promoted by Black Power has forestalled the development of a radical critique of existing social/economic structures, the kind of critique that would adequately respond to the needs of the masses:

Black unity, elevated to an end in itself, became an ideology promoting consolidation of the management elite's expanded power over the black population. In practice, unity meant collective acceptance of a set of demands to be lobbied by a leadership elite before the corporate-state apparatus. To that extent, "radical" Black Power reproduced on a more elaborate ideological basis the old pluralist

---

[1] Adolph L. Reed, Jr., "Black Particularity Reconsidered," in Eddie S. Glaude, Jr., ed., *Is It Nation Time?: Contemporary Essays on Black Power and Black Nationalism* (Chicago and London: University of Chicago Press, 2002), pp. 39–66.

brokerage politics. ... having internalized the predominant elite-pluralist model of organization of black life, the radical wing could not develop any critical perspective. Internal critique could not go beyond banal symbols of "blackness" and thus ended up by stimulating demand for a new array of "revolutionary" consumer goods.[2]

I have certain problems with this narrative, and one of my problems is with Reed's understanding of class, an understanding I see as too static.[3] Reed assumes the existence in the 1960s of a black elite who managed to consolidate its elite status in the period following Black Power through the political agenda that Black Power advanced. But as I noted in chapter 4, the period beginning in the 1960s was one where at least a significant number of African Americans *became* middle class. Black Power may have facilitated that process, but what is problematic about that? A similar obscuring of this facilitative aspect of Black Power is accomplished by describing the advocates of "Black Power" as "petit bourgeois." Such descriptions, besides being needlessly derisive, also obscure the dynamic aspects of class formation taking place at this time.[4]

Reed is correct in pointing to the limited benefits of Black Power. Forty years after Black Power, the great majority of African Americans still live in dire economic straits, cut off from opportunities for integration into United States political and economic life as much, if not more, than they were forty years ago. Black Power, like its successor policy of affirmative action, has only benefitted some, with many left behind. But the question

---

[2] *Ibid.* pp. 53, 51.

[3] While I am questioning Reed's analysis by focusing on his static understanding of class, one could also question his claims about the managerial functions of the black middle class. Charles Hamilton disputes this kind of managerial critique by arguing that both the black middle class and the black poor rely heavily on public funds. Because this is so, the black middle class and the black poor significantly share public policy interests. See Alex Poinsett on Charles Hamilton's research in *Ebony* 28 (August, 1973), pp. 35–42. See particularly, p. 38.

[4] Cornel West frequently uses the phrase "petite bourgeoisie" in his essay "The Paradox of the African American Rebellion," pp. 22–38 in Glaude, Jr., ed., *Is It Nation Time?* West argues that the transformation of African American politics during the 1960s represented the rise to leadership of a new African American "petite bourgeoisie" in place of an older one. This use of this phrase is found, for example, on p. 31 where West describes Black Power as projecting "the aspirations and anxieties of the recently politicized and radicalized black petite bourgeoisie."

I have concerns about West's use of this term in this context. Marx used the term pejoratively and the negativity in his description stemmed from his belief that this social grouping – i.e. owners of small capital – was historically on the way out. Are the people that West describes owners of small capital? But then, by using Marx's term, aren't we merely taking advantage of the negativity without gaining any attendant analytic content? West could be interpreted as using this phrase to describe people who are marginally middle class. If that is the case, I would prefer that he say that explicitly as that might make us more rather than less sympathetic with the economic situation of this group.

is how we explain this limited benefit. Reed talks about the 1960s as a
period where there existed an "openness to alternative possibility" and
where there was a "contest of tendencies."[5] He combines this description
of a world where many outcomes were possible with the claim that the idea
of black unity presupposed by Black Power was responsible for narrowing
those options. Thus he claims that the idea of "black community"
"blocked development of a radical critique in the civil rights movement"
and that "this phony unity restricted possibilities for development of a
black public sphere."[6]

Reed's story about the 1960s possesses similarities with other leftist
complaints one sometimes hears about identity politics: if only women,
black people, and gays and lesbians had not come along and pushed the
left to focus on issues of cultural politics, a politics focused on class
inequalities could have come about. Richard Rorty voices a similar com-
plaint when he argues that the left in the last several decades has too
extensively focused on issues of culture and that it is time now to right
the balance by focusing more on issues of economics.[7] And Walter Benn
Michaels has recently put forth a similar type of argument. Michaels'
focus is not so much on Black Power as it is on the kind of emphasis on
racial diversity that has been one of the legacies of Black Power. The title of
a recent book by Michaels reveals his position: *The Trouble with Diversity:
How We Learned to Love Identity and Ignore Inequality.*[8] Michaels claims that
the emphasis that we in the United States have placed on diversity in the
recent past is "at best a distraction and at worst an essentially reactionary
position."[9]

A problem with all of these arguments is that they make identity politics
responsible for problems in the society and/or on the left that were present
before these politics came along and would have continued to be present
even without the existence of these politics. A question that can be
reasonably posed to Reed, Rorty, and to Michaels is the following: How
likely would it have been for there to emerge a politics committed to
radical income distribution in the United States in the 1960s or in the

---

[5] Adolph Reed, Jr., "Introduction," pp. 5–7 in Adolph Reed, Jr., ed., *Race, Politics, and Culture: Critical Essays on the Radicalism of the 1960s* (New York: Greenwood Press, 1986).
[6] Reed, Jr., "Black Particularity Reconsidered," pp. 51, 53.
[7] Richard Rorty makes this argument in *Achieving Our Country: Leftist Thought in Twentieth Century America* (Cambridge, Mass. and London: Harvard University Press, 1998). I've responded to Rorty's argument in ways similar to the way I have done here in a review of his *Achieving Our Country* in *Constellations* 5, no. 4 (December, 1989), pp. 575–79.
[8] Walter Benn Michaels, *The Trouble with Diversity: How We Learned to Love Identity and Ignore Inequality* (New York: Henry Holt & Co., 2006).
[9] *Ibid.* p. 16.

decades following, even had there not been the "distraction" of an emphasis on culture and diversity?

For a political idea to "block" or to divert a particular development requires that that development would be ready to flourish if only some leaders were expressing the right, rather than the diverting, political idea. But the failure of a politics based on class inequality to emerge in the 1960s, and in the period since, seems to me less about the absence of leaders expressing the right slogans, and more about the political climate of the country. Though Lyndon Johnson's "war on poverty" in the 1960s indicated a certain concern with poverty in the United States, that concern remained limited to strengthening certain governmental programs, rather than with combating social inequality in a more extensive way. The lack of societal interest in an extensive attack on economic inequality was evidenced in the 1960s by the inability of Dr. Martin Luther King, Jr., before he was shot, to create a powerful political movement focused on poverty.[10] This lack of interest was not surprising as, in the 1960s, there existed no set of institutions that could successfully mobilize constituencies outside of the left around such a program. The American labor movement had lost its radical leadership during the anti-communist purges of the late 1940s and 1950s. By the 1960s, the US labor movement had become narrow in its goals and conservative in its politics. The Democratic Party was at that time dominated enough by its commitments to anti-communist, big business; to racist, southern politicians; and to fearful, sometimes racist, northern, ethnic communities, to keep its support of radical income distribution limited. Such constituencies, with their racism, strident anti-communism, and fearful views about social change, made up a large part of the population outside of the New Left. The rise of identity politics did not prevent the New Left from developing a successful politics of radical income redistribution. The conservative climate of the country did.

Thus, when civil rights and anti-Vietnam work stopped being possible avenues for political activity, the New Left merely faced the same kind of inhospitable political climate to radical income redistribution that an older left had faced in earlier decades. Without the emergence of radical feminism, Black Power, and a vibrant gay and lesbian movement in the late 1960s, there would have been the same absence of a left presence in US politics at this time as there had been in the 1950s. And, in the period

[10] Robert C. Smith points out the many factors indicating the likely failure of this movement even if King had lived, in *We Have No Leaders: African Americans in the Post-Civil Rights Era* (Albany, N.Y.: State University of New York Press, 1996), pp. 190–91.

following the 1960s, with the growing legitimacy of a conservative movement emphasizing small government and lower taxes, the viability of a
political movement emphasizing radical income redistribution became
even less likely. Indeed, one might say that in the period from the 1960s
up until the present, identity politics has often provided some of the few
spaces in America of the 1970s, 1980s, and 1990s where left economic
proposals have been advanced.[11]

What about the effectiveness of another form of identity politics in
changing the social reality of late twentieth-century America, that of
radical feminism? Here also one might, at first glance, point to a variety
of failures. Forty years after radical feminism, many American women still
struggle in reconciling full-time wage labor with the demands of domestic
life. Moreover, radical feminists' many claims about female objectification
seem to have done little in stopping the growth of the beauty industry.
Today, that industry appears to affect female consciousness even more
than it did prior to the emergence of radical feminism.

But these failures have had less to do with radical feminism's analysis of
the causes of problems it saw women facing, as they have had to do with
some of the solutions radical feminism proposed for dealing with these
problems. By the late 1960s, many in the country were supportive of the
idea that women possessed dual identities: feminine identities enabling
them to be good mothers and wives and gender neutral identities enabling
success in the world of work. It is because so many supported this idea of
women's dual identity that the early 1960s women's rights version of
feminism has been highly successful. Few today in this country would
argue that women should not participate in paid work and political life in
all of the ways that men do.

And, since the 1960s, many have even become supportive of the more
radical feminist claim that "the personal is political." I noted in chapter 5
that as increasing numbers of women have come to face extended work
lives where they need to reconcile participation in the paid labor force with
expectations that they bear significant responsibility for the tasks of private
life, many of the problems raised by radical feminists have become part of
ordinary public discourse. Issues of housework, of childcare, of sexuality,
and of power relations within private life have become talked about in
ways that they were not prior to the late 1960s. Problems first raised by
radical feminists – such as date and marital rape, workplace sexual harassment, and the politics of housework – have seeped into the discourse of

---

[11] This point also replicates a point I made in my review of Rorty's *Achieving Our Country*,
p. 578.

ordinary life. Thus, in many respects, radical feminism has never died but instead has become institutionalized in such places as rape crisis centers, women's studies programs, and sexual harassment offices in public corporations.

On the other hand, some elements of radical feminism have retreated from public discourse. As I earlier noted, radical feminism not only raised concerns about private life but also attacked many aspects of the feminine identity associated with women's private lives. And this attack was one most American women have not been willing to endorse. Most American women continue to derive as much pleasure, if not more, from their roles as wives and mothers as they do from their roles as wage earners. Consequently, most try to develop strategies for reconciling the demands of each rather than sacrificing the role of wife and mother to that of full-time worker. Indeed, the pleasure that most women derive from their actual or potential roles as wives and mothers helps explain the ability of capitalist enterprise to make the beauty industry such a profitable one. That industry has been aided by a culture that places ever greater importance on outward appearance, a factor that explains also the ability of that industry to extend its reach to men. As there has not been in the United States from the 1960s to the present a social base ready to support socialist calls for radical redistribution of wealth, so also has there not been a social base ready to support the kind of radical transformation of sex roles that radical feminism called for.

If the institutionalized consequences of identity politics must be assessed in complicated ways, so must a similar assessment be made about the ideological consequences of this turn in American politics. On the one hand, these movements made it possible for gender and race to be talked about in more complex and reflective ways than was the case before the rise of these movements. In the mid 1960s, many liberals avoided being racist or sexist by denying the significance of race and sex. Since all claims about race and sex differences were assumed to be about the biologically caused limits of blacks and women, avoiding racism or sexism could only mean denying the reality of such differences. Black Power and radical feminism, however, asserted such differences, but now as positive attributes and as possibly environmentally caused. By emphasizing the fact of group differences that were possibly environmentally caused and sometimes positive, race and sex differences could become the object of public discussion in ways they could not prior to the emergence of identity politics.

Since the late 1960s, there has been a barrage of discussion about such differences. Discussions of race and gender differences are everywhere, from assessments about how blacks and women might vote for any particular political candidate or issue, to whether the "culture" of particular workplace environments are black or female friendly. Political campaigns are assessed as to their hidden gender or racial messages. The potential audiences of marketing campaigns, television programs, music and film productions, are all now analyzed in terms of their gender and racial content. Blacks and women have become groups whose specific needs, voting preferences, values, etc. are thought about, talked about, and explicitly addressed.

This self-consciousness about racial and gender differences is annoying to some. The argument here is that we have become *too* gender and race conscious. Many maintain that in this extended focus on what separates us, we have lost sight of what ties us together. Those who make this argument claim that this extensive focus on gender and racial differences has inaugurated a kind of tribalistic mentality where all of our differences are highlighted.

This argument is valid only if it can be assumed that without this attention to race and gender, or indeed to issues of identity in general, our culture would express what is common among us. But the instruments of cultural influence are still unevenly distributed. And those with existing cultural power cannot be relied upon to incorporate the perspectives of others for the simple reason that cultural privilege tends to blind the holder of such privilege to the particularities of their perspective. So blinded, such holders tend to assume that their perspectives are commonly shared. Thus, commonality is an attribute too often claimed about values and perspectives that in fact are more narrowly held. Partly as a consequence of identity politics, the country has become more self-conscious about the possibility of falsity in claims about commonality. Statements about "we Americans" are put forth more cautiously, with greater recognition of the pluralistic and ever-changing nature of what being a citizen of the United States means. This recognition does not deny the value of commonality as a goal; it simply assumes that such commonality can be truly achieved only after difference is first recognized.

But, on the other hand, that we are more comfortable acknowledging differences around identity does not mean that we have succeeded in figuring out how best to discuss such differences. Those who espoused identity politics in the 1970s and 1980s often treated identity categories in homogeneous ways. This meant that they viewed those who possessed a particular form of identity as all possessing a uniform set of attributes – including values, perspectives, desires, and experiences – that were believed to follow from that identity. Advocates of identity politics recognized that human beings possessed multiple identities. However, they also tended to assume that each form of identity had a content that was independent of other forms, and that content was applicable to all who possessed it.[12]

This way of thinking about identity was not unique to the advocates of identity politics. It represented an understanding of identity that has been endemic in popular thought. Older "naturalistic" models of identity had also assumed commonality among all members of a particular identity. Even when "culture" supplanted nature in explaining different "ways of life," first among anthropologists and then within wider circles of popular discourse, "culture" was often treated as common among all those who participated in it. Anthropologists of the 1930s, and in the decades following, have sometimes tended to associate "culture" with whole regions, reinforcing a tendency within the discipline to think of "culture" in "spatial" terms.[13] This tendency to think about "culture" spatially has sometimes inclined anthropologists, and even more so commentators within popular discourse, to talk about "culture" as something manifest equally among all members of a region or group.[14]

Consequently, when spokespeople for identity politics began to talk about the "culture" of African Americans or when radical feminists began to talk about the "culture" of womanhood, both tended to assume something applicable to all those who possessed that identity. Black Power advocates argued that while black men and women experienced life differently as a consequence of their gender, both groups shared experiences *as* blacks that were as politically oppressive for women as for men and could be struggled against independent of gender. According to this way of thinking, "gender" was a social identifier that could, at least temporarily, be set aside while racial issues were first addressed. Similarly, radical feminists argued that while women of different races experienced life differently as a consequence of their racial identification, all women *as*

---

[12] Elizabeth Spelman uses the metaphor of a pop bead necklace to capture this approach to identity. The metaphor captures the independent and separate nature of particular forms of identity suggested by this approach. See Elizabeth Spelman, *Inessential Woman* (Boston: Beacon Press, 1988), pp. 114–32.

[13] See Susan Hegeman's chapter, "Terrains of Culture: Ruth Benedict, Waldo Frank, and the Spatialization of the Culture Concept," pp. 93–125 in Susan Hegeman, *Patterns for America: Modernism and the Concept of Culture* (Princeton University Press, 1999). See also pp. 29–30.

[14] Clifford Geertz makes this point about "culture" in the discipline of anthropology in his essay, "The World in Pieces: Culture and Politics at the End of the Century," pp. 218–63 in Clifford Geertz, *Available Light: Anthropological Reflections on Philosophical Topics* (Princeton University Press, 2000). As he states: "But that, too, is much more difficult now that the way in which we have become accustomed to dividing up the cultural world – into small blocks (Indonesia, say, in my own case, or Morocco), grouped into larger ones (Southeast Asia or North Africa) and those into yet larger ones (Asia, the Middle East, the Third World, or whatever) – no longer works very well on any of its levels" (p. 223).

women shared certain common experiences around which they could unite. Thus, in response to a claim I once wrote contesting this position, a reader angrily replied that I was surely wrong since "all women are equally rapable."[15]

But, all women are *not* equally rapable. Class, race, and age differences make some women, as well as some men, more susceptible to rape than others. Potential dangers, like experiences, perspectives, and values are not shared equally among all those who possess a particular identity. Recognition of this lack of uniformity has sometimes led people to the other view of identity still common today, "that we are all just individuals." This view is equally problematic, since it denies the fact that different identities are also associated with distinct patterns of experience, perspective, values, etc. The denial of such associations is not just theoretical; it suggests that there exists no need for changing, celebrating, or in any way politically addressing the patterns of association that do exist.

Since the late 1980s, theoreticians have been attempting to develop ways of thinking about identity that fall into neither of these two extremes. These attempts have begun with the recognition that identity categories are social constructs whose meanings possess the same kind of flux and variability as do other social categories. Some theorists draw upon Wittgenstein's claims about language to elaborate how the meanings of identity categories, like the meanings of many other words in a language, are neither strictly individual, and thus not private, nor uniform across contexts or constant across time. Yes, there are patterns in the meanings of identity categories, as there are patterns in the meanings of other words in a language, but, following Wittgenstein, these patterns are better thought of in terms of "family resemblances" rather than in terms of identical replicas.[16]

This idea of degrees of commonality interspersed with difference in the meaning of identity categories has helped us understand how particular identities will both vary among members of any particular identity grouping while also expressing elements of similarity. If we think of identity categories like threads in a tapestry that is the social whole, then the

---

[15] This claim was made in a book review I wrote of Catherine MacKinnon's *Toward a Feminist Theory of the State* published in *The Women's Review of Books* 7, no. 3 (December, 1989), pp. 11–12. The response was in the following issue in January, 1990.

[16] I made this analogy with Wittgenstein's claims about meaning in my essay "Interpreting Gender," in *Signs: Journal of Women in Culture and Society* 20 (August, 1994), pp. 79–105. Cressida Heyes elaborates it in "Back to the Rough Ground: Wittgenstein, Essentialism, and Feminist Methods," pp. 195–212 in Naomi Scheman and Peg O'Connor, eds., *Feminist Interpretations of Ludwig Wittgenstein* (University Park, Pa.: Pennsylvania State University Press, 2002).

meaning of any identity category will change as it intersects with other identity category "threads" and as it changes across contexts and across time.[17] Tying together all of these analogies is the idea of rough common-alities, where neither similarity nor difference is absolute.

This view of identity is difficult to promulgate politically. It is much simpler to talk about identities as either simply individual or homogene-ous among members of groups. But this more complex view is also what is most politically needed. This view of identity would enable us to address those patterns that do exist in more subtle and complex ways. For exam-ple, rather than asking such non-productive questions as whether class or race are more important determining factors in the lives of African Americans today, we might try to differentiate the contexts where class supercedes race and vice versa. Rather than trying to figure out "what women want today," we might focus on the diverse conflicts that different groups of women face at different points in their lives and how these conflicts are themselves effected by changing historical circumstances. In short, while we would continue to acknowledge the fact of group specific problems, we would also acknowledge how those problems are themselves mitigated or amplified by diverse contexts differently faced by different members of such groups.

Identity politics, in its early and most public manifestations, did not promulgate this complex view of identity. However, identity politics did make it possible for us today to begin to think about identity in such terms. Identity politics stretched our notion of what constituted a legitimate political issue. It forced us to recognize that since identity affects life possibilities, it needs to be addressed on a political level. While identity politics often expressed a view of identity that was crude and simplistic, it also inaugurated a discussion about identity that we continue to need today. Therefore, identity politics represents neither a lost nirvana nor a simple wrong turn. Rather it is best viewed as a useful beginning of a discussion in which we still need to be engaged.

---

[17] Nancy Fraser and I used the metaphor of "tapestry" to suggest this view of identity in our essay, "Social Criticism Without Philosophy: An Encounter Between Feminism and Postmodernism," in *Communication* 10, nos. 3 and 4 (1988), pp. 345–66. Geertz uses the following language to express a similar idea: " If it is in fact getting to be the case that rather than being sorted into framed units, social spaces with definite edges to them, seriously disparate approaches to life are becoming scrambled together in ill-defined expanses, social spaces whose edges are unfixed, irregular, and difficult to locate, the question of how to deal with the puzzles of judgment to which such disparities give rise takes on a rather different aspect. Confronting landscapes and still lifes is one thing; panoramas and collages quite another" (*Available Light*, p. 85).

Index

Page numbers in italic indicate a reference to authors who are quoted in the text but their actual name is only given in a footnote. Page numbers with an 'n' prefix refer to notes.

Cambridge Cultural Social Studies

Roger Friedland and Richard Hecht, *To Rule Jerusalem*

Suzanne R. Kirschner, *The Religious and Romantic Origins of Psychoanalysis*

Linda Nicholson and Steven Seidman, *Social Postmodernism*

Ilana Friedrich Silber, *Virtuosity, Charisma and Social Order*